A
Reporter
Here
and There

A
REPORTER
HERE
AND THERE

E.J. Kahn, Jr.

Random House

New York

Most of the material in this book appeared originally—some of it
in different form—in *The New Yorker,* to which acknowledgment
is gratefully made. The author extends similar thanks to *Vogue,*
in which parts of one chapter were first printed.

Manufactured in the United States of America

For my favorite travelling companions—
Jinny, Terry, Joey, Tony, and Barge

Here

There

HERE

Gilroy
Was Here

I was born and raised in New York City, near Columbia
University, but my old neighborhood is one of those that, in
a mere generation, has changed considerably. I was amazed
to read in 1960 that the police had picked up a loiterer on
the block where I used to play, simply because he looked suspicious. When I was young, there was nobody in the area
who looked any more suspicious than I did, and I cut a figure
of such innocence that the Barnard girls, whose dormitory
was directly across the street from my apartment, scarcely
ever bothered to lower their window shades.

As an adult, I have become a statistic in the emigration of
native Manhattanites to the suburbs—in my case, to the
unincorporated village of Scarborough, in Westchester
County. My wife and I moved into a two-story cottage there
in 1947, after the first of our three sons, Terry, was born.
We were hardly settled when, the day after Christmas, the

great blizzard of that year swept over the city and its environs. Once we were dug out, I couldn't wait to get together
with my maternal grandfather, then going on eighty-nine,
and match my experiences in the storm against his recollections of the blizzard of 1888.

It wasn't until after the New Year that I had a chance to
drop in on Grandpa at his Manhattan apartment. He said
right off the bat that he hadn't paid too much attention to
the great snow of '47, having spent December 26th and 27th
happily and comfortably absorbed in his fourteenth reading
of *Nicholas Nickleby,* but—and here he seemed to be following the line that most old-timers, according to the newspapers, hastily adopted when they woke up on the 27th—it
was altogether meaningless and misleading to make com-
parisons in terms of official estimates of totals of snow-inches,
and we youngsters couldn't possibly begin to imagine the
cutting wind and the biting cold of '88, not to mention the
drifts. Ah, those drifts! Why, he said, half closing his eyes,
he could remember a ten-foot mountain at the corner of
Broad and Beaver—or was it Maiden Lane?—that was so
formidable that when a man with a pair of brewery horses
tried to . . .

I brashly started to relate my own adventures, but
Grandpa quickly interrupted me. "How come you didn't
spend the night of the twenty-sixth on one of those stalled
commuters' trains, as everybody else in Westchester did?"
he asked sternly. I replied that I hadn't gone to my New
York office the day after Christmas, having made plans to do
some skiing with my wife. "Didn't go to work!" said Grandpa
triumphantly. "When I was your age, I worked twelve hours
a day six days a week, and a man who didn't even *try* to get
to his office during the Blizzard wouldn't have dared admit it
to a stranger, much less to a member of his own family." To
change the subject, I asked Grandpa to tell me what he considered the biggest difference—aside, of course, from wind

velocity and temperature—between the two storms. "Machines," he said firmly. "In my day, we didn't have Sno-Gos or any mechanical plows, and we didn't have subways, or trucks, or automobiles. You should have seen those brewery horses at Broad and Beaver. The driver was a big, beefy chap in a fur hat that covered his whole face except for his eyes, and there were icicles hanging from his eyebrows that must have reached nearly to his nose, and those horses were snorting like dragons when they breathed, and while I was standing there, next to that twelve-foot drift, the fellow with the icicles down to his chin and I suddenly heard this faint little baby cry come from somewhere, and . . ."

Grandpa was certainly right about the machines. But for the gasoline engine, my experiences in the great snow of 1947 would have been so embarrassingly trivial that I could hardly have counted on them to lure my own grandchildren to my knee and hold them there, wide-eyed, while, between chuckles, I reminisce. As it is, because of machines, I have some hope of being able to keep the little beggars' mouths agape. December 26th began quietly enough in Scarborough. When my alarm clock went off at eighty-thirty and I reluctantly got up (my grandfather never stayed abed later than seven-fifteen in his life, he had often told me), it was snowing hard, and there were three or four inches of the stuff on the ground, according to an unofficial estimate I made from the bathroom window. I was so little impressed, however, that when I drove to the railroad station at nine to pick up the morning papers, I didn't even stop at the local gas station to have my chains put on. Traffic was flowing smoothly on the old Albany Post Road, which was only twenty feet from our house, and, besides, I had always figured I could put the chains on myself if I needed them, a theory that had never, incidentally, been confirmed. We really did live only twenty feet from the Post Road. A spry crow

would hardly have had to take to wing to leap from our bedroom, upstairs, to the Post Road. On many nights, in fair
weather, when the upstate trucks came thundering down the
road on their way to New York, our beds would actually quiver.

Anyway, as the snow piled up that White Friday, we
dropped the notion of going skiing, and I kept myself occupied by shovelling a footpath from our front door to our
garage, a hundred feet away. Every couple of hours, I went
outside and worked on my path, and as the walls of snow
flanking it increased in height, I became aware of the seriousness of the situation. On one of my trips to the garage, I
tried to put my chains on. No luck. By then, it didn't matter
much, because our driveway was already impassable, but I
wanted to keep a path clear from the house to the garage;
living in a motorized age, I had, I suppose, a blind faith in
my machine, and even if the machine couldn't perform its
customary services for me, I was determined not to be out of
touch with it. So I shovelled diligently through the afternoon
and early evening.

My wife fed Terry and put him to bed, and then she
cooked dinner. The groceries we had ordered over the telephone that morning hadn't been delivered, but we had
enough canned food, we figured, to last us for three or four
days. We finished dinner at about nine o'clock, and Jinny
said she thought she'd wash her hair, and went upstairs. A
few minutes later, she called to me to come up, and when I
did, she pointed out the bathroom window to the Post Road,
where, through the still-falling snow, we could dimly make
out a half-dozen motionless vehicles. "Some people are walking around out there," she said, "and it seems to me that I
haven't felt any traffic moving for quite a while. Maybe
the road's blocked." We put on ski boots and tramped out to
the highway. Traffic had stopped, all right, some of it in the
middle of the road; trucks and cars were stalled all over the

place. As we approached one giant truck-trailer with "Ruppert's Beer" prominently inscribed on it, a fellow got out of the truck cab and shuffled toward us, blowing on his hands. We asked him what was up. Well, he said, he'd been stuck there for a couple of hours. Some other drivers and passengers had taken refuge in a nearby church, he told us, but he had decided to wait around, in the hope that a snowplow would come along and open up the road. While we were talking to him, four other men climbed out of three other trucks, stalled not far away, and walked over. We invited them all in to have a cup of coffee, assuring them that if a plow came by, they'd be able to hear it from our house. They waded back home with us. There were, in addition to the Ruppert man, a man driving a moving van to its base in New Jersey and his helper, a boy of around eighteen; the driver of a tobacconist's truck heading south from Peekskill; and an old man. During the night, which the inadequacies of the machine age were to permit us to spend together, the old man never said anything, so I have no idea who he was or where he was going; all I know about him is that he was, when my wife and I first saw him, entirely blue. He was wearing dark-blue clothes, he had a heavy beard of dark blue, and the unshaven portion of his face was light blue.

When the five men got inside our house, we noticed that the Ruppert man was shivering and that his clothes were wet. He had been fussing with his chains, he said. Jinny told him to go up and take a shower and, while his pants were drying, to put on some gray flannel slacks of mine. He didn't want to at first, but she was insistent. I took him upstairs, gave him the pants, and remarked that I'd been having some trouble with my chains, too. Meanwhile, downstairs in the kitchen, Jinny had started making coffee and sandwiches. By the time they were ready, the Ruppert man had bathed, changed, and joined the rest of us. After a while, the tobacco man reported that from the bathroom window he'd seen

somebody else walking on the Post Road. I went out to investigate and ran into another beer driver—a Schaefer man.
I told him he might as well come in and get warm. He
seemed reluctant, but when I said that we already had
a Ruppert man in the house, he brightened and said that in
that case he'd be glad to. Then we saw, staggering toward us
through the snow, a woman, two little boys, and a man carrying something wrapped in a blanket—a baby boy, it turned
out. The father was a used-car dealer from Schenectady.
They didn't have to be urged to join us. As I was leading this
squad past our garage, I saw a flickering light inside it. I
went in. The moving-van driver was holding a flashlight, and
the Ruppert man, back in his own pants and down on his
knees, was putting my chains on my car.

Back in the house, my wife, who had seen us coming, was
heating a big caldron of soup. Assorted soup, I guess you
could call it, since the ingredients consisted of all the cans
we had on hand—one cream-of-asparagus, two split-pea, a
vegetable-with-beef, a black-bean, two pepper-pot, and a con-
sommé. When I told her we had another beer-truck man,
she reflected for a moment and then insisted that he go upstairs, take a shower, and put on my gray flannel pants. He
didn't particularly want to take a shower, and his pants were
reasonably dry, but he didn't argue.

The tobacco man soon went to sleep on a living-room sofa,
with his hat on. The rest of the group began feeding the
three little boys. I went outside to see how everything was
going in the garage and, having got that far, decided to make
one more survey of the highway. I came back with an Army
officer from Virginia, his wife, and their daughter, aged five.
By the time we got inside the house, Jinny had inserted all
the leaves in our dining-room table, put chairs around it,
lighted some candles, and turned on the lights on our Christmas tree, and was presiding over a lively supper party, the
menu of which included the assorted soup, canned compote

of fruit, and some mince pie left over from Christmas. Since
there were truck drivers present, the meal began, of course,
as well as ended, with coffee.

It was midnight when our group finished drying the
dishes. The radio had been announcing repeatedly that driving conditions were terrible, but we all still felt that the road
was bound to be opened up soon. A couple of the truck
drivers telephoned their dispatchers and said they expected
to be rolling again shortly. The Ruppert man put the dishes
away. The Schaefer man and the mother of the three boys
got into an earnest chat about progressive education. The
Army officer revealed that he was in the Signal Corps, and I
suggested that he might be able to do something about a de-
fective string of lights on our Christmas tree. He replied,
apologetically, that he was a cryptographer. The wife of the
Schenectady man told us that her name was Gloria, that her
husband's name was George, and that their sons also had six-
letter names beginning with "G"—Gerald, Gordon, and Gil-
roy. Jinny seized an opening to tell about how the speeding
trucks on the Post Road made our beds rattle at night. The
drivers listened thoughtfully, and the moving-van man said,
"You know, once a cop stopped one of our boys and dragged
him off his seat and into a house along a dip on the
Post Road, a house even closer to the highway than yours.
The cop didn't say anything to the driver, just shoved him
inside the front door, and the driver looked around, and it
was awful what he saw—cracked mirrors, and broken cups
and plates, and goodness knows what all else—and he
thought to himself, 'My God, this might be *my* home,' and
he got back on his seat and drove away, and pretty soon the
word got around, and not any of us have gone by that house
ever since at more than twenty miles per hour."

At twelve-thirty, I called the police and told the sergeant
on duty that if he wanted to move any of the nearby vehicles

abandoned on the Post Road and couldn't find the drivers, our house would be a likely place to make inquiry. I asked the sergeant when he thought traffic would get going. "Not before morning," he said. I asked him what I should advise the drivers to do. "Tell 'em to stay put," he said. We didn't have quite enough beds, couches, and cots in the house, so three men had to sleep on the floor. Jinny got everybody billeted, and at one-thirty she and I decided to go to bed ourselves. Fifteen minutes later, we heard the roar of a motor outside and rushed to a window. A snowplow was lumbering south on the Post Road, weaving in and out among the stalled vehicles. It got abreast of our house, stopped, turned around, and headed back north. I went downstairs, with the idea of reporting that the road was now partly open in one direction. Everybody was asleep except the Ruppert man, who was fixing the lights on our Christmas tree. I didn't disturb anyone.

My wife and I were awakened by our baby at six-forty-five. I dressed and went downstairs. The Ruppert man and the blue man weren't in sight, but our party was otherwise intact. The tobacco man was still asleep on the sofa; his hat had fallen off, or someone had taken it off. The Schaefer man had two pots of coffee percolating on the kitchen stove, and Gloria was cooking oatmeal. A moment later, the Ruppert man came in from outside; he had been shovelling snow off my footpath. The blue man never did turn up again; he had presumably walked to Ossining. I went out to the Post Road. No cars were moving, but a pedestrian said that he thought it was passable as far as Ossining. I reported this intelligence to our truck drivers, and they called their dispatchers and passed the word along, as if transmitting a front-line message to headquarters. Jinny said that we were practically out of food. I made an announcement to this effect, whereupon the truckmen went outside and, with what looked like almost no effort, dug out my driveway. Then they piled into my car and we drove, quite easily, to Ossining, where we picked up a batch of supplies. On the way back, we slithered around a stalled Ruppert truck with a driver sitting in it. My Ruppert man requested me to stop, got out, chatted briefly with the other driver, and then asked me if it would be all right if the fellow came along with us. Ruppert No. 1 explained that Ruppert No. 2 was supposed to be following him into New York and that it wouldn't look good if No. 2 got in ahead of him. When we reached home, I found that Jinny had collected two more truck drivers, sporting the colors of the A. & P., who had spent the night on the road, in their cab. One of them was eating breakfast, and the other soon joined him. He had been upstairs taking a shower, and was wearing my gray flannel pants.

We had lunch at eleven-thirty, and then sat around listening to weather reports on the radio until two o'clock, when the road magically opened up. My wife and I went out to the highway with our guests and waved goodbye to them as they drove off. They all promised to stop in and say hello when they next came by.

Soon, everything was almost back to normal at Scarborough. The Post Road had been cleared, and traffic was moving along it at a brisk rate. One odd thing that both Jinny and I noticed, however, was that after dark the trucks didn't seem to roar by as fast as they used to; our furniture hadn't trembled since the night of the storm. I tried to tell my grandfather about this several times, but I never could get him out of his damned old snowdrift.

A Bear
at
Large

My sons—not unlike most fathers' sons, I daresay—constantly seem to be getting me into situations that, left to my own devices, I could avoid, if not indeed evade. It is not necessarily always the boys' fault. On the day that Terry was born, for instance, in the spring of 1947, I began to keep a diary. I would scribble notes during the day, and each evening, after visiting my wife and baby at the hospital, would diligently type out the notes, in the interest of, if not permanence, permanent legibility. On Jinny's return home from the hospital, things got kind of hectic around the house, and I missed an occasional nightly stint of typing. Then I began to type my notes once weekly. Then I began not to type them at all. Then I began to scribble them once weekly. At the end of six months, my diary had petered out, and that may have been just as well, for there appeared to be not much more to my productivity than the self-conscious pride and awe of a man who has successfully weathered reproductivity.

A decade or so later, on the advice of a tax counsellor, who said the only way a self-employed writer without secretarial assistance could hope to avoid, or evade, the onslaughts of the Internal Revenue Service was by keeping a running account of his dubious activities, I started anew on a diary. Each morning, at my house, twenty-eight miles from New York City, I would sit at my desk and try to remember anything that had happened the previous day of a conceivably tax-deductible nature.

But it was hard to concentrate. My home is certainly not in the forest primeval. Indeed, on a clear day, from the heights of Scarborough, you can see the Empire State Building, and on any old day you can see Sing Sing. Yet there is a gratifying, if not particularly unusual, abundance of wildlife in our neighborhood, and as I gazed out the window, brooding over the lunch tab I'd picked up the day before, my attention to duty would be diverted by some mallards frisking on our pond, or, even better, by some plump Canadian geese, who would march up onto the lawn and sun themselves between dips, until Barge, my friendly Labrador retriever, would run over in the hope of getting better acquainted with them.

In addition to the fowl, squirrels, rabbits, raccoons, woodchucks, skunks, and possums roam in uninhibited freedom across our fields; and the sight of anywhere from one to half a dozen lovely, white-flanked deer walking gracefully across our lawn is not uncommon. (One fall, a big buck sauntered right into our driveway, and might have nuzzled the front door open if Barge hadn't chased him away.) We've had red foxes around, too, and the banks of the pond, alas, have been ravaged by a resident colony of muskrats.

All in all, though, we had to concede that when it came

to fauna the folks over in Connecticut, who were once hosts
to a stray moose, had the edge on us. In the winter of 1957,
however, an extraordinary series of events occurred in Scarborough, which is part of the incorporated village of Briarcliff Manor and the township of Ossining, and I found on
leafing through my diary soon afterward that they all but
dominated its pages. I can best relate them, in more or less
orderly sequence, by presenting some excerpts from that
pre-empted journal:

FEBRUARY 2ND—Cold today. This evening's Ossining *Citizen Register* reports no groundhog shadow-casting, owing to
snowfall. On arising from an afternoon nap, learned from
our maid, Sarah, that two men in hunting clothes had come
to the kitchen door asking leave to set traps for muskrats.
Sarah, wonderful maid that she is, told them I was busy working and suggested they return tomorrow.

FEBRUARY 3RD—Trappers back. I asked them if traps
could hurt dogs, cats, children, or other wildlife. They assured me there was no danger of that, so I granted them
permission to go ahead. Feel sorry about harassing the muskrats, but damn near broke my neck in January stumbling in a
hole they'd dug. It's a case of my neck against theirs. As the
trappers were departing, one of them mentioned casually
that they might catch mink in the traps, too. Mink!

FEBRUARY 5TH—*Citizen Register* says Briarcliff cops are
searching for a 150-lb. black bear seen last week on Sleepy
Hollow Country Club grounds. Hmm. Probably just a big
dog. I remember how as a kid I was once chased across a golf
course by an English sheep dog that I would have sworn at
the time was a dragon. Strange, though, that just last August,
Carroll Colby, the *Cit. Reg.* Adventure Editor, wrote in his
column that it would not be utterly fantastic for a bear to
turn up in Westchester. Out of curiosity, I checked to see
what Ernest Thompsom Seton had to say in his classic *Lives*

of *Game Animals*, and found that he estimated there were a few hundred black bears left in the Adirondacks—thirty years ago, that is. Come to think of it, Bear Mountain, across the Hudson and twenty miles north of here, must have got its name from bears. And Briarcliff public-school column in *Cit. Reg.*, called "Bear Facts," mentions student publication *Bruin*. Must be some reason. Seton also says that the black bear (*Ursus americanus*) is elusive, speedy, a good swimmer, a loner, a nomad, and harmless. Glad to hear the last, just in case.

FEBRUARY 6TH—Paper reports bear tracks in the Sparta section of Ossining, near the river, a couple of miles from my house. Adds that Colby, who is a special game protector for the State Conservation Department—and a many-faceted man, being, in addition to game protector and Adventure Editor, a Briarcliff village trustee, the fire commissioner, and an author and illustrator of juvenile books—had photographed the tracks and said they looked to him like those of a year-old black bear. Seems incredible.

FEBRUARY 7TH—Went to New York to straighten out a mess at the bank and heard much bear talk on the commuters' train. Awful jokes. A Merrill Lynch partner was hailed raffishly as an expert on bear habits. Ribald speculation that the bear was simply an excessively hairy neighbor taking a constitutional in the buff. Etc., etc. Became the victim of innuendoes myself as friends pointed out that bears are related to raccoons, that coons raid garbage cans, that my Barge is black and big (85 lbs.) and raids garbage cans. Ridiculous! Anyone can tell a bear from a dog. *Cit. Reg.* published one of Colby's photos of the Sparta animal tracks, showing them to be bigger than a child's hand. Tracks look peculiar.

(This is a P.S. written March 6th: Learned today the photo was printed upside down.)

FEBRUARY 9TH—The trappers inspected their traps. No

muskrats. No mink. Sarah brought me the *Cit. Reg.* and pointed—with relief, I sensed—to an item from Irvington, ten miles to the south. A game warden there pooh-poohs our bear, saying that several dogs in his area were killed by an animal that he suspects is a rambunctious bull mastiff. In other words, our beast is probably canine, not ursine. Spoilsport.

FEBRUARY 11TH—The killer dog, a giant bull-mastiff bitch, was shot in some Irvington woods yesterday. Trouble there apparently is over. Hope so, because the dog show is on at the Garden, and killer dogs are terrible publicity. Funny thing—a Briarcliff resident with a bear background insists he heard a bear galumphing in his yard last night, *after* the Irvington slayer was slain. Went to monthly fire-company meeting, and heard more bear talk. Someone asked Chief Bowers when he was going to catch the bear. Big joke. In oblique reply, he informed us that the hook-and-ladder was dispatched this afternoon to break up a fight between a dog and a raccoon in a culvert. The firemen smoked the dog out, then put a 2½-inch line in to flush the coon out, but the coon just straddled the hose. The chief said that many side bets were made on who would prevail—coon or firemen. Coon money won when the firemen left, with their prey still in the culvert. This is getting to be a very animal-conscious neighborhood. Read the *Cit. Reg.* on getting home, and found the Hunting & Fishing Editor in a debunking mood. "Yarns of Westchester bears have a point in common with the Loch Ness monster," he wrote. "No one has managed yet to come up with a corpus delicti." Erudite but morbid. H. & F. Editor added that it seemed odd to him that no hunters had seen the bear—if there is a bear—during the hunting season, but omitted the pertinent fact that the hunting season ended December 15th, long before the bear was spotted. If there is a bear.

FEBRUARY 16TH—A clipping of one *Cit. Reg.* bear story

has been pinned to the post-office bulletin board, alongside the circulars describing wanted criminals. Seems uncharitable toward what E. T. Seton called one of the friendliest animals anywhere—"timid, shy, and inoffensive." Murray Goodwin, whose house is less than a quarter mile from ours, told me at the post office that he had seen some outsize tracks in his rock garden yesterday. I said maybe my dog had made them. "Not Barge," he told me. "I know *his* tracks. They've been around our garbarge cans for years." Bade him a curt good day.

FEBRUARY 19TH—The paper reports that the organist at All Saints', directly across the road from the Goodwins', saw a bear through the church window a few days ago. For goodness' sake! The bear, or whatever it was, skedaddled into the woods. Can't remember where Barge was when the bear was seen at All Saints'. The children, home from school, announced a sudden revival of local interest in Davy Crockett. No shooting is allowed here, of course, even in the hunting season. Bows and arrows only.

FEBRUARY 21ST—The bear story is getting around. The *Westchester News,* a White Plains weekly, says a bear has been pawing garbage cans all the way from Ossining to Tarrytown. Seton wrote that bears are omnivorous—that they "prefer all things eatable at all times." Just like Labrador retrievers.

FEBRUARY 24TH—Great to-do this afternoon on River Road, a mile and a half southwest of here. Jane Homes' maid was walking a baby carriage, accompanied by a pack of dogs, when, she claims, she saw a young black bear in the woods at the edge of the road, not fifteen feet from her. The dogs lit out after the bear, and the bear vanished. The police were summoned, but found nothing. Jane says she asked maid, "Have you ever seen a bear before?," and maid answered "Yes." What is one to think?

MARCH 1ST—Fresh snow last night. Out after breakfast

with Barge, I found the ground already covered with animal tracks, much larger than Barge's and quite unlike them. Suspect imagination is getting the better of me. Today's Colby column in the *Cit. Reg.* is devoted to bears. Says he has had several letters about them. "And I am glad, for they are fascinating creatures, even if we seldom have a chance to see them outside of zoos." Colby also discusses tracks. The dog is a digitigrade, he explains, meaning it walks on its toes; the bear is a plantigrade, meaning it walks on the soles of its feet. I learn something every day.

MARCH 4TH—Bear! On going down to breakfast, I found Sarah in a swivet. Said she was awakened at 4:30 A.M. by sounds of something heavy nudging the garbage cans right outside her bedroom window. She thought at first it was a prowler, but then she became convinced it was an animal. She was too scared, understandably, to lift her head from the pillow. I knew it couldn't have been Barge, because he was snoring at my bedside then. Rushed outside and saw fresh tracks—big as my hand—in the snow near the garbage area. Plantigrade. Tried to call Colby, but he was out of town. Damn! Our breadman spread the word, and pretty soon some neighbors came over to gawk at the tracks. Robie Bucci brought along a Boy Scout handbook. The tracks resembled the bear-print pictures in it. Sarah was not cheered by the thought that a wild bear was only three feet or so from her pillow, even though separated by a wall.

MARCH 5TH—The trappers came by to check their traps. No muskrats, no mink, no moose, no nothing. Who cares? I drove over to Briarcliff Police Department and dropped in on Chief Johnson. He's been here, man and boy, most of his life, serving on the force for thirty-one years and as chief for twenty. Rock of probity. He told me there were several reports of the bear that hadn't reached the general public. For instance, it was thought to have been seen at Briarcliff College, but at the request of the college authorities, who were evidently reluctant to alarm the students' families unnecessarily, the story was hushed up. A snow-removal crew had also claimed to have seen the bear, at 4 A.M. on March 1st, a mere hundred yards from my driveway. That was the morning of the fresh snow—the morning I was puzzled by the tracks. The chief and I were soon deep in bear gab. He is sure the bear is a bear. Thinks maybe it wandered south out of the Catskills and crossed the Hudson while the river was frozen, but he admits that's just a guess. No matter; he is convinced that wherever the bear came from, it's here. I asked what the procedure would be if the police came face to face with the bear, and he said the only thing they could do—unless the bear acted ornery—would be to rope it; a 50-foot lasso is standard equipment in all police cars. The local cops did shoot a man once, back in the prohibition era, when a bootlegger acted ornery and pulled a gun on them. Self-defense. Same rule for bears. Johnson recalled that he and his fellow-cops used to rope a couple of runaway horses a week—twenty or thirty years ago, before the territory got built up and grew tame. He's proud of the way the local citizenry has behaved with a bear in its midst. No panic. Said I ought to talk to Colby, the ranking bear authority of the village.

MARCH 6TH—Colby back. Got him on the phone before breakfast. Told me he was just leaving to investigate two bear visits reported last night. Evidence of a real bear is piling higher almost daily—circumstantial, certainly, but then there's nothing shameful about circumstantial evidence. Ask any lawyer. Finally got to see Colby in person at his home. A real outdoor type, he has a den full of hunting licenses, woodsy relics, rifles, shotguns, bows and arrows. Has known bears since boyhood. Books he's written include *Who Went There?*, a juvenile about animal tracks. "There seem to be two classes of people in Briarcliff right now," he told me, "those who are dying to see the bear and those who don't

want any part of it." He paused, presumably waiting for me
to classify myself. I remained coolly noncommittal. Then he
told me that he had sent some of his bear-track photos to the
Museum of Natural History for possible authentication, but
that the pictures were too fuzzy for positive identification.
He showed me a letter from a mammalogist at the museum
saying, "It would not surprise us to get reports on bear in
this locality." Scientific open-mindedness. Colby said that
when he first scrutinized the Sparta tracks, he was tempted
to pass off the whole affair by announcing that they were
probably those of a big dog—a St. Bernard, say, or a Lab, or
a Newfie. But then his conscience nagged him, and made him
confess the animal might be a bear. Told me that bears are
not true hibernators, being often up and about during the
winter, especially after a lean fall. He was not surprised that
the bear was still at large. "A bear can outrun a dog, outrun
a horse, outrun a deer, and beat a chipmunk up a tree,"
he said. "The way I feel about our bear is that so many mature, responsible people here have reported seeing it that the
story *must* be true." I admitted sharing his slant. Sarah's
hearing is both mature and responsible. Colby said that when
he got the first bear report he called a game farm north of
Pawling, where there are seven bear cubs in captivity.
Thought maybe one had escaped. The owner said hold on,
and went out and counted. Seven. Colby now thinks maybe
our bear floated down the Hudson from the Adirondacks on
an ice cake. Just a theory. "This is the most interesting thing
that's happened in Briarcliff since I became a special protector," he told me. "I only wish I could find a perfectly beautiful paw print." I invited him down to have a gander at
mine, and he accepted with alacrity. Declined a drink when
we got to the house—sober, mature, responsible citizen.
Guided him to an unmelted patch of snow outside Sarah's
window. The ground was horribly trampled by now—dogs,
cats, squirrels, skunks, deer, Boy Scouts, trappers, breadman,

milkman, garbage men, Sarah, me. But two distinct, unmangled prints were still visible. Not perfect, not beautiful, but they looked persuasive to Colby. He was unwilling to make an unequivocal pronouncement on the basis of such skimpy evidence, but conceded that they were very possibly the footprints of *Ursus americanus* and, if so, the tracks of the closest wild bear there has ever been to New York City since it stopped being a village. Imagine! The most adventurous bear of them all, right in my own back yard!

With that last hysterical entry, my diary came to an abrupt and inconclusive halt. (I had occasion to regret this a couple of years later, when an Internal Revenue Service auditor asked for my records of the period.) And the furor the bear had aroused stopped almost as quickly. He was spotted twice more in Briarcliff, but he did no damage to anyone, and no one, I was delighted to learn, did any damage to him. I talked to a few big-city sophisticates afterward who, like the warden in Irvington, refused to take our bear seriously. Mainly to fortify myself with arguments against any more such skeptics I might encounter, I telephoned Dr. W. J. Hamilton, Jr., Professor of Zoölogy at Cornell and New York State's most eminent mammalogist. Dr. Hamilton had never previously heard of a wild bear nearer to New York City than the Catskills, but he said it seemed quite likely to him that our bear was the real thing, and, in terms of proximity to Times Square, it was therefore certainly a record-breaker. "Bears are wide-ranging creatures, and where they're concerned, nothing is impossible," he told me. "Heavens, there've been copperheads in Bronxville, so why not a bear in Briarcliff?"

Why not?, I thought, and "Why not?," I kept telling those doubting Thomases in our vicinity who spoofed the whole notion. Nobody claims to have seen a bear in our area since then, and from time to time I, who seem to have acquired the reputation of a pro-bear man in this lingering neighborhood controversy, have been subjected to ridicule, if not abuse, from the anti-bear forces. But there have been comforting voices mingled in with the chorus of contempt. During a debate on the subject at the Scarborough post office one day, when I was being cruelly badgered by pro-bear-baiters, a sweet, gentle, middle-aged woman who lives across the road from me sidled over and said, "Don't let them get you down. Why, with my own eyes I once saw an elephant in Scarborough."

In
the Quiet
of
Truro

Back in the days when a motor trip from Manhattan to the Yale Bowl was a journey not to be undertaken lightly, my family treated me, contemporaneously with my reading Longfellow's recapitulation of Myles Standish's odd courtship, to a ride all the way to Massachusetts, so I could gaze with suitable reverence upon Plymouth Rock, which I innocently believed for the next twenty-five years or so to be the site of the Pilgrims' first landing in the new world. We were supposed to go on to Cape Cod the next day, but something happened—conceivably, our car ran out of steam—and we didn't make it.

On my own, I almost made it to the Cape when, fresh out of college, I decided at noon one sunshiny autumn day to drive there, along with an adventurous bachelor friend. We headed northeast from midtown Manhattan, and on drawing abreast of the Yankee Stadium recalled that Bob Feller was pitching for the Cleveland Indians that day against the

home team. By the time the game was over and we'd retrieved our car, the weather had changed, it was cold and
damp, and the prospect of Cape Cod seemed uninviting. So
we turned around and drove to Miami instead.

My wife had been to Cape Cod often before we were married, and she had acted in a summer theatre there for several
seasons. So she was enthusiastic—as indeed, following my
earlier disappointments, was I—when in the winter of 1950
some close friends told us they were renting a house on the
Cape for a month that summer, at Truro, and why didn't we
rent one, too? They gave me the name of a local real-estate
agent, and after some correspondence I was able to report
that we had signed a lease, sight unseen, for a Truro house,
and how were our friends coming with theirs? "Oh, we forgot to tell you," they told us. "We've decided to go to Europe." They went to Europe and have been there ever since,
perhaps being embarrassed to face us.

That was how Jinny and I became summer residents of
the Cape, and I've been grateful ever since to our absent and
absent-minded friends for having lured us to the lovely spot.
Truro, along with Chatham, Orleans, Eastham, Wellfleet,
and Provincetown, is part of the Lower, or Outer Cape. Cape
Cod, which makes up most of Barnstable County, Massachusetts, is shaped like an arm. The upper arm, which is called
the Upper Cape, even though it's south of the Lower Cape,
is the seat of, among other communities, Oyster Harbors, an
island colony with gates and a uniformed sentry; Hyannis
Port, with John F. Kennedy; and Hyannis, which is the
Cape's hub and has on its outskirts a frowzy swarm of motels,
fried-clam shacks, pizza palaces, bowling alleys, and souvenir
shops. We go there as infrequently as possible.

Except for Provincetown, which is *sui generis,* the Lower
Cape, a narrow, spindly, thirty-mile-long spit of land, is a
more or less uncluttered area, and we go there as often as we

can. After traipsing over this bewitching stretch a century ago, Henry David Thoreau wrote, "If it is merely a ten-pin alley, or a circular railway, or an ocean of mint-julep, that the visitor is in search of—if he thinks more of the wine than the brine, as I suspect some do at Newport—I trust that for a long time he will be disappointed. . . . A man may stand there and put all America behind him." Thoreau's account of his briny stroll through the Lower Cape has just one puzzling aspect—his disclosure that he carried an umbrella. It must have been a nuisance to lug along the beach, and in a gusty Cape Cod rainstorm it couldn't have kept a clam dry.

Truro, where in Thoreau's day land was selling at twenty-five cents an acre, and where not long ago half an acre fetched twenty-five hundred dollars, is a small and unimposing town, but we love it. In 1954, we bought a house there, on a knoll in the Pamet River valley, after we had come to realize how fond we were of Truro, with its solid, plain old homes, its astonishingly smooth white beaches, its rolling dunes and moors, and its genial inhabitants—both the year-rounders and the "foreign element," as native Cape Codders sometimes refer to us summer people. (A Cape Cod paper said of a woman who died there, at the age of eighty-six, "While she was not one of us, she did much for the community during her eighty-four years on the Cape.")

The *Cape Codder,* a weekly paper published in Orleans, has called Truro "the most native town on the Cape." However that may be, it is certainly unpretentious. Almost every summer day, a tourist will pull in at the gas station in the center of town and ask, "Where's Truro?" "You're in the middle of it, Mister," is the conventional reply. The year 1959 was a big one for Truro, which was incorporated in 1709. On August 15th, the town's two-hundred-and-fiftieth anniversary was celebrated, with a communal picnic at midday and a ham-and-bean supper at the elementary school that evening (my wife was asked to contribute a pie, and baked a

blueberry one, using our own berries), followed by fireworks. These were launched by a Wellfleet man, Charles E.
Frazier, Jr. He is a licensed fireworks operator and usually
gets paid for putting on a show, but on this occasion, as a
neighborly gesture, he declined to accept a fee. Frazier was
born in Boston, but his parents were Wellfleet folk, so the
natives accept him as one of their own. He has been a Wellfleet selectman for over twenty years, as well as its leading
lawyer and one of its leading real-estate men. In addition, he
has been president of the Lower Cape Ambulance Association.

Versatility is characteristic of year-round Cape Codders.
Our town clerk in Truro, Thomas A. Kane, who lives a few
hundred yards from us on South Pamet Road, is also a schoolteacher and a newspaper columnist, and at one time or another in the last decade he has driven the ambulance, played
the trombone, tended bar, mowed lawns, and taken care of
the graveyard. Another Jack-of-many-trades is Arthur S. Joseph, who lives directly across the road from us. He is the off-
season custodian of most of the summer homes in the
vicinity, and has built or remodelled quite a few of them. He
drives the school bus, is a special police officer, and has the
garbage-collecting concession. Moreover, he was at last reckoning Truro's fire chief, tree warden, moth agent, and one
of its two fence viewers (arbitrating boundary squabbles),
field drivers (taking in stray cattle), and poundkeepers.

The year-rounders in Truro have to be many-sided to
keep the town going, for at the most recent formal count
there were only eight hundred and fifty-one of them. Truro
used to be much bigger. A hundred and twenty-five years
ago, the Pamet River, now a narrow, shallow, swamp-edged
stream, was broad and navigable, with a spacious harbor.
Truro then had a population of over two thousand and, to
‑tain it, a fleet of more than a hundred whalers and
‑rel boats, as well as dozens of flourishing saltworks. But

the river's harbor shoaled up, and salt deposits were found elsewhere, and one terrible October day in 1841 fifty-seven Truro fishermen were lost in a single storm. This boosted the number of widows in the town to a hundred and two, and houses like ours were to be had pretty much for the asking.

In Truro, as in the five other towns from Chatham out— which, all told, have a winter population of fifteen thousand and a summer population of seventy thousand—there is hardly any industry today save the furnishing of services to tourists and vacationers. The Cape Cod Chamber of Commerce makes a distinction between these two transient species; a tourist is someone who comes without a reservation and stays less than a week, whereas a vacationer books ahead and sticks around. Truro has a Chamber of Commerce of its own, which puts out a modest promotional booklet every year. The last edition I saw said, "Here in the quiet of Truro, we have no insomniacs. We guarantee the best night's sleep you've had since you were a baby."

Jinny and I always sleep well enough at Truro, but our first couple of summers there we had some unsettling moments. We had barely arrived, in 1950, when the manager of the summer theatre she'd worked in, discovering that she was back in the neighborhood, asked her if she would appear in one play, for old times' sake.

At first, I was opposed to this proposition. We had two sons by then—the oldest, Terry, was three; and his brother Joey was only eighteen months—and I pointed out to her that she had enough responsibilities as it was, without taking on any additional ones. She said in rebuttal that perhaps the trouble with our household wasn't so much that she had too many responsibilities as that I had too few.

"Don't be silly," I said. "What about the flag?"

Upon moving into our rented house we had found in front of it a lofty flagpole, at least fifty feet tall. Inside the house we had found a handsome flag of sufficiently ample size to fit the pole. I resolved at once to hang it there. I was excited at the prospect, partly because the Fourth of July was only a few days off and partly because I had never presided over a flagpole before. But on examining the pole closely I discovered that there wasn't any rope attached to it.

Fortunately, the caretaker of our place came by to ask if everything was satisfactory. Everything was, I replied, with a single exception—no rope for the flag. He received this news sympathetically, and the next day a man who had not only the versatility of a Cape Codder but also the agility of an acrobat showed up, shinnied to the summit of the pole, coaxed a rope over a pulley affixed there, and, after he had descended, knotted the two dangling rope ends together with an accomplished flourish.

After he'd departed, I realized that he hadn't put any clamps on the rope, to be attached to the metal grommets sewn into one end of our flag. I set off in our car and tried to buy a pair of clamps at every hardware store within twenty miles of Truro. No flag clamps anywhere. (This is not to insinuate that Cape Cod is unpatriotic. Indeed, it was my deduction at the time that the shortage of flag clamps was the result of an overabundance of flagpoles; the supply of clamps had been exhausted, that was all.)

Consequently, I had to resort to a rather inefficient method of flag-flying. Before breakfast—I shared then the prevalent belief that the flag may be flown only between sunrise and sundown—I would untie the rope, thread one end through the grommets, retie it, and then secure the flag with diaper pins to prevent it from sliding down. It took me quite a while to perform this operation every morning and to perform its reverse every evening, but the spectacle of my own flag fluttering proudly in the breeze off the dunes was reward enough 'or my expenditure of time and effort. Besides, our boys seemed to approve highly of the flag, and I was anxious not to inhibit this precocious manifestation of allegiance.

My wife finally convinced me that, despite the demands the flag was making on me, I could manage without her during a week of rehearsals and a week of performances, and she took the job. She was a trifle distressed, and so was I, when we looked over the script of the play. I had hoped to take Terry, at least, to see her in it, but it was patently unsuitable for him, since it had his mummy cast as an alcoholic dope fiend of sensationally wanton habits.

During one scene, she was called upon, after a vigorous scuffle with a gentleman friend, to stab herself, fall to the stage in a heap, and then be picked up bodily by her vis-à-vis and flung into a wooden chest. The producer had provided the chest with a mattress, but nonetheless she suffered some painful bruises during rehearsals. The actor who'd been assigned to manhandle her was a puny fellow, and he kept dropping her against the unpadded edges of the chest, rather than into its cushioned depths.

All this exercise seemed potentially hard, what was more, on Jinny's favorite evening dress, which, summer-theatre budgets being what they are, she had agreed to wear as her costume. She had made it herself the year before, and she was especially fond of it because it had figured in an odd colloquy at a fashionable supper party we'd attended during the winter. I had found myself seated alongside a handsome, dazzlingly accoutred woman, whose name I hadn't caught when we were introduced. When our small talk began to ebb, she'd looked over at Jinny and said, "That's a pretty dress your wife has on."

"Made it herself," I said, proudly. There was a pause, and then, to keep the conversational ball rolling, I said, "That's a pretty dress you have on, too."

The lady smiled graciously.

"Bet *you* didn't make *it* yourself," I said.
"I did, too," she said.
She'd turned out to be Valentina.

By opening night, my wife's co-player had learned fairly
well the knack of disposing of her humanely—though her
dress was as buffeted as driftwood—and as a result her spirits
were relatively high. So were mine; three people I had met
at the beach that morning had complimented me on the fine
appearance of our flag. Jinny was due at the theatre at seven
o'clock, in order to have plenty of time to make up. We were
just about to drive away from our house when I realized that
it would be dark long before we got back home and that I'd
better lower the colors right then. Jinny told me to hurry;
we were late as it was, she said. I ran to the flagpole and gave
one strand of rope a sharp tug. To my horror, instead of the
rope's sliding over the pulley and bringing the flag with it,
the knotted ends flew apart, leaving the flag still firmly
moored to the top of the pole, and on the short-rope-end side
of the pulley. There was obviously no way of getting the flag
down except to climb the pole.
"Hurry!" my wife yelled from the car.
"The flag's stuck!" I yelled back.
"Then leave it," she said.
"I can't," I said. "The flag's got to come down."
"The curtain's got to go up," she retorted.
What does one do, even in the most smoothly adjusted of
domiciles, when two such inviolable traditions crash head
on? I took one last, mournful look at the flag, crawled despairingly into the car, and drove off toward the theatre.
Maybe, I thought, it will be an uncommonly dark night—so
dark that anyone passing our house won't be able to see the
᾿gpole, much less the huge emblem of my dishonor being
᾿nly flaunted at its peak. But this rosy hypothesis was
        superseded by another: The moon would be full

and bright, the flag would be visible for miles around (as it was on a clear day), and within an hour after sunset a posse of vigilantes would gather at my house, waiting grimly to teach proper respect to the heretic in residence there. I didn't mention any of this to my wife, however; I figured she had enough on her mind.

I was in a bad way by the time we reached the theatre. My ebbing morale wasn't improved any, either, by a chat I had backstage with the actor who was scheduled to wrestle with Jinny an hour later. He had appeared in the same role once before, he told me, and on that occasion the knife in use had accidentally pinned his fellow-player's dress to the floor, obliging him, in order to dislodge her preparatory to crating her, to rip a couple of yards of material off her frock. I thought fleetingly of my wife's gown, wondering if Valentina would still like it cropped, and then I remarked that I didn't understand how a situation like that could occur, as I assumed they were going to employ a rubber dagger.

"Oh, no, we've got a real one," he said airily.

My wife gave an excellent performance. She played her part with such realism and verve, and so much ketchup, that I was sure she had actually been nicked, if not pierced clean through. She was impressively limp when the actor hauled her up from the floor (I was delighted to see that her entire dress came up with her) and dumped her into her repository. It was a good, clean shot, without recourse to any backboards. As soon as the play ended, I dashed backstage to make certain she was all right and, upon ascertaining she was, to congratulate her.

"I'm afraid I was too preoccupied to give much of a performance," she said. "I was so worried about you and the flag."

When we got home, the night was clear and the moon was brilliant. In its shimmering light, I saw one of the loveliest sights imaginable—our towering flagpole standing straight and firm without a scrap of flag appended to it, as bare as the Cape Cod dunes themselves.

Jinny sighed with relief. "I didn't dare mention it before now," she said, "because I didn't want to arouse any false hopes in you, but the acrobat must have made it all right."

"What do you mean?" I asked.

"Just before the curtain went up, I telephoned the care-taker and asked him to get his man over right away," she said. "I explained that it was an emergency. I guess he found him, all right."

I had a wonderful, peaceful night's sleep, just the kind the Truro Chamber of Commerce crows about, and I don't ever again want to hear anybody suggest that a woman can't suc-cessfully combine marriage and a career.

Our second year in Truro, my sister, who is a painter, came to spend a couple of weeks with us. She found the place and its environs so inspiring that she soon ran short of the ma-terials she'd brought with her. She borrowed our car one afternoon so she could stock up, nine miles away, in Province-town, a summer haven of countless salty painters and psy-chiatrists, not to mention an even vaster number of tourists who are curious about the summer habits of painters and psychiatrists. While she was gone, my wife took Terry into the bathroom to wash the sand out of his hair. Joey in the interim had begun to play with some toys in the door-way to my sister's room. I had a lot of reading that I was anxious to catch up on, so, during this lull in the household's activities, I went out on a porch and settled down con-tentedly with a reprint from the *Southern Medical Journal* of an article by a doctor of our acquaintance, entitled "Psy-osomatic Aspects of Cardiovascular Disease." I had d a provocative passage about a cardiological symptom spnea (difficult or labored breathing marked by a flattening of the diaphragm induced by emotional turmoil) when I heard my wife shout, "Bring Spock, quick!"

Just as a single wail of the village siren propels a volunteer fireman out of bed and into his pants, so did that familiar curt summons jerk me from my chair and to the living-room mantel. What Jinny had reference to, I knew, was *The Common Sense Book of Baby and Child Care*, by Dr. Benjamin Spock, a primer of practical advice on which parents slavishly rely in times of anger, fright, or bewilderment. I grabbed Spock from the mantel, where we had enshrined it, and raced to the bathroom. There I came upon my wife apprehensively regarding Joey, who was plastered with what appeared to be blood and had the stuff running out of his mouth.

"It's paint," Jinny said comfortingly. She held out a lacerated tube that Joey had filched from his aunt's room and chewed through. "I don't know how much he's eaten. What's Spock say to do?"

Fumblingly, I riffled through Spock's usually dependable pages. Only once had the book failed us—when Terry, after making friends with a stray dog, had skipped home bringing with him a colony of fleas; Spock had dealt appropriately with lice and worms but had ignored fleas. Now the Doctor seemed to be lax again; he listed antidotes, some of them quite drastic, for ammonia, arsenic, benzene, drain cleaner, ink, kerosene, lye, Lysol, mothballs, and shoe polish, but didn't mention paint. I conveyed this information, or lack of it, to my wife.

"What's the label on the tube say?" she asked, with astonishing calmness. "Maybe it contains something that's also in ink or mothballs."

" 'Grumbacher genuine casein color, cadmium red light,' " I read hoarsely. " 'Gouache tempera, artists' quality. Permanent. Pure cadmium sulfoselenide on barium sulfate. Vehicle: stable casein emulsion. Please, after your day's work, clean brushes with Grumbacher's Brush and Hand Cleaning Fluid or soap and water.' "

"What's all that mean?" cried Jinny.

"I don't know," I said. "I'll ask Dr. H——."

Dr. H—— lived just down the road from us and we had met him on the beach. I telephoned him. "What do we do for a child who has apparently eaten some pure cadium sulfoselen—" I began.

"I'm sorry, old man," he interrupted, "but I haven't practiced in ten years. I'm a hospital director, you know."

I rushed from the phone to the bathroom, where my wife was cleaning off our son—externally—with soap and water, as the Grumbacher label had suggested. The paint had a very unpleasant odor.

"Try the beach," she said. "It's probably crawling with doctors. Take the tube with you. Hurry."

It was lucky for me that the bathing beach we generally use was only a quarter of a mile off, considering that my sister had our car. I ran all the way, and was breathing heavily when I got there. I realized as soon as I tried to identify the bathers that I had left my glasses behind. Without them, I can't recognize faces too well at a distance. So I stumbled, panting, across the sand, peering under beach umbrellas in the hope of spotting a familiar physician, and probably causing not a few people to conclude that I needed the ministrations of one, what with my dyspnea and my being by then liberally smeared with the bloody contents of the tube. Finally, I staggered to the umbrella of a lady I knew and gasped out my predicament. She took the tube, tasted the paint, made a wry face, and said we shouldn't worry; a child would instinctively reject anything that tasted as dreadful as Grumbacher's gouache. I was momentarily cheered, but I knew ʼey's eccentricities; had I not seen him, three days earlier, ʼ dead horsefly off the porch floor and gobble it down? ` this disagreeable picture was flashing through my mind, the lady, who has better vision than I have, espied one of the summer-resident psychiatrists, an eminent émigré from Budapest or Bucharest or Vienna or some such place. She called to him and he came over. She introduced us. He bowed stiffly. I bowed limply. She explained the situation. "If you please," said the doctor, and reached for the tube of paint.

I handed it to him, and he began to read the label, or what little of it hadn't been obliterated by Grumbacher's oozing gouache. Suddenly he noticed that the paint was coming off on his fingers. Aghast, he returned the tube to me, stooped and picked up a bit of driftwood, and tried to clean off his hand with it. He merely got paint on the other hand. He slashed at his palms with mounting frenzy, and then scampered off toward the ocean, holding both hands carefully away from his body, as if he were a surgeon tidying up for an operation.

I ran back home and found Joey clean and placid, though still exuding a repellent odor. My wife told me that in my absence she had managed to get another doctor on the phone, and that he had told her that if the paint had produced no ill effects during the first few minutes, it wasn't likely to ever. We decided we might as well forget about it and all go to the beach for a swim, which turned out to be a sound decision. On our way, we met the lady who had gallantly eaten the paint on my behalf. She was heading for our house with a message from the psychiatrist, and she delivered it to us through vermilion-flecked teeth. The doctor had left the beach hurriedly, she said, a few moments after my consultation with him. "He said," she went on, "that he thought warm water would probably be a help." She wasn't sure, and I don't know to this day, whether he meant for Joey's stomach or his own hands.

Our own medical problems that trying day were insignificant, though, compared to those of another psychiatrist who once, but only once, vacationed briefly in Truro. He had some consultative connection or other with prisons, and after a particularly debilitating year of rehabilitative toil he came to the Lower Cape for a rest. He hadn't even un-packed his car when he was questioned, rather severely, by the local police, who detected in him a striking resemblance to the description a young girl had given them a few hours earlier of a man who'd tried to molest her. A few hours later, fortunately, the real culprit was flushed, but not before the doctor's mind had visualized the grim headline, "SING SING PSYCHIATRIST HELD ON ATTEMPTED RAPE CHARGE."

While the psychiatrist was still breathing heavily after that ordeal, he got a phone call from the house next door. Emergency. The tenants' daughter's cat had just been in a dreadful fight, and they couldn't find any other doctor, and would he please come right over and save the pet before it bled to death. He sat up all that night with the cat, and, somewhat to his surprise, pulled it through. The *next* night, he was the guest of honor at a welcome-to-Truro party, and while he was chatting amiably with a perfectly sober man he'd never laid eyes on before, the fellow suddenly keeled over in what, near as the psychiatrist could recall from his dimly remembered medical-school training, had all the symptoms of a massive heart attack. No sleep that night, either. A day or two after that, the psychiatrist quietly left Truro, and he hasn't been seen there since. Somebody told me he went to Minnesota, permanently, and I don't blame him.

The Soil
Where
First They
Trode

Usually, our family travels to and from Truro by car. It is easier now than it used to be; the Connecticut Turnpike has opened, and, even better from our viewpoint, we no longer have a cook who used to abash us by bridling angrily every time that, just east of Providence, Rhode Island, we traversed the Segregansett River. Flying to Cape Cod is quick, but chancy, on account of fog; and the only time I ever essayed to make the trip by railroad, I got into a terrible fix.

I happened to be on the same train with several carloads of Fresh Air Fund children, en route to a seashore holiday. As I passed through one of their cars on my way back from the diner, an engaging urchin grabbed my sleeve and asked if I'd fetch his bag down from the luggage rack overhead. "Why, sure, sonny," I said, and did his bidding.

"Hey, Mister," cried a child across the aisle, "gimme mine, too!"

"Mine's the blue one up there!" his seatmate called out.

"Here, Mister, here!"

"Please, Mister, that one!"

Soon the car rang with admonitions, while I tugged and hauled like a longshoreman, consumed with self-admiration for my good deeds. I had about half the suitcases in sight down at floor level when a chaperon who'd been dozing at one end of the car lurched to her feet and yelled, "What do you think *you're* doing?"

"Just giving the kids a helping hand, ma'am," I said self-deprecatingly.

"They're not supposed to get their paws on that stuff till they get off the train," she wailed.

An instant later, I could see what she meant, but by then it was too late, for the children had opened up their bags, and apples, oranges, and balled-up socks were flying through the air in one of the merriest free-for-alls I ever witnessed. Under cover of the barrage, I withdrew hastily to my own car, and hid in a compartment.

In some ways, the most enjoyable excursion we regularly make to the Cape is an annual Thanksgiving pilgrimage with our own fresh kids, now three in number. Since establishing ourselves as warm-weather residents of Truro, my wife and I have found that our interest in the Pilgrims and their traditions has increased enormously. Though we live there not far from the Pamet River, this once broad but now modest stream is hidden from us by the high-bush blueberries, poison ivy, and other native flora that border it; and no one ventures from our house to the Pamet, aside from an occasional boy, on exploration bent, or an agent of the Cape Cod Mosquito Control Project, on business. Still, even though we cannot see the Pamet, we find it agreeable to reflect that in the late fall of 1620, a month before they touched the soil of Plymouth, a band of armor-clad Pilgrims, led by Myles Standish, tramped this river's banks, within musket shot of a patch of land where we pick blueberries and the mosquitoes pick on us.

From Corn Hill, a bluff in Truro where the hungry Pilgrims unearthed, and appropriated, a cache of Indian corn, one can look down to the end of the Cape and there see Provincetown, whose skyline is dominated by a giant granite shaft. Modelled on an Italian campanile, the tower soars up two hundred and fifty-two feet from the crest of a hundred-foot hill right in the center of the town. Many newcomers to the Cape are puzzled to learn that this eye-catcher, a little over twenty miles from Plymouth across Cape Cod Bay and eighty miles overland, is a monument to the Pilgrims. The simple explanation is that Provincetown is where the Forefathers first stepped ashore after sixty-six dismal days on the Atlantic. This welcome event occurred on November 11, 1620—November 21st, according to our present calendar —on a stretch of sand that is now marked by a simple, five-foot-high block of stone. Near it, on a brick wall, is a bronze plaque inscribed with several lines from the renowned poem "The Landing of the Pilgrim Fathers," written in 1825 by Felicia Hemans. Mrs. Hemans, an Englishwoman, did not identify her "stern and rock-bound coast" beyond alluding to it as a wild New England shore, but it can reasonably be inferred that she was thinking of Plymouth as the Pilgrims' initial port of call. The citizens of Provincetown who put up the plaque declined, however, to make any such inference, and among the lines they immortalized in bronze, with obvious pride in their own shore, not Plymouth's, are these:

> *Ay, call it holy ground,*
> *The soil where first they trode.*

The Pilgrims spent five weeks on Cape Cod, or anchored just off it. The Mayflower had hardly come to rest in Provincetown Harbor when most of the adult male immigrants assembled in the ship's cabin and subscribed to the celebrated Mayflower Compact, by which they pledged themselves to adopt a fairly democratic way of life in this country. (Thomas Kane, our town clerk in Truro, is also a local historian, and he argues that the Compact was signed in Truro Harbor, but not many scholars share this chauvinistic view.) The following day—Sunday, November 12th— everybody stayed aboard the Mayflower, at worship. The day after that, the Pilgrim women went ashore for the first time and set about scrubbing the salt and grime out of their families' clothing. It was thus that Monday became this nation's traditional washday.

All in all, the Pilgrims had a wide range of experiences during their sojourn on the Cape. Dorothy Bradford, the wife of William Bradford, who was one of their leaders and later became their Governor, drowned in Provincetown Harbor; Peregrine White, who lived to see the eighteenth century, was born on the ship while it was at anchor there. Expeditions fanned out from Provincetown to Truro, where they found not only the corn but also a freshwater spring, now called Pilgrim Spring, and on to Eastham, another ten miles up the Cape, where a brief and bloodless skirmish with some Indians took place, on a beach now called First Encounter Beach. Finally, on December 20th—December 30th, by present-day reckoning—the Mayflower began letting off its passengers at Plymouth, which, as some Provincetown people are fond of pointing out, was then also known as Thievish Harbor. (Several expeditions had previously explored that stretch of the coast, and an Indian had stolen a harpoon from the members of one of them.)

Since the Mayflower was a bulky vessel, ninety feet long and with a displacement of about a hundred and eighty tons, she could hardly have come close to Plymouth Rock. Whether the small boat in which her passengers were ferried ashore got anywhere near the Rock is debatable. Even in

Plymouth it is admitted that the tradition of the Pilgrims' landing on Plymouth Rock hangs on nothing more substantial than the conceivably faltering memory of a resident named Elder Thomas Faunce, who in 1741, at the age of ninety-five, suddenly recalled that as a boy he had heard someone say they did. That sort of evidence would never stand up in court—at least, not in a Provincetown court.

Anyway, whether or not the nonagenarian's testimony is regarded as decisive, Provincetown has little respect for the Rock. To Provincetown, a second landing, no matter where, is a pitiable anticlimax. One Provincetown official, a baseball fan, told me that the Plymouth landing stands in relation to the Provincetown landing as a post-season barnstorming tour by the two teams in a World Series would stand in relation to the Series—the same dramatis personae, perhaps, but none of the significance. To this contention, Plymouth could, of course, retort that the Pilgrims' stay on Cape Cod was analogous to spring training, and that the landing at Plymouth, where the Forefathers chose to make their home, was the start of the regular season. The Plymouth people could also retort that if in Provincetown eyes the Rock is just a rock, why do Provincetown fishermen keep threatening to sneak across Cape Cod Bay some moonless night in one of their squat and sturdy vessels, tear the Rock from its moorings with grappling hooks, and haul it back to their own thievish harbor?

Naturally, no one in Provincetown tries to contest Plymouth's one great, unimpeachable claim to fame—that of being the scene of the Pilgrims' first permanent colonial settlement. What Provincetown laments is that few people distinguish between the first landing and the first colony. Most Americans—facts or no facts, campanile or no campanile—believe, as I used to, that the Pilgrim Fathers sailed straight from Plymouth, England, to Plymouth Rock, and the myth is now so deeply rooted in the national consciousness that it could probably never be pried out. (In the Midwest, a few years back, the jackpot question on a quiz show was "Where did the Pilgrims first land?" A whole flock of contestants flubbed it by confidently answering "Plymouth," before somebody came up with a hesitant, prize-winning "Provincetown.") As a rueful editorial in the weekly Provincetown *Advocate* put it not long ago, "Plymouth is in an enviable position."

In 1956, a replica of the Mayflower—or, rather, what purports to be a replica, for nobody knows exactly what the ship looked like—sailed across the Atlantic, theoretically duplicating the voyage of its forefather, as a good-will gesture to the United States. It was built, at a cost of some three hundred thousand dollars, under the auspices of a British group called Project Mayflower, Ltd. Good will? Not around Provincetown. Project Mayflower was thought up by a couple of British public-relations men, one of whom, on a preliminary visit to Plymouth, may also have strained the good will of that town's patriots, by placing his bowler squarely on top of the Rock and having himself photographed beside the embellished shrine.

The British, as a matter of fact, can be held chiefly accountable for all the confusion about the landing. While evacuating Boston during the Revolution, they took along the principal source of reliable information about the Pilgrims' early movements—the manuscript of Governor Bradford's history, "Of Plimoth Plantation," which gives Provincetown its due. From 1775 to 1855, this work appeared to have been lost. Then it was discovered in the library of the Bishop of London, and after forty-two more years had passed, it was returned to the United States. (It is now in the Massachusetts State House, in Boston—a location that Provincetown views as hardly ideal but considerably more palatable than Plymouth would be.) Many of today's history books give the impression of having been written while Bradford's text languished in obscurity. Not that there is any conformity among the historians. The Encyclopædia Britannica, for example, careens wildly on a pro-Provincetown tack, going so far as to assert that Provincetown sheltered a Pilgrim settlement from 1620 on—a claim that not even the Provincetown Chamber of Commerce would dare make. Webster's Dictionary, on the other hand, ignores Provincetown entirely in its entry for the Pilgrim Fathers. (It does mention the Pilgrims under "Provincetown," in its Gazetteer, but what uninformed student in search of Pilgrim lore would think of looking there?) And some contemporary reference works don't commit themselves one way or the other. The Encyclopedia of American History, published in 1953, has its Pilgrims sighting Cape Cod and deciding to land "nearby." It doesn't say nearby what.

School children in Provincetown are fed the story straight, for among their textbooks are some written by Lewis Paul Todd, a historian who lives in Truro and can stare at the Provincetown monument any time he wants to get his bearings. But the thirst of youngsters in many other regions for the facts about their nation's history is often strangely slaked. The kind of thing that makes Provincetown people writhe is a passage like this, from *The Making of Modern America,* a high-school textbook: "Finally they landed far to the north on the bleak shores of Cape Cod Bay in December of 1620. The Pilgrims made friends with some of the neighboring Indians and soon laid the foundations of a small community, which they called Plymouth." (The place had first been called Plymouth by Captain John Smith in 1614, long before the Pilgrims left England, much less laid any foundations.) Even *A Basic History of the United States,* by the usually dependable Charles and Mary Beard, declares flatly that the Mayflower Compact was signed as the Pilgrims' ship "rode in the harbor of Plymouth."

Needless to say, there are plenty of textbooks that have the
landing story right, but for every one of these there is one
like *A History of Our Country,* by the reputable professor
David S. Muzzey, who says that the Pilgrims "reached the
shores of Cape Cod . . . but instead of proceeding south-
ward they decided to stay where they were and, landing on
the low, sandy shore of Plymouth harbor. . . ." In Provincetown, the most charitable interpretation put on this version
is that Muzzey is fuzzy.

In 1955, *Holiday* published an article entitled "Where the
Pilgrims Landed." Among its two thousand and some words,
"Provincetown" never once appeared, but among those that
did appear were a freewheeling handful asserting that the
Pilgrims "first set foot in the New World" in Plymouth.
Provincetown is used to that sort of thing. A year earlier, another monthly, *Family Circle,* had carried in its Thanksgiving issue an article about the Pilgrims, prepared with the
assistance of the Plymouth Chamber of Commerce, in which
Provincetown was not mentioned, either, and in which Plymouth was described as "jealously guarding its Pilgrim heritage."

Most people in Provincetown will grimly agree that Plymouth does guard its Pilgrim heritage jealously, and some of
the more cynical among them would substitute the adverb
"avariciously." "Why do they have to name hens and hot
dogs and gelatine and everything after Plymouth Rock?" a
Provincetown civic leader asked me bitterly one day, making
it clear that there exists a potential market of at least one
for a product called Provincetown Sand Gelatine. One of the
reasons Plymouth guards its heritage so diligently is economic in origin. "Frankly, this place would be a ghost town
without the tourist business," the secretary of the Plymouth
Chamber once told me, and it's not hard to understand why
tourists flock to the town, for, as the distinguished historian
Samuel Eliot Morison has written, "The landing of the Pil-

grim Fathers on Plymouth Rock is perhaps the best known event of American history." (Morison is an anti-Provincetown—or, perhaps more accurately, a non-Provincetown—historian. In *The Growth of the American Republic*, on which he and Henry Steele Commager collaborated, the authors state that on November 11, 1620, the Pilgrims landed "in the harbor of Cape Cod," and when they first identify any harbor at all, a page later, it is "the harbor already named Plymouth.")

The town of Plymouth is too upright to make any false claims for its Rock, but on the cover of a Chamber of Commerce brochure bearing the phrase "See Historical Plymouth Mass. First," the word "first" is blown up and is juxtaposed with a photograph of the Rock in such a way that a careless reader might easily just associate those two and overlook everything else. At the Rock itself, signs proclaim it as "Landing Place of the Pilgrims." Not *"First* Landing Place," honorably enough, but not *"A* Landing Place" or *"Another* Landing Place," either. Just "Landing Place." (Apparently, no one has thought of borrowing the tactful expression "final landing," which Calvin Coolidge applied to the Rock in 1920, when, as Governor of Massachusetts, he had friends in both Plymouth and Provincetown.)

In Plymouth there is a detachment of young men in Pilgrim costume on hand during the summer to enlighten visitors about the Rock, and they, laudably, make no attempt to hedge. Their forthright set spiel goes, in part, "Now, contrary to the popular belief that has sprung up in recent years, the Pilgrims did not first land at Plymouth Rock." ("Recent," in Plymouth, is apt to be applied to any year subsequent to 1741.) This confession by the guides usually causes consternation among some tourists, and one can almost hear them mutter, "In that case, what am I doing here?" Then the guides, possibly motivated by a sense of civic guilt, take a deep breath and rewrite history in Provincetown's favor. They say that the Pilgrims stayed there for two whole months, thereby landing them in Plymouth in the lustreless year of 1621.

The cascade of historical literature with which the present-day pilgrim to Plymouth finds himself deluged is, on the whole, fair enough to Provincetown, although the latter town is sometimes assumed to have had a rather low place in the Forefathers' esteem. "Plymouth Rock—Its History and Its Significance," a pamphlet the Pilgrim Society of Plymouth published in 1954, states, "The Pilgrims' first problem after casting anchor in Provincetown Harbor was to find a suitable place to settle," thus implying that after one look the Pilgrims decided Provincetown was no place for them. The literature, as I discovered during a landing of my own at Plymouth, often leaves it up to the reader to deduce for himself what's been what. I had barely finished reading a monograph put out by the Massachusetts Department of Commerce, in which I read that "Plymouth is the birthplace of the town meeting form of government," when a lady in Colonial costume handed me a booklet called "The Pilgrim Story," which informed me that the signing of the Compact, in Provincetown Harbor, is "generally accepted as the first New England town meeting." This booklet referred to Provincetown as a "haven of refuge" for the Pilgrims, a description that to many Plymouth ears must sound downright subversive, for Plymouth boosters like to stress the fact that the death of half the Mayflower's passengers in Plymouth during their first winter in the New World was the direct result of respiratory and other afflictions they had acquired on the inhospitable sands across the Bay. This emphasis reflects Plymouth's condescending attitude toward Provincetown. "Sure the Pilgrims landed in Provincetown," a Plymouth Chamber of Commerce man told me. "But the Cape had nothing to offer them. It still hasn't much to offer. We get a much higher class of visitor here."

Nearly three-quarters of a million people, of all classes, visit Plymouth Rock each year; about twenty-five thousand visit the Provincetown tower. These figures are perhaps as good an explanation as any of Provincetown's discontent. But there are other galling circumstances. The Compact was signed in Provincetown Harbor, yet where is the table on which it was signed? In Plymouth. Peregrine White was born in Provincetown Harbor, yet where is his cradle? In Plymouth. (The best Provincetown can boast is a small-scale reproduction of it.) Provincetown has a stone from a wall in the yard outside the church, in Austerfield, England, where Bradford was baptized; Plymouth has a slice of molding from the church itself. Bradford declared in his history, "All great and honorable actions are accompanied with great difficulties, and must be both enterprised and overcome with answerable courages." Provincetown is doing its best to keep its chin up in its battle for recognition, but new difficulties are forever arising. A few summers ago, the Cape Cod Chamber of Commerce, an outfit whose sympathies would presumably be on the side of Provincetown (its headquarters are in Hyannis), ran a newspaper advertisement that gave prominent display to a map of the Cape and some of its environs, including Plymouth. On the map appeared the figure of a lone Pilgrim. And where was he perched? On Plymouth. A couple of years before that, the nonpartisan, or so one would expect, Commonwealth of Massachusetts got out a road map on which Pilgrim Spring, in Truro, was labelled "Plymouth Spring." And the *Cape Cod Guide,* a piece of tourist literature widely distributed on the Cape, has far more to say about Plymouth and the Pilgrims than about Provincetown and the Pilgrims, perhaps because the *Guide* is edited and published off the Cape—specifically, in Plymouth.

Provincetown has not taken all this lying down. The head of its own Chamber of Commerce has a plucky way of saying, when someone mentions Plymouth, "Plymouth—where's that? You mean Plymouth, Oregon?" But he couldn't have been thinking about Oregon in 1955 when his Chamber put up a large billboard within the town limits of Plymouth, Massachusetts. "Come to Provincetown, FIRST Landing Place of the Pilgrims," it read, and it showed a picture of the Provincetown campanile. When the secretary of the Plymouth Chamber of Commerce, a man who wore Pilgrim dress in President Eisenhower's first inaugural parade, saw this, he exclaimed, in pure John Aldenese, "Jeez, they got a hell of a nerve putting up something like that in Plymouth!" Some outraged custodians of Plymouth's Pilgrim heritage tried to have the word "first" stricken from the signboard, but Provincetown, having bought the space, wouldn't stand for that. Plymouth ultimately got its revenge for this affront. A radio station, WPLM, began broadcasting from there, carrying plug after plug for Pilgrim Plymouth. "It's beamed right into Provincetown!" a Plymouth man told me, cackling hilariously. "They get wonderful reception there!"

Given enough of a start, a fast-rolling legend can usually stay comfortably ahead of any plodding fact, and it is one of Provincetown's handicaps that in seeking its share of Pilgrim glory it got going too late, and with too little. Whereas, even on the hottest days, Plymouth abounds with natives in Pilgrim dress, Provincetown, as a rule, has only one—the Town Crier. Provincetown's simple, five-foot-high memorial at the first landing place wasn't put up until 1917, while Plymouth has been honoring the Rock practically ever since Elder Faunce's memory was jogged.

The Provincetown campanile, it is true, has a fairly long

history. As far back as 1852, there was talk in Provincetown of putting up a lofty landmark along the line of the present one, but nothing much was done about it until the beginning of this century, when a concerted drive to raise money for the monument got under way. In 1906, Congress appropriated forty thousand dollars toward the ninety-two thousand needed for the campanile, thereby proving that the government of the United States, if not many of its citizens, has long been aware of Provincetown's rightful place with respect to the Pilgrims. (The appropriation was voted after some hearings during which a director of the Cape Cod Pilgrim Memorial Association, a nonprofit organization that sponsored and still maintains the tower, said, "There is no rivalry nor ill-feeling between Provincetown and Plymouth. We recognize the importance of Plymouth as the place of the Pilgrim settlement, and Plymouth people are generally cordial to this project.") President Theodore Roosevelt visited Provincetown in 1907 to lay the cornerstone of the tower, and three years later President Taft came along to dedicate the finished job. (It is indicative of the paucity of authentic Pilgrim mementos in Provincetown that its historical museum exhibits a one-dollar bill hallowed merely by the fact that Roosevelt gave it as a tip to his carriage driver that day.)

Set in the inside walls of the tower, and visible from a winding ramp by which sightseers can climb to the summit, is a series of stone tablets, each presented to Provincetown by a friendly community or by a regional branch of the General Society of Mayflower Descendants, and each inscribed with the name of its donor. A hundred and thirty-three of these stones were installed at the time the tower was built, and since then thirty-nine more have been contributed and put into place, including one from Plymouth. By design or accident, the Plymouth slab is so placed that unless a visitor looks hard for it, he is almost certainly bound to miss it.

Of all the gadflies Provincetown ever hatched to buzz at Plymouth, indisputably the peskiest was Harry Kemp, the eccentric, imaginative, and effervescent poet, who died in 1960, aged seventy-six. Once a ruggedly bohemian ornament of Greenwich Village, Kemp lived in Provincetown for more than forty years. He called himself the Poet of the Dunes, and often wrote with a quill plucked from a sea gull's wing. His reflections on Pilgrim history inspired him to compose, among hundreds of other verses, a number of taunting couplets that the Provincetown Town Crier can sometimes be heard reciting. A sample goes:

> *Ring loud this story from coast to coast:*
> *Provincetown's true glory is Plymouth's*
>   *false boast.*

Kemp belonged to the old Provincetown Players, and was a friend and drinking companion of Eugene O'Neill in the playwright's Cape Cod days. Subsequently, when Kemp was not living in a driftwood shack on the rolling dunes near the town, he made his home in a grubby storeroom back of a real-estate office on its main street. He found the latter setting congenial partly because he paid no rent and partly because O'Neill's former lodgings were directly overhead. (Provincetown once put a plaque there honoring the playwright, but, being an eccentric community, spelled his name "O'Neil.") Kemp championed Provincetown's cause and propagandized against what he called "the hoax of the Rock" for more than a decade, not always with the unanimous approval of his fellow-townsfolk. He came in for criticism once when he used a bottle of gin to christen a roadside sign showing the way to the Pilgrims' first landing place. The poet calmly defended himself by saying that the Pilgrims were gin drinkers and that he could conceive of no beverage more appropriate for the ceremony. Later, he tried hard to find a sponsor for a twelve-foot granite statue of a Pilgrim laundress he wanted to have set up in Provincetown in commemoration of the first Monday Washday. He invited the nation's soap companies to get together and become joint patrons of this project, but their reactions were lukewarm. Since his death, Provincetown has been raising funds to have the statue put up—if only in plaster—as a memorial to *him.*

Kemp looked upon his struggle to educate other Americans about Provincetown as a crusade, and, like many crusaders before him, he was not only militant but often quite lonely. He presided over the Provincetown Pilgrims' Association, which he founded in order to give his crusade institutional dignity, but it attracted only a dozen or so members, and even within this limited group there was strife. A vice-president resigned after President Kemp, miffed at something or other this subordinate had said, rapped on the door of his home at one o'clock in the morning and challenged him to come out and fight.

The Association has never been highly thought of in Plymouth. On its stationery, which has a flamboyant letterhead bearing the inscription "Provincetown—Where the Pilgrims First Landed," Kemp once wrote to the chairman of the Board of Selectmen of Plymouth, calling upon him to issue a formal proclamation of Provincetown's priority in the Mayflower's itinerary. Kemp received a frosty reply stating that the Board "has no desire or intent to deviate from the recorded pages of the established history of the United States." The Board failed to indicate which of the conflicting recorded pages of established American history it had no desire or intent to deviate from.

Every now and then, Kemp would stride boldly into Plymouth, usually wearing a flowing toga and a wreath of wintergreen—a plant he regarded as better suited than laurel to his kind of poetry. He made one such trip, thus attired, in 1952, to attend the première of *Plymouth Adventure,* a Metro-Goldwyn-Mayer motion picture about the Pilgrims. The film was a grave disappointment to Kemp. While it was being made, he had written a spirited letter to Dore Schary, its producer, urging him not to slight Provincetown, and had backed this up by getting five hundred and fifty-one Provincetown school children to sign a petition imploring Schary to pay strict attention to history and also to please hold the world première of the picture in Provincetown. To the children, Schary replied sonorously, "You may be sure that we will spare no effort in this challenging enterprise to bring faithfully, and with integrity, to the screen such great moments as the Signing of the Mayflower Compact and The First Landing of the Pilgrims," and added that he was seriously considering holding the première in Provincetown.

When M-G-M decided to hold it in Plymouth instead, Kemp was angry. On seeing the film, which gave Provincetown the brushoff, he was incensed. He went home and composed a poetic diatribe entitled "Agenda for the Denunciation of Dore Schary," which he later intoned in the streets of both Provincetown and Plymouth. In Plymouth, too, Kemp once got into a fiery debate with a man who told him that the Pilgrims' stopover in Provincetown had been so transitory that it couldn't really be called a landing. "If that wasn't a landing," Kemp shouted, nearly tripping over his robe in his agitation, "you'd better dig Webster up from his grave and have him redefine the word."

Kemp was an exceptional swimmer. He took a dip in the ocean every day, summer or winter. It was his notion that an annual swimming event—the American Channel Swim, he called it—over the twenty miles or so of water from Provincetown to Plymouth would do much to remind people that the Pilgrims followed the same course, and in 1954, in an effort to stir up interest in his proposal, he staged a preview of what the Swim might be like. Kemp was unable to recruit anyone who could negotiate the entire distance, but he assembled a handful of reasonably proficient swimmers, including four attractive young ladies. With the poet, dressed as Neptune, leading the way, the party plunged into the water at Provincetown and struck out for Plymouth. "We took off with no previous concatenation of effort, but we swam like an aquacade, even though one of the girls had a terrible hangover," Kemp once told me. After several hundred yards of splashing and groaning, the aquacade was hauled up onto the deck of an accompanying fishing boat, which then chugged on across the Bay. Half a mile off Plymouth, the swimmers, revived and fortified by red wine, took to the water again, and made their way to the Rock. Kemp had hoped to be met and thrown into stocks by a throng of irate Plymouth officials dressed in Pilgrim costumes, but Plymouth, not wanting to participate in any stunt that might publicize Provincetown, totally ignored the dripping invaders. The following summer, Kemp persuaded a survivor of the previous year's incursion to strike out for Plymouth once more, on a non-stop basis. But after covering almost half the course, Kemp's man had to be pulled from the water. His ribs hurt, and it subsequently developed he had broken one of them the day before. Such is the poet's lot in the modern world.

Kemp had diabetes, and, of course, kept going with the help of insulin. "It makes me feel glorious!" he said to me. "My God, it's by a miracle of science that I can write my great poetry and enjoy the adventure of life!" He found a gratifying use for the little glass containers his insulin came in. He would fill them with sand from the beach the Pilgrims first landed on and send them to eminent citizens, along with this homemade couplet:

> *Not on Plymouth Rock but on Province-*
> *town sand,*
> *The Pilgrim Fathers first came to land.*

Kemp was conscientious about the sand he shipped out. "I'm no paragon of virtue, but you've got to do the right thing," he would say. "If I used sand from any old place, instead of from right where they landed, I'd soon be doing something even more corrupt, and eventually I'd be thoroughly corrupted. So I go straight to the landing place and get my sand there, and I have somebody watch me to make sure." He sent his grainy tokens to the governors of all the states and of Hawaii, when it was still a territory. He hoped Hawaii would send him in return some long-distance swimmers for his American Channel Swim, and pointed out that Hawaii could benefit hugely from the publicity it would derive from the affair. "If you want statehood, come and swim for it," he wrote. But Hawaii begged off. To deliver some Provincetown sand to the Governor of Massachusetts, Kemp, wearing a Pilgrim costume, flew to Boston in 1950 in a plane operated by the Provincetown-Boston Airline, which runs a direct shuttle service between the two ports and has the inexact, if heartfelt, slogan "The Route of the Pilgrims." On this particular flight, however, the plane did not follow its regular route. Instead, it detoured to Plymouth, where it dived low over the Rock. Leaning out of a window and taking careful aim, Kemp gleefully bombed Plymouth Rock with Provincetown sand. He thought he hit his target, and felt sure that even if he didn't, the Forefathers would have understood and appreciated the gesture.

On every November 21st from 1947 on, Kemp duplicated, after a fashion, the Pilgrims' first landing. He would dress a few men, women, and children in Pilgrim trappings, which a fisherman's wife made for him, take the party off shore in a fishing boat, and then row them in to the stern and sand-bound coast of Provincetown, where they all struck suitable poses of thankfulness and Kemp read a poem—a different one every year—that he composed for the rite. "God, what words!" he was heard to exclaim after one recital. "Did they come out of me? They're good!"

After one reënactment, Kemp took a jagged piece of streaky brown wood, roughly two inches square, out of his pocket and reverently floated it on the water. This object, which he usually kept in a cigar box, was, he believed, a fragment of the Mayflower. It was given to him in 1950 by the late Hamilton Holt, for many years president of Rollins College, in Florida. One of the dormitories there is called Mayflower Hall, and has a much larger hunk of similar wood embedded in it. Both pieces of wood were taken from a barn in Buckinghamshire, England, whose rafters, many people maintain, were once part of the Mayflower's hull. Another school of thought holds that the Mayflower sank, and was lost for all time, in the North Sea in 1623. It is known, though, that in 1624 some surveyors appointed by the High Court of the Admiralty appraised the Pilgrims' ship at around a hundred and twenty-five pounds sterling, so even if she sank, it would seem that part of her, at least, was salvaged. Whatever the case, it has been established that there were a score or so British ships named Mayflower afloat around 1620, and there is no proof that the timbers in the Buckinghamshire barn, if they did come from a Mayflower, came from *the* Mayflower. Kemp was not bothered by such quibbles. "Plymouth hasn't got a piece of the Mayflower," he would say. "We have!"

One ambition of Kemp's Provincetown Pilgrims' Association was to get a full-scale replica of the Pilgrims' Mayflower. This was also a primary goal of a more influential group, in Plymouth—the Plimoth Plantation, which has been responsible for constructing a number of Pilgrim-style buildings there. When the sponsors of the English-built replica of the Mayflower not only implied that she might bypass Provincetown after crossing the Atlantic but disclosed that they were going to turn her over to the Plimoth Plantation, Kemp was furious. He dashed off indignant cables to Sir Winston Churchill and Queen Elizabeth, neither of whom replied—in her case, possibly because he had couched his protest in Elizabethan language.

After a time, Kemp prevailed on the Selectmen of Provincetown and the president of the Cape Cod Pilgrim Memorial Association, a neighbor who was also president of Provincetown's principal bank, to cable additional protests. The banker got an answer: The Queen, a royal secretary had been commanded to inform him, felt that the issue under discussion was outside her province. Kemp then declared that if the new Mayflower bypassed Provincetown, he'd have a band of robust fishermen standing by to go after her in an armed trawler, fire a shot across her bow, and compel her to come about and follow the Pilgrims' course. He won out, after a fashion; on its way to Plymouth, the ship did briefly poke its squat nose—it had to be tugged—into Provincetown's expectant harbor. But despite the port's valiant efforts, the facts about the Pilgrims are unlikely ever to catch up with the legends their peregrinations inspired. Maybe it doesn't matter too much, and maybe some day the people of both Plymouth and Provincetown will eventually heed the metrical summation that Kemp, evidently caught by his Muse with his guard down, wrote with his sea-gull's-quill pen a few years before his death:

> *What matter where they landed first,*
> *Or where the infancy was nursed*
> *Of this our great and favored land—*
> *Whether upon the Rock or sand?*

The Man
Who
Cried Wolf

For years, I've been reading enviously about other people's children and the special treats they enjoy—Queen Elizabeth's riding in state coaches, Leonard Lyons' playing ball with Joe DiMaggio, and so on down the privileged line. When my son Terry became eight, in 1955, and could read himself, he also became just as aware of the perquisites of the élite as I had long been, and he began nagging at me to cut him in on the star dust—dinner at the White House, Davy Crockett's autograph, *anything*. I sensed that my big chance had arrived one day when I bumped into a college classmate who turned out to be a public-relations man for General Dynamics, and who remarked casually during a reunion lunch that perhaps I'd like to take my family to the launching of the second atomic submarine, the Seawolf, which a subsidiary of his outfit, the Electric Boat Company, was then whipping into shape in a shipyard at Groton, Connecticut.

At dinner that evening, I referred offhandedly to this proposal, and the reaction was so enthusiastic that I realized I
had got onto something fairly hot. The next morning, I
called my General Dynamics chum and said I'd like to take
him up on his kind offer. He advised me that a formal invitation would be forthcoming.

In the weeks that followed, the launching of the *Seawolf*
became a major conversational topic in my household. Night
after night, Terry and Joey, who was then six and could not
read, but knew more about fission than I did, badgered me
for details about our prospective adventure. Having had no
further traffic with General Dynamics, I had to fall back on
my imagination, and the boys somehow got the notion that
they were to be key figures in the launching.

Finally, the invitation arrived, as arresting and fancy a
document as any invitee could wish for. Accompanying it
was a yellow card admitting bearer "and party" to the
launching site at Groton. At this point, bearer and party consulted a road map and discovered that Groton is a hundred-
and-seventy-mile drive from Truro, where by that time we
were in summer residence. Since the do at Groton was scheduled to start at eleven in the morning, bearer was smitten
by the realization that he was in for a real early start.

And a real early start it was—five-thirty, to be exact, on a
bleak and foggy day. We'd have been off five minutes sooner
if my wife, who had declined to accompany us, on the ground
that she had nothing suitable to wear, hadn't insisted that I
come straight back into the house and put on a tie. It took us
around four hours to get to Groton, and we passed the
time pleasantly enough, by speculating on the other guests
we'd be rubbing elbows with. I allowed as how there'd
surely be a flotilla of admirals, possibly the Secretary of the
Navy in person, and almost certainly Lewis L. Strauss, a fellow who could hardly have been absent on such an occasion,

since he was both an admiral and the head of the Atomic
Energy Commission.

The temperature had been rising throughout our voyage, and as we hove into Groton, we knew that the launching, whatever else it might be, would be sweltering. I began
furtively to loosen my tie, but was halted by a brusque reminder of what Mummy had said. At Groton, to our amaze-
ment, we found the road leading to the Electric Boat Company jammed with cars. What did people think this was, I
wondered irritably—the Danbury Fair? How were we
V.I.P.s supposed to get to the place if every Tom, Dick, and
Harry was to be allowed to clutter up our access route? It
took us nearly an hour to negotiate the last couple of miles.
Eventually, we squeezed into a parking lot and entered the
shipyard, grandly flashing our yellow pass. We were
handed a printed program, which Terry read as we moved
along. "You were right, Dad!" he exclaimed. "Strauss is
going to speak, and Secnav, too!"

Meanwhile, we were nearing a giant cradle in which
nestled the *Seawolf* herself, a huge, gray, sharklike vessel
decked out with gaudy bunting. Directly ahead of us were
some gates leading to a grandstand that had been set up at
the bow end of the ship to accommodate a few hundred spectators. I marched nonchalantly toward this haven, but was
quickly stopped by a badge-wearing fellow. "Green tickets
only this way," he said firmly. "Yellow tickets *that* way."
He pointed toward the stern of the submarine. Presently,
we found ourselves standing on a dock alongside the stern of
the ship. The only trouble was that there were people packed
twenty deep between us and the *Seawolf*. My children
couldn't even see her conning tower unless I lifted them up
on my shoulders. Through a loudspeaker we heard a hospitable voice announce that the ceremonies would get under

way in ten minutes. During that blistering interval so many more people crowded into our area that we were soon standing shoulder to shoulder, except for the boys, who were shoulder to knee.

"Where are the admirals, Daddy?" a small voice piped up from below.

With some difficulty, I raised Joey on high and drew his attention to a naval officer mopping his brow nearby. (He and I were the only two men in that vicinity inane enough to be wearing ties.)

"That's only a lieutenant j.g.," said Joey scornfully.

By eleven o'clock, it seemed as though there must be twenty-five thousand people sharing our oven. (The *Times,* the next day, estimated the crowd at only twenty thousand, but its correspondent was probably sitting up forward with the admirals and couldn't see all the children who, like mine, were wedged between adults' legs.) The voice of orator after orator—none of them visible from where I stood— droned out of the amplifying system, and occasionally some phrase about atoms for peace or the glorious traditions of our gallant Navy would seep into my consciousness through the heat. (By this time, two would-be spectators within fifteen feet of us had keeled over and had been dragged away.)

What concerned me most was: How was I going to enable my kids to see the *Seawolf* slide into the Thames? I was damned if I was going to cart them three hundred and forty miles on one of the hottest days of the summer to gaze at a great historical event, and then have that event elude their gaze entirely. I finally decided that the only thing to do, once the sub began to move, was to grab a child, hoist him high for a second or two, drop him, grab the other, and repeat this operation until the ship was out in the river.

That was what I did. Each son had three fleeting glimpses of the *Seawolf* as it glided past us. I was far too occupied

with stooping and lifting to view any of the launching myself, but I gathered it was an impressive, inspiring sight.
That's what my wife said; she watched it at a neighbor's
house on television.

The
Government
and
the People

Up to the election of President Kennedy, few Cape Codders wanted to have much truck with the federal government, or with any other authority that had its seat outside the narrow confines of their peninsula. By and large, they have kept their noses out of other people's business, and they expect non–Cape Codders to reciprocate. In the last decade, though, their expectations have frequently been dashed. In the summer of 1960, for instance, a team of federal architects was moseying around Truro taking photographs and measurements of some of the old houses, for enshrinement in the Library of Congress. One might think that nobody could object very strenuously to this, but an architect who came around to our place to sketch a mantel said that one crusty Cape Cod woman had sent him packing with "You're a government man, you don't get to enter *my* house."

Our house dates back to 1800 or thereabouts, and it has had many owners. Next to one of the four fireplaces that sprout from its central brick chimney is a small wall cabinet, mysteriously boarded up. My wife and I, for reasons we would find it hard to define, have never pried into this recess. A man once stopped by who'd been born in our house and had lived in it until forty-seven years before we bought it. We asked him if he knew what was or had been in the cabinet. He didn't, but anyway he seemed glad that we hadn't broken into it. Some folks, he complained, rip the guts out of the fine old Cape Cod houses they acquire. They have a perfect right to, of course—their property is their property—but most Cape natives hate to see the old ways and wainscottings altered.

Saturday is the only day of the week on which we residents of Truro may go clamming—and then only if we have obtained a shellfish license at the town hall (a dollar a year a family). One summer Saturday in 1960, a retired Army colonel went out on the flats and marched back in with a ten-quart bucket of steamers and an eight-quart bucket of quahogs; he had assumed, as many of us had, that this was the legal weekly limit. So, evidently, had our old shellfish warden, but he had died the previous winter, and his successor flagged the colonel down and said he couldn't take ten quarts *and* eight quarts; the limit was ten *or* eight. Having served in the Military Police Corps, the colonel meekly dumped one pail, and then sought clarification of the law from his brother-in-law, one of Truro's three selectmen. The selectman, though, was too busy to look up the shellfish regulations (ten *or* eight turned out to be right), because he was rushing off to Washington to testify at a Congressional-committee hearing on a proposed national park that the Department of the Interior has been trying for several years to establish on Cape Cod.

Thus, on Cape Cod these days, has the national interest impinged on the local interest, in a few instances amid turbulence that has shaken the Cape as violently as any of the

northeasters that used to be the principal beclouders of its
customary tranquillity.

The Cape's name goes back to 1602, when an English sea-
farer named Bartholomew Gosnold sailed close by it and
was impressed with the abundance of a species of fish in the
seas that lapped against it. Today, as then, the Cape waters
teem with fish—not only cod but halibut, whiting, flounder,
and other nourishing varieties. Inevitably, they now also
teem with fishing boats. Some of the present-day boats are
berthed at Provincetown, where the catching and processing
of sea food is the major industry and practically the only
year-round one; other boats chug over from Boston, New
Bedford, Plymouth, and Gloucester to join the Provincetown
fleet in dragging their nets through the profitable waves off
the Atlantic Ocean side of the Cape, or, as this part of the
coastline is known locally, the back shore.

To Cape Codders, the Atlantic is a very special entity. For
them, it has long meant life and death. From the fish and
the tourists who swim in it, they have filled their bellies and
their pockets, and its waves have filled their graveyards. During the Second World War, the Cape shoreline became one
of the many spots in the United States where the armed
forces pitched their tents, and the Army also took to pitching
a considerable amount of practice ammunition seaward,
into the fishing waters. In the summer of 1951, the often dis-
parate interests of the fishing industry, the vacationers who
spend what the *Cape Codder* once called "the easy summer
dollar," and the military became entangled in a controversy
that reached its peak at a spirited New England town meeting at Wellfleet attended by more than three hundred representatives of the various factions concerned.

It was a brisk, no-holds-barred meeting, attended by quite
a few of the fishermen, who had declared a "no-fish" day so
they could tell the Army face to face how sometimes they

might be excluded from its target area for hours and at other times be told to proceed on through and then, whap!—a shell or two would scream out over their heads. One fisherman said he'd once been stopped by Army patrol boats for as long as five and a half hours, and when a military spokesman said, "The boats don't stop you," the fisherman said back, "The hell they don't." The fishermen told off the government in such certain terms—ultimately causing it to shift its sights—that one Massachusetts official at the hearing was moved to observe, "The Army will leave here with the thought that they will never want to hear of a fish again, or eat a fish." Then, being a true-blue Cape Codder, he added, "But if they do anyway, I hope they'll eat fish from this area, because they're the best fish you'll find anywhere in the United States."

A national park has been much on Cape Codders' minds, and in some cases has attracted much of their spleen, since 1956, when the Department of the Interior proposed creating a Cape Cod National Seashore. What this meant was that the federal government would take over nearly thirty thousand acres of the Lower Cape, including the entire ocean front, for a national park. (A national seashore, the National Park Service has explained, is a national park that is not quite as strictly regulated as an ordinary, inland national park.) It was on November 1, 1956, that most Cape Codders learned what the Park Service was up to. That day, the *Cape Codder* ran the headline "TAKING OF BACK SHORE IN EASTHAM, WELLFLEET, TRURO AS A NATIONAL PARK RECOMMENDED IN FEDERAL REPORT." The Park Service had long been perturbed over the way the beaches of the Atlantic and Gulf coasts were being gobbled up by developers, and it had resolved to preserve some of the shoreline for future generations to look at and loaf on. The Park Service already controlled twenty-five million acres in close to two hundred lo-

cations all over the country, but the only sizable stretch of
beach among them was the Cape Hatteras National Seashore Recreational Area, in North Carolina, which was authorized by Congress in 1937 and was formally dedicated in
1958. In 1954, the *Cape Codder* reported, the Park Service
had made a survey of thirty-seven hundred miles of eastern
shoreline, from Maine to Texas, and had found only fifty-
four coastal areas unravaged enough to warrant preservation.
Of these, Lower Cape Cod, with its practically unbroken
thirty-mile sweep of dune-fringed ocean beach, from Chatham to Provincetown, was the finest—"an irreplaceable
treasure," as the Park Service later acclaimed it.

According to the first news story, the boundaries of the
proposed park—how much more land it would embrace,
that is, than the ocean beach itself—had not yet been spelled
out. Cape Cod is not, like so much of the Northwest, a wilderness out of which vast hunks of national park can be
carved without seriously disturbing any human being's domestic routine, and therefore many Cape Cod homeowners
were curious to learn whether their property would be included in a park and, if so, what their status would be. The
Park Service, for the time being, was holding its peace, and
while the homeowners waited, they began spiritedly debat-
ing the pros and cons of a national park. The debate swelled
into a storm. Some of the opponents of the park found themselves not on speaking terms with lifelong friends who had
become its proponents. When the program for Truro's two-
hundred-and-fiftieth birthday was in preparation, in 1959,
it was suggested to John C. Worthington, the chairman of the
town's board of selectmen and also the dean of the town's
softball players, that a ball game be held between a pro-park
squad and an anti-park squad. In the interests of community harmony, the idea was not pursued.

If it had been, Worthington, a gentle, reflective man, who
is in the fishing business, would presumably have played

on the pro-park team. He believes that a strong, authoritative hand is needed to keep the Lower Cape from being ruined by commercial developers, as so many other seashore areas—including much of the Upper Cape—have been. "If we don't have a park, sooner or later some real-estate operators are going to cut the Lower Cape all to pieces with their bulldozers," Worthington told me. "That's what the Cape can't bear." Already, Worthington and other advocates of a park have noted, the Lower Cape has been cruelly marred. In North Truro, for instance, astride a hill where as a boy Worthington shot quail, there now stands a restaurant-cocktail-lounge-motel-gift-shop compote that at night blazes with neon signs. Some Cape Codders think this enterprise particularly deplorable because it adjoins a cemetery, though others have argued that the ideal spot for an eyesore is one where the neighbors have had their lids permanently sealed.

The opponents of the national seashore have argued just as keenly as Mr. Worthington has. Some of them have observed that if public ownership of the ocean beach is the main desideratum, why, some five-eighths of the shore already belong either to the federal government, in the form of military posts and fish and wildlife sanctuaries, or to the state or the Lower Cape towns. One man who has made this point is Joshua A. Nickerson, a great-great-great-great-great-great-great-grandson of William Nickerson, who bought much of what is now Chatham from some compliant Indians in 1656, and whose descendants have been so numerous on Cape Cod that up to a few years ago more Nickersons than Smiths were listed in the Cape Cod phone book. (Some Nickersons think, or hope, that Richard M. Nixon is a Nickerson, and, perhaps partly as an antidote to all the attention the Kennedy family was focussing on Cape Cod, they once invited Mr. Nixon, while he was vice-president, to a Nickerson clan reunion, but he couldn't make it.) There are still a couple of hundred Nickerson listings, including the Nickerson Drug Company, Nickerson Fish & Lobsters, the Nickerson Funeral Home, the Nickerson Lumber Company, Nickerson's Service Station, and Nickerson's Tourist Cabins—a roster that fairly accurately reflects the economy of present-day Cape Cod.

Joshua Nickerson, the president of the lumber company, believes in public ownership of the beaches but decidedly not in federal ownership. He and his kin have already given thousands of acres of land, including more than three miles of ocean frontage in Chatham, to Cape Cod towns, and one of his relatives presented to Massachusetts the Roland C. Nickerson State Park, in Brewster. Joshua Nickerson thinks the Cape's beaches should be regulated by the Cape's natives, because the natives understand them best. "I have a strong feeling that I represent a certain continuity of a way of life," he told me one time. "Your ordinary tourist walks along a clam flat at low tide and he just sees sand and water. I see the clam holes, and all kinds of marvellous things. You've got to live here for three hundred years, as I have, before you can see Cape Cod, let alone understand it."

Like Nickerson, Charles Frazier, the Wellfleet lawyer and selectman, has been a strong anti-park man. Wellfleet puts on a parade every Fourth of July, and its selectmen traditionally have a float in the line of march. In 1959, they entered two floats, both with an anti-park motif; on one, which was supposed to show what life on Cape Cod would be like under a park administration, Frazier lay curled up in a sleeping bag. Another lawyer—Silas S. Clark, a former mayor of White Plains who moved to Truro, where each summer he patiently coaxes a dazzling array of flowers from the sandy soil—is pro-park. Clark made an intensive study of part of South Truro, and he was disheartened at the manner in which builders sheared the tops off some of the undulating, scrub-covered hills there; he predicted that as a result the hills would gradually wash away. A pro-park Provincetown artist complained that the Cape had already become so overdeveloped that skunks no longer dwelled beneath his porch. The Barnstable County Beach Commissioners and the Cape Cod Association of Planning Boards came out against a park, as did the *Saturday Evening Post,* but the American Forestry Association and the National Parks Committee of the Garden Clubs of America were pro-park, as was the *Atlantic Monthly.* So were the Cape Cod Park Commissioners Association (preponderantly) and the Massachusetts Beach Buggy Association (unanimously). And both houses of the Massachusetts legislature endorsed a park, in identical resolutions, containing eight Whereases and three Resolveds.

From the start, the battle lines were drawn in, among other places, the newspapers—and notably in the letters-to-the-editor column of the *Cape Codder.* "Creeping socialism!" one correspondent said. "Uprooting of home life at the pleasure of socialist-minded and dictatorial leaders!" In rebuttal, another man asked, "If this be socialism, then what of Boston Common and Central Park?" A letter from two persons who identified themselves as "Wellfleet Clam-Diggers" suggested cynically that if the National Park Service was so eager to conquer new rural realms for urban Americans to enjoy, it should set aside urban realms, notably Manhattan Island, for rural Americans: "We country people, and there are millions of us all over the nation, have as much right to enjoy, gratis, the unspoiled attractions of the Bowery, Fifth Avenue, Broadway, Liberty Island, and the Empire State Building as the Gothamites have to free access to the charms of Yellowstone and Cape Cod."

Probably the most prolific letter writer on the Cape, year in and year out, is a Provincetown lawyer, S. Osborn Ball, whose family owns several hundred acres of ocean-front land in Truro, bought by his father seventy years ago. A public beach on the ocean side of Truro, donated to the town by the Ball family, is called Ballston Beach. S. Osborn Ball, an unpredictable man, who as a rule is vehemently anti-federal government but has been pro-national park, pointed out in one of several letters to the *Cape Codder* that all the fuss everybody was making was of little long-range consequence, for had not Rachel Carson predicted that in four thousand years the sea will swallow up the Cape entirely?

The longest published letter anyone wrote on the subject was a six-thousand-word diatribe against a park signed by Mrs. Walter P. Chrysler, Jr., whose husband in 1958 bought an abandoned church building in Provincetown and converted it into an art museum. (The institution became informally known as the First Church of Chrysler.) Mrs. Chrysler's massive blast, which was published *in toto* by several Cape Cod papers, and in part by the *Cape Codder*, was addressed not to any editor but to President Eisenhower. (His reply, if any, was not made public.) In it, she declared that if the Cape Cod National Seashore went through, the fate of the individual homeowner on the Cape would be not unlike that of Cardinal Mindszenty in Hungary. It was indicative of the confusion that prevailed on the Cape that at the time Mrs. Chrysler wrote her letter, she was head of the ticket-sales committee for the Provincetown Symphony Orchestra, whose conductor's wife, Mrs. Joseph Hawthorne, was busily circulating a pro-park petition.

Most of the newspapers published on or delivered to the Cape have been pro-park. A columnist for the weekly Yarmouth *Register* wrote, "In our shrinking, defiled, and exploited continent we must hold on to the few remaining miles of unspoiled beaches. Whose side are you on, God's or man's? The Creator's or the destroyer's? Is this a difficult choice to make? We must not diminish the Great Outer Beach by the length of one gull's wing or the shadow of one beach plum. Let America come here and replenish its soul."

The *Cape Codder* hedged for a few weeks after breaking the park story ("Locally, we are going to have to play a canny and intelligent game in order to steer events in a way which will be to our best advantage," was its first reaction), but by February, 1957, it had made up its mind. "The Cape has a responsibility to itself and to the country in general to preserve what is essentially a national resource," it said. "We have concluded that the National Park is the best alternative in keeping with this responsibility." On the other hand, the weekly Provincetown *Advocate*, which had also been dragging its feet, kept on dragging them for twenty-eight months longer, and then, in July of 1959, said, in an editorial entitled "We Don't Like the Park": "The Cape is not a seashore. It is a quintessence of old New England, and more important, by far, is the imprint of its people, past and present—mostly past."

Once the *Cape Codder* took a stand, it began beating the drums hard for a park. It commended to its readers the example of France, where, it said, "*Le littoral appartient à l'état*," and it asserted, "Let's face it! We—the people who own and live on Cape Cod—are losing a little more of it each year, each month, each week. Are there any who cannot see the creeping desecration, the impinging blight that chews like disease into area after area?" Everybody was facing it, though not everybody agreed about just where the desecration would come from. An anti-park group, the Eastham Citizens Committee, announced, "Let's face it. Do the people in these towns want to be pushed off a substantial area of their lands, like the poor Indians from their reservations, just so hordes of people can flock in for two short months of the year to desecrate the area with vast tent camps foisted onto us in the sacred name of conservation?"

In 1957, a good many Cape residents refused sulkily to shingle their roofs or patch their pipes, on the ground that

it was fruitless to maintain homes from which, as they reckoned it, the government was about to oust them. In 1958,
many of the same people, with the perversity so characteristic of Cape Codders, planted trees. In its first issue that
year, the *Cape Codder* ran an editorial predicting the events
of the next twelve months. Sometime in the spring, it said
boldly, the Park Service would finally issue a detailed report on Cape Cod. "Reactions will be immediate and vocal,"
the editorial went on. "The National Park Service will be
alternately praised as the conservator of the last of Cape Cod
as she used to be and damned as the socialistic agency of a
foreign power, namely, the Republicans in Washington.
Congress will pass the measure." The report was not forthcoming in 1958, but the reactions were. An Upper Cape
bank president told a citizens' meeting, "The type of people
who come to national or state parks are not the type we want.
We want the solid kind, like those at Oyster Harbors." (In
a subsequent newspaper account of a dinner dance at the
Oyster Harbors Club, the only two guests mentioned were a
writer and a press agent.) The *Cape Codder* began running
a long series of articles by a seventy-seven-year-old pro-park
naturalist, Dr. William Gould Vinal, who had just finished a
biological-research stint for the National Park Service, and
who before that—back in 1909—had made an exhaustive
study of the sex life of Cape Cod bivalves. Two installments
in Dr. Vinal's series were devoted to "The Rise and Fall of
the Long-Necked Clam." He urged Cape Codders to "keep
your fin up"—which he said was an old Cape phrase meaning "go at something cautiously" and derived from the behavior of the bull whale when wary.

Meanwhile, without waiting for the Park Service's detailed report, three Massachusetts congressmen introduced
Cape Cod park bills in the House of Representatives. Senators Saltonstall and Kennedy were biding their time. Cape
Cod is a Republican stronghold, Kennedy nothwithstanding.

(Some of his Lower Cape constituents were flabbergasted when, in a letter to one of them, he referred to the Lower Cape as the Upper Cape.) Staunch Republicans on the Cape say bitterly that there were no hurricanes in the area until Franklin Roosevelt became President and no sheep ticks until Harry Truman took office. (They have tended to gloss over the fact that there were no April snowstorms prior to the Eisenhower administration.) The winner of the Republican primary in any Congressional contest in the Ninth District, which includes all of the Cape (as well as Martha's Vineyard, Nantucket, New Bedford, and most of Plymouth County), is as sure of election as a Democrat in Georgia. The representative from the Ninth District retired in 1958, and how the candidates to succeed him felt about a national park was significant, inasmuch as Congress customarily does not pass any park bill over the vigorous objections of a member whose constituents are immediately affected. On the eve of the 1958 Republican primary, therefore, the aspirants to the Congressional seat were urged to state their views on the park question. To a man, they kept their fins up. One unsuccessful candidate was the finniest; appraising a national park, he managed to say that its effect would be either beneficial or disastrous. The eventual winner of the primary, Hastings Keith, a West Bridgewater man, did not let his triumph becloud his prudence. "I want to be sure the public has its say before I have mine," he declared.

At the start of 1959, the *Cape Codder* refrained from speculation about the park situation, but its readers did not. One of them was heard to mutter that the whole concept of a national park was a plot foisted upon a Democratic Congress by organized labor, whose leaders coveted recreation areas for the rank and file. Some disaffected residents of Truro launched a rumor that their beloved Ballston Beach was destined to be converted into a bird watchers' haven, and one

Ballston Beach habitué let it be known that although he had nothing against birds, he didn't like alien bird watchers, and was thinking of selling his Truro house and moving to Nova Scotia. On March 5th, the *Cape Codder* complained editorially that the Park Service had been intolerably poky in issuing its report, and in less than a week that agency released two documents, one a white-covered paperback tome called "Cape Cod—A Proposed National Seashore Field Investigation Report," and the other a neat blue brochure called "Cape Cod National Seashore—a Proposal." The second, an abridgment of the first, was widely distributed on the Cape, and at cocktail parties housewives who used to swap beach-plum recipes began swapping views on it. The bulkier report was obtainable, too, but only on request, from Washington. The existence of the two documents, and the fact that the heavier of the pair was harder to come by, led some Cape Codders to deduce that the Park Service was pulling a fast one—that there were grim objectives in the larger document that were slyly left unstated, or were muted, in the smaller. Quite a few Cape Codders who got their hands on the unexpurgated text read it as searchingly as, in other sections of the country, their fellow-citizens were reading the unexpurgated text of "Lady Chatterley's Lover."

Actually, there was not much difference between the two documents, except that the abridged one was fancier and more poetic. Both quoted Thoreau, both declared Cape Cod to be of national significance as an area of scenic, scientific, and historic interest, and both pointed out that the Cape is within a day's drive of nearly a third of the population of the United States, and is thus a splendid recreational Mecca. (On a sunny summer-weekend day, the Cape has attracted half a million visitors, not counting the White House correspondents; sixty million of them might tax even its broad and hospitable beaches.) The Park Service, now that the truth was out, envisaged a national park of 28,645 acres,

17,830 of these to be acquired from private owners. In addition to ocean frontage, much inland territory was ear-marked for inclusion; in sections of Truro and Wellfleet the proposed park would have cut all the way across the Cape and taken in some Cape Cod Bay frontage. Of the Lower Cape towns, Truro and Wellfleet were slated to cede by far the largest tracts—9,875 and 7,854 acres, respectively.

My wife and I were pleased at reading that our part of Truro is "an area of geological interest." We had never known that. "Cape Cod is a well illustrated chapter in geologic history, setting forth the story of glacial deposition in gigantic but simple form," the main report said. Tacked onto it was a bulky geological appendix, and there were also biological, archeological, and historical appendixes. But while considerable attention was paid to the Cape's strata, flora, and fauna (the co-authors of the biological appendix, one of whom was Dr. Vinal, disclosed that they could not agree on whether there are squirrels on the Cape), the human inhabitants got short shrift, and this omission didn't escape notice. "People are more important than geological formations," it was later stated by Joshua Nickerson. (He said nothing about squirrels.)

The reports also touched lightly on the fact that the proposed park would engorge six hundred homes in Truro and Wellfleet (including ours), not to mention a few dozen in the other Lower Cape towns. "Parks haven't made America great—but HOMES have," a man wrote the *Cape Codder*. "My little home is doomed!" cried a Truro woman at a community meeting, and she added, "Who will protect us from rape and murder when those thousands who have never heard of us come wandering in?" "The rape of the Cape" became a rallying cry for the disenchanted. But there was no unanimity among home-owners. Some who lived outside the proposed boundaries, anticipating that it would be years before the park authorities got around to evicting anybody, if they ever did, bewailed the fickle fate that had denied them the protective aegis of the government against bull-dozers. One Truro neighbor of ours, Arthur Joseph, who was anti-park, calmly began building a house, for a relative, in-side the proposed park. Our town clerk and local newspaper columnist, Thomas Kane, who was pro-park, said that he would be quite content if the government would let him occupy his home for twenty-five years. In a lighthearted mood, he added, "We'll dress the kids in tattered clothes, wrap our good child bride in a moth-eaten blanket, shove a short-stemmed clay pipe in her mouth, decorate her hair with seagull feathers, and have her sit out on the front lawn, staring in stony silence at the passing tourists. Around her we'll display all her hooked and braided rugs, and perhaps some of our wood carvings."

Few of Kane's fellow year-rounders found the situation amusing. There was so much grumbling, in fact, that within two weeks of the release of the reports the director of the Park Service, Conrad L. Wirth, decided to go to the Cape and try to clarify matters. Wirth has been in the Park Service since 1928 and has been its director since 1951, but his at-tachment to parks is lifelong. He was born in one—a park in Hartford, Connecticut, where his father, a park man be-fore him, had a house on the grounds and established the nation's first public rose garden. Late in March, 1959, Wirth, a soft-spoken but self-confident man, gamely presented him-self at two open forums, in Chatham and Eastham. A total of around seven hundred Cape Codders attended these meetings, as did a *Life* photographer, whose pictures were never published, perhaps because many of the women in the audience turned up in mink coats instead of oilskins. Rep-resentative Hastings Keith was there, too, in a business suit.

Wirth patiently coped with a barrage of questions typical of those that were worrying Cape Codders. When would the park come into being? Probably not for ten or fifteen years after Congress passed a suitable appropriations bill. What would happen to the homes in the park area? People could give them to the government, as a tax-deductible contribution, or they could sell them to the government, at a price to be fixed by negotiation, and after selling they could, if they wished, have life tenancies. But wouldn't the Park Service have the right of eminent domain? Yes, but the agency hardly ever exercised it. What would keep the parts of the towns not within the park from being overrun by commercial developers? Local zoning. How would the towns be compensated for the loss of tax revenues from the property usurped by the government? Well, Congress might vote a special grant, as it had done for Teton County, Wyoming, when the Grand Teton National Park was created, and in any event the towns might well boom, since within the park itself no food or lodging would be provided for visitors.

And so the questions went, for two choleric evenings, the second of which, at Chatham, was spiced by a brief but lively oration from an anti-park man who identified himself as Keeper of the Town Pump in South Orleans. This was Kenrick A. Sparrow, who could also have identified himself as Judge of Probate and Insolvency for Barnstable County, or as Moderator of the Town of Orleans, or as a native whose family has been on Cape Cod for at least three hundred years —maybe longer, since one of his mother's grandmothers is reputed to have had Indian blood. (The family has Nickerson blood, too.) Judge Sparrow, whose great-grandfather was also Keeper of the Town Pump, and who is proud that he now sleeps in a bed a great-uncle died in, tries, as a rule, to maintain judicial detachment about Cape Cod controversies, but at Chatham he got carried away and delivered a blunt attack on the government. "I had no intention of saying anything when I arrived at the meeting," he said afterward. "Why, I didn't even take my overcoat off. But I sensed that the general feeling in the hall was that the little people had no chance to fight Washington, and after that I just couldn't keep from firing that old 1812 powder that I've had stored up in me since the time my great-grandfather Joshua Crosby manned a quarter-deck gun on the *Constitution*. Those nice old ladies and innocent teen-agers who go in for bird watching hope that a national park will keep the Cape from changing. I'm afraid it may bring change more quickly than anything else that could happen. To me, it's important that the Cape stay the Cape, and that my boys grow up in a house that was built by their great-great-great-grandfather and is shaded by trees planted by their great-great-grandfather."

Conrad Wirth's personal appearances did little to allay the Lower Cape's misgivings. As our Truro selectman, John Worthington, said a few weeks afterward, "It appears to me that everybody who attended those Eastham and Chatham meetings got a different idea of how each question was answered." Many Cape Codders were anxious, and some weeks later, on May 20th, their anxiety increased when the late Senator Richard L. Neuberger, of Oregon, an ardent conservationist, introduced a bill that would have authorized the Secretary of the Interior to take over three unspecified seashore or lake-shore areas, totalling a hundred thousand acres, for national parks, and to do so without holding any preliminary hearings whatsoever—that is, without consulting local inhabitants. Inasmuch as the Park Service had made far more thorough studies of Cape Cod than of any other waterfront region, it was taken for granted by Cape Codders that their land would be among the areas tapped. Neuberger was a Democrat, of course, but he announced that he was introducing his bill at the request of the Eisenhower administration. What was more, the bill had the blessing of both the Department of the Interior and the Bureau of the Budget—meaningful endorsements that no previous Cape Cod bill had been accorded.

To many Cape Codders, regardless of what their feelings about a park had been up to then, the Neuberger bill was anathema. They feared Congress might pass it, if for no other reason than that the Senate and House Committees on Interior and Insular Affairs, which handle park legislation, are dominated by Westerners; Westerners were presumed to have little knowledge of Cape Cod. (The easternmost member of the Senate committee then was from Iowa.) Congressman Keith came out flatly against the Neuberger bill. Joshua Nickerson called it "unwarranted usurpation of power," and Charles Frazier warned against "outright confiscation of property—government by decree, not of law."

An especially articulate decrier of the bill was Francis Biddle, onetime Attorney General in President Roosevelt's Cabinet, who has a thirty-acre place in Wellfleet, with a stout old Cape Cod house that was built in 1790. Biddle, who has been spending about half of each year on the Cape, has given up the practice of law, but he volunteered to serve as informal unpaid counsel to the citizens of Eastham, Wellfleet, and Truro when, or if, it turned out to be necessary. As a matter of fact, Biddle had already swung into action. In the spring of 1959, the Park Service had announced that it imagined it could buy up all the private property it wanted on the Cape for between sixteen and eighteen million dollars. Many Cape Codders immediately became indignant; the prevailing view was that forty million would be more realistic, and one Lower Cape civic leader pushed the estimate up to a hundred million. So Biddle went to the agency's regional headquarters, in Philadelphia, to obtain a breakdown of its calculations. It took Cape Cod to send a Biddle *to* Philadelphia.

In a letter to the *Cape Codder,* Biddle besought the paper to oppose the Neuberger bill, which he had earlier described as "more of a wartime measure than either I or Harold Ickes would have ever dared to propose." The *Cape Cod-*

der, which had been so friendly to the Park Service that Conrad Wirth had affectionately called it "the good little weekly paper," promptly denounced the bill. In July, Senator James E. Murray, of Montana, chairman of the Senate Committee on Interior and Insular Affairs, introduced an even broader omnibus park bill—Neuberger was one of seventeen other sponsors of it—that would have permitted the Secretary of the Interior arbitrarily to choose not three but ten shore areas for parks. The Neuberger bill, however, remained the Cape's bête noire. At a public meeting held in Orleans to discuss the park, a woman asked from the audience, "Is it American to tolerate Neuberger?" The chairman, a minister, paused for a moment before replying "Yes."

During Wirth's visit in March, he had talked to several selectmen from the Lower Cape towns, and urged them to find out how their constituents felt about a park. In June, Truro's selectmen wrote to all the town's taxpayers, resident and non-resident, and asked them to indicate, by sending in postcards, whether they favored a park for Truro and, if so, which of several theoretical park plans they liked best. The results of this poll were disclosed at a special town meeting, on the evening of June 24th. This was an exciting occasion for some of us summer people, because town meeting is traditionally held in February. To be sure, we were not allowed to vote at the summer session any more than we would have been at a winter one, but at least we had a chance to watch our neighbors in political action.

The meeting, held in the gymnasium of the Truro School, drew about two hundred people—a good turnout for such affairs—but the oratory was somewhat less impassioned than many of us summer folk, who comprised half the crowd, had anticipated. Almost without debate, the voters present instructed the town's planning board to draw

up a zoning bylaw for consideration at the next winter meeting. This was an unprecedented move for Truro, where the
electorate had steadfastly frowned on zoning proposals for
twenty-five years. Then John Worthington, sitting up front
with his two fellow-selectmen, arose to bring the body
politic up to date on the national-park situation. He looked
a bit flustered; later we learned that an hour before the
meeting a car with faulty brakes had driven through the side
of his house and into a room occupied by—but, happily, not
at that moment containing—his eighty-eight-year-old
mother-in-law. Worthington reported that of six hundred
and eighty postcard replies received by the selectmen, two
hundred and seventy-seven were against any kind of park,
and four hundred and three were for some kind, although
only a hundred and thirty-eight of these were for the kind
proposed by the Park Service. He interpreted this to indicate that sixty per cent of the taxpayers were for a park. The
town's foremost real-estate man, Antone Duarte, Jr., took
another view, saying that inasmuch as only twenty per cent
of the postcards favored the one kind of park that had been
officially proposed, eighty per cent of the community could
be said to be against a park. After an hour's discussion, a
good deal of it statistical, the meeting adopted two resolutions, both of which Duarte had forehandedly written out.
The first, a condemnation of the Neuberger bill, was passed
without dissent. The second, a condemnation of the earlier
park bills before Congress, was passed by a vote of fifty to
thirty. It carried despite several speeches against it, one by a
man who said fervently he was for a national park even
though the proposed one would encompass almost all the
land he owned aside from the spot his house stood on. He
was L. Thomas Hopkins, a professor who used to be Moderator of the Town of Truro. When he stood up to speak,
though, I heard him identified by one native merely as "the

fellow that married Hester Rich." The Riches are an old Truro family.

In the fall, the two Massachusetts Senators, in conjunction with Representative Keith, wrote an open letter to all Cape Codders, saying that they were going to put forward a park bill of their own—one that would make everybody happy, and one that they hoped to get passed soon in order to prevent the park controversy from becoming "a lingering issue which creates unfulfilled hopes or barren dispute." On September 3rd, they introduced their bill, which Kennedy, who presented it to the Senate on behalf of Saltonstall and himself, said penetrated "some uncharted areas of park legislation." The park that he and his fellow-sponsors visualized (Hyannis Port was not within its bounds) would "meet the legitimate interests and sentiments of existing residents," he declared, and went on, "We have tried to set up this proposal in the perspective of history and against the knowledge that an enterprise of this sort is precisely the kind of activity which characterizes a free people. We are confident that as a result of the protections which are clearly written into the law and the spirit which we know animated both the authors of the original proposal and of this legislation . . . it will be possible to establish a great national park in an area which may otherwise be increasingly blighted by the relentless and sweeping advance of commercial development."
The park that the three Massachusetts legislators had in mind did not differ much in size from the one mapped out by the Park Service, but they invested it with novel protections. Previous park bills had granted property owners occupancy of their homes either for twenty-five years or for life; the Saltonstall-Kennedy-Keith bill went beyond that, stipulating that if the towns concerned adopted and enforced for their park lands zoning bylaws that were satisfactory to the Secretary of the Interior, the property owners and their

descendants might sit tight, like stalactites, forever. In other words, no eminent domain. Never before had Congress fooled around with zoning, or authorized such potentially cozy oases within a national park. Provision was made in the new bill for reimbursement to the six Lower Cape towns concerned of lost tax revenues for three years, and each of them was to be allowed to use ten per cent of its expropriated private acreage—in the case of Truro, seven hundred and ten acres—for future residential developments inside the park boundaries. An advisory committee, to include one member from each of the six towns, was to be set up to serve as a liaison between the Park Service and the park. What was more, the three legislators pledged that before any bill was passed, hearings were to be held on Cape Cod itself.

Kennedy had hardly stopped talking about his new bill on the Senate floor before people were talking about it on the Cape. John Worthington, for instance, found it dandy, but Charles Frazier had his doubts—still thought the proposed park was too large. So did Antone Duarte. The Cape Cod *Standard-Times,* of Hyannis, said editorially, "Obviously, there's going to be a Cape Cod Seashore—the snowball has become too big to halt." The *Cape Codder* endorsed the new park bill heartily, and continued to publish Dr. Vinal, who was pointing out that under the terms of the Pollution Act of 1924 the pumping of bilges within the territorial waters of the United States is taboo. A Massachusetts representative who had introduced one of the early Cape Cod park bills said he was going to confer with Frazier, and afterward might throw still another Cape Cod park bill into the bulging Congressional hopper.

The National Park Service was unruffled. "There's nothing we're doing that can't afford to wait," Wirth told me. "We're building a long-range program. We as individuals are just a few minutes in the passage of time. We don't own this earth.

We're merely custodians of it. We owe it to future generations to pass along to them the inheritance we got. I don't
care which bill is passed. All I know is that I'd like to save
some seashore." Whatever the outcome might be, most Cape
Codders would probably have agreed that the Provincetown *Advocate* was talking sense when it said, "Many a tide
will wax and wane on Cape Cod's great shore before the proposed National Park becomes a reality." My wife and I had
just about decided when the fuss began that if we should
have to yield up our house, we'd open that secret cabinet
first. But as the months passed by and the federal government and Cape Codders merely sniffed at each other warily,
like contentious puppies unwilling to take the first nip, Jinny
and I decided, like so many others who love Cape Cod, that
there was really nothing to be done but keep our eyes and
ears open and keep our fins up.

When it hasn't been Interior or Defense that has ruffled
the Cape, it has been some other arm of distant government.
Quite a few Cape Codders have lately been in a swivet, for
instance, about what they consider the intrusive presence in
their midst of one of the most powerful outside forces of all
—the atom in process of fission. This presence has come
about because the radioactive wastes that are by-products of
nuclear-energy operations have to be disposed of somewhere and somehow—efficiently, economically, and, above
all, safely. A third of a recent annual report made by the
United States Atomic Energy Commission was devoted to
waste disposal. The transcript of some hearings that the
Joint Congressional Committee on Atomic Energy held in
1959 on the disposal of industrial radioactive wastes ran to
more than three thousand pages. In 1960, the International
Atomic Energy Agency, a United Nations adjunct, published
two volumes, running to six hundred pages each, about a
conference it held on radioactive wastes the previous Novem-

ber in Monaco. The consensus of the conference was, as the opinion of most scientists had been all along, that there is no danger to human beings from low-level radioactive wastes that are carefully put in the ocean—wastes, that is, with a radioactive content of between a thousandth and a millionth of a curie per gallon (a curie being the amount of radiation emitted by a gram of radium).

The United States has been using the high seas as a receptacle for low-level wastes ever since the atomic age began, and during the last few years dumping operations have been governed, for the most part, by procedures spelled out in a handbook issued in 1954 by the Committee on Radiation Protection of the National Bureau of Standards. The Committee prescribed that ocean disposal of packaged waste should take place in waters at least a thousand fathoms, or six thousand feet, deep, which in the Atlantic generally means at least two hundred miles offshore. Moreover, according to the handbook, "any recommendations concerning the disposal of radioactive wastes in the ocean shall not only provide adequate safety but also be such that they will minimize (or, if possible, eliminate) the possibilities of undue public alarm."

Way back in 1946, a Boston firm was authorized to dump low-level radioactive trash into the Atlantic, and by mid-1959 this outfit had, without duly or unduly alarming the nearby public, disposed of about twenty-five hundred curies' worth in a segment of the ocean that the Committee on Radiation Protection would seem to have frowned on, for it was only fifteen miles from Boston and thirty from Provincetown, and the water was only about three hundred feet deep. Still, the A.E.C. obviously did not consider the dumping dangerous, pointing out that much of the stuff that had been put over the side consisted of mops, rags, gloves, boots, and other equipment used in atomic-energy installations. This mildly radioactive dross was sealed in

fifty-five-gallon steel drums encased in concrete to make
them sink and stay sunk. The drums would hold together
for around ten years, it was reckoned, by which time many
of the radioisotopes within them would have decayed. Even
if a drum should spring a leak immediately, the ocean would
so diffuse and dilute the radioactivity emitted by its contents that the effects would be negligible. And, in any case,
radioactivity is not alien to the sea. Nature herself has endowed the oceans of the earth with a total of five hundred
billion curies.

There was nothing secret about the dumping off the Massachusetts coast, but for thirteen years hardly anybody paid
it any heed. As one of the many dozens of treatises on this
phase of sanitation has put it, "What is everyone's business
often becomes no one's business." Sooner or later, all the
same, it was inevitable that Cape Codders would find out
what was happening and get mad. They belatedly sat up and
took anxious notice of this latest federal nuisance in the summer of 1959, when their local papers reported that the
Atomic Energy Commission was on the point of granting a
license to another offshore Atlantic dumper. What had
been no one's business suddenly became everyone's business. Many Cape Codders realized for the first time that
bulky depth charges were already in the Atlantic—irre-
trievably, and a lot nearer shore and in a lot shallower water
than the 1954 handbook had held proper—and the protests
began.

True, the stipulated disposal site for the new dumper was
to be two hundred miles out at sea, in a thousand fathoms,
and the Boston outfit that had been dumping closer to
land was also going to have to move its operations out there.
True, a panel of eminent scientists—including some of the
oceanographers at the Woods Hole Oceanographic Institution, on the Cape itself—had not long before issued a report
on pelagic dumping, with recommendations, presumably

acceptable to the A.E.C., that would preclude the depositing in the Atlantic of radioactive substances in sufficient quantity to render its waters any less pure than drinking water. But had not Dr. Bostwick Ketchum, one of the Woods Hole oceanographers who worked on that report, written elsewhere that knowledge of the problems involved in the addition of radioisotopes to the ocean was still very incomplete? And had not the A.E.C. itself called one of its Pacific Ocean dumpers on the carpet for several infractions of its rules? And had not scientists time and time again asserted that certain organisms can absorb radioactivity in far greater concentration than their watery environment can—the ratio for scallops, for instance, being seventeen thousand to one, and the ratio for the egg yolks of some water birds more than a million to one? And was it not perhaps pertinent that two years after the 1954 Bikini atomic-bomb tests some clams were found on the shores of Rongelap Island so lethally laced with radioactivity that the Navy called them "killer clams"? And, moreover, had not the general manager of the A.E.C. himself told the Joint Congressional Committee, in July, 1959, that further studies would be required before his agency could categorically assert that if a single steel drum burst and if a fish came into contact with its contents and if a human being ate that fish, no harm would result?

The more Cape Codders learned, the more agitated they became, and, in that summer of 1959, even though they were pretty busy worrying about a national park, a good many of them had enough energy left to decide that it was imprudent to have any more people licensed to meddle with their ocean. Enough, they felt, was enough—if not, indeed, too much. Several articulate Cape Codders, including some resident scientists, began to express misgivings. From the start, the most outspoken dissident was a tough-minded middle-aged Truro woman named Grace DesChamps, who has been regarded by some of her acquaintances—including, in

all probability, the A.E.C. functionaries she has harried—
as a pest, and by others as a latter-day Paul Revere. A news-
paperwoman for years and most recently a stringer for the
Boston *Globe,* Miss DesChamps was raised on a Truro
farm, and she resettled there, for good and all, in 1953.
When she was a child, one of the few decorative touches in
her home was a print of the landing of the Pilgrims on the
Cape Cod dunes. Sitting beneath this picture, she would read
aloud to her mother from Governor William Bradford's old
history "Of the Plimoth Plantation." "Those Pilgrims were
heroes to me," Miss DesChamps once told me. "Because
of them, something extraordinary happened, and what
they accomplished became part of my own folklore. I was
kept pretty busy as a girl, tending pigs and cows, and working in the cranberry bogs, but I never felt any sense of de-
privation, because I was on Cape Cod and I loved Cape Cod.
I still love it. It's both a shrine and a friend to me. It has always seemed to me that Cape Cod was the place God made
first, and I don't ever want to see anybody playing any dirty
tricks on my revered old friend."

Miss DesChamps knew hardly anything about atomic
energy and its ramifications until early in 1959, when she
happened to pick up a copy of the boating magazine *Skipper* that contained a piece about Atlantic waste-dumping.
Her curiosity piqued, she began to look into the situation,
and she soon concluded that the A.E.C. had gone too far too
fast, and too haphazardly. "I kept being told by scientists I
talked to that it's a long-standing tradition of theirs to move
slowly in the absence of indisputable knowledge," Miss Des-
Champs told me. "It seemed to me that the tradition wasn't
being universally respected—in fact, that the A.E.C. didn't
even know for sure exactly what was being dumped where."
Her own knowledge of radioactive-waste disposal soon became well-nigh encyclopedic. "Do you know what it says on
page two-four-three-five of the Joint Committee hearings?"

she might ask a startled acquaintance, and she would then provide the answer: "Why, this oceanographer was talking along glibly about how good the safety tests were that the A.E.C. had been making at existing dump sites—he didn't mention this, but I have it on good authority that the Commission has only sixty inspectors to cover the entire country, for heaven's sake—and when the Committee's counsel interrupted him and asked a few pertinent questions, the scientist confessed that the tests were inadequate, preliminary, and uncertain. Some tests! Or take page one-oh-four-five, where they print the bibliography for a paper submitted by a man who had been dumping wastes into the Columbia River, next to the big Hanford reactor out in Washington. Of the fifteen sources cited in the bibliography, twelve are marked either 'Secret' or 'Confidential.' How can a layman check up on something like that? The pollution of the Columbia River strikes me as having precious little to do with national security. The people have the right to know. I'm not against atomic energy, but I'm for information."

Once Miss DesChamps, who is fond of clams but was so busy absorbing and emitting radioactive information that in 1960 she didn't even bother to get a shellfish license, went into action, she amassed a lot of allies. Shortly after reading the article in the *Skipper*, she attended an informal meeting in Provincetown called to protest the A.E.C.'s plan to let another company dump low-level waste off the Cape. That meeting spawned a propaganda group with the title of the Lower Cape Committee on Radioactive Waste Disposal, and this attracted a couple of hundred members, including some from the Upper Cape. Its principal working members, though, have been an unflagging triumvirate—Miss Des-Champs, and Mr. and Mrs. Ned Lehac, who live in Wellfleet, five miles up Cape from Truro. Lehac is a retired junior-high-school science teacher from the Bronx whose avocation is songwriting; he wrote the melody for, among other numbers, "You Forgot Your Gloves." He and his wife, who used to be a dancer, bought an old Wellfleet house in 1956. "Jane and I searched around for the ideal retirement spot," he told me one day, "and we finally decided on Wellfleet and put all our money in our house, and practically the next thing we knew they were dumping atomic junk in our back yard. Every time I think about it I get angry. I've been thinking about it for over a year and I'm still angry. Anger is a luxury, you know, but I can afford to indulge myself, because I sleep only four hours a night."

One might have supposed that a local phenomenon like the Lower Cape Committee would not be able to disconcert the mighty A.E.C. One would have been wrong. As early as 1956, a nongovernmental association called the Atomic Industrial Forum sponsored a meeting on public relations, during which one participant advised his audience that "a hostile public has recourses in the nuclear field not otherwise open to them," and explained this statement by saying, "Small community groups, aroused to vocal opposition by fear or apprehension, can appeal to their state government or to their representatives in Congress, with an excellent chance of at least delaying progress. Such action, even if it is promptly squelched, still can lay a foundation of suspicion and doubt not easily dispelled." He went on to say that a good way to allay doubt and suspicion was to get to "the little guy," by which he meant the small-town newspaper editor. "Swing him and you'll probably swing the community," he said. The Lower Cape Committee proved unsquelchable; not only did it make the conventional representations to its elected representatives, but it went in for some vigorous swinging itself, sometimes of the roundhouse variety and sometimes—or so the A.E.C. seemed to think—aimed below the belt. Almost at the start of the battle, the Boston *Globe,* a relatively big-guy paper, ran a dispatch from Miss Des-Champs indicating that some wastes incidental to the production of the Hiroshima bomb were among those resting on the sea bottom off Boston and Provincetown. Hiroshima wastes are not necessarily any more potent than anonymous radioactive wastes, but they sound scarier. The A.E.C. subsequently denied this particular allegation, but Miss Des-Champs insisted that she got the news straight from the man who deposited that historic cache of trash. She and Lehac, moreover, began to peck away at the A.E.C. through a flurry of letters, full of fear and apprehension, to two small-guy weeklies, the Provincetown *Advocate* and the *Cape Codder.* "The editor of the *Advocate* was terrific," Lehac told me. "We got him so worked up *he* couldn't sleep nights, either, and he's no four-hour man." The *Cape Codder* also got edgy, and, on one occasion, ran an editorial putting some of its anxieties into the mouth of a talking sea gull, which said, "That's our ocean out there. We live out of that ocean. And you use it as an atomic wastebasket."

In September, 1959, the Atomic Energy Commission deferred to the entreaties of the Lower Cape Committee and other vocal Cape Codders to the extent of holding a round-table discussion in Boston on the license it wanted to grant. (The A.E.C. also dispatched half a dozen of its officials to Truro, to give the Lower Cape selectmen an authoritative briefing on waste disposal. One selectman observed that the A.E.C. might have forestalled all the fuss if instead of identifying the location of its Atlantic dump site as "east of Massachusetts" it had resorted to "west of the Azores.") At the instigation of Lehac, who thought it "incongruous and ironic" that one branch of the federal government should have been dumping radioactive wastes near an area that another branch wanted to conserve as an ornament of nature, the National Park Service sent an observer. A parade of witnesses testified at the hearing that there was nothing dangerous about either the dumping that was contemplated or the dumping that had already been carried out. Dr. Ketchum, the Woods Hole man who had helped alarm Cape Codders by stressing the incompleteness of scientific knowledge, said dramatically that if a person obtained all his proteins for thirty years off fish taken from one of the disposal areas, he would consume less than one-tenth of the radioactive substances generally deemed safe for human ingestion. Even this, however, failed to tranquillize many Cape Codders, and presently they learned that their concern about radioactive waste disposal in the high seas was not unique. "We didn't think anybody gave a good gosh damn about what was happening," Miss DesChamps told me, "but we found we had friends everywhere."

One crony materialized in the person of a Boston lawyer named James B. Muldoon, who, in one of a series of articles he wrote for the *Massachusetts Law Quarterly* on the legal aspects of radioactivity, declared, "The fatal and inexcusable defect in the public health philosophy of the nuclear scientists is that they are primarily concerned with how much radiation a man can stand, and not how perfectly can he be protected against all radiation." (Muldoon, who, like Miss DesChamps, is a self-taught nuclear-energy expert, added a learned footnote to the waste-disposal issue when he revealed that in 1624 Sir Francis Bacon, in *The New Atlantis,* had anticipated the whole problem by speaking of a future world with furnaces spewing forth "wildfires burning in water and unquenchable.") Other friends turned up in Texas. The A.E.C. had already had a handful of curies dumped into the Gulf of Mexico and hoped to deposit more there—a prospect that not only riled a lot of Texas fishermen (fishermen are not to be trifled with anywhere) but provoked the Mexican government into lodging a demurrer with the State Department, which told the A.E.C. that its scheme could have "seriously harmful effects" on international relations. Loath to be a party to creating seriously harmful effects, the A.E.C. stayed its hand, though not before the Houston *Chronicle* had run several waspish dispatches from Miss DesChamps, one of them headed "Echo of Hiroshima Bomb Stirs Cape Cod Area."

Miss DesChamps was by this time rolling along in fine fettle and high gear, not to mention high dudgeon. Less than a year after she first learned about waste-dumping from the *Skipper,* she was writing about waste-dumping for the *Skipper.* She was also writing for the *Nation,* in which she painted the picture of her crusade in broad strokes: "For the first time in the history of Cape Cod—a stronghold of conservative political thinking and a birthplace of the democratic procedures—Cape Codders will weigh their venerable heritage against the power of a government agency from whose rulings it would appear there is no appeal." When the New Bedford *Standard-Times,* which has a daily Cape Cod section and is normally a stronghold of conservative journalistic thinking, although it endorsed President Kennedy, ran an interview with the offshore dumper from Boston in which he was quoted, or perhaps misquoted, as saying that ninety-five per cent of the radioisotopes he handled were dead before they left his wharf and that cesium 137, for example, had a half life of a mere 2.6 minutes (meaning the amount of time it took that element to shed half its radioactivity), Miss DesChamps pounced hawklike on the statement. Cesium 137, she pointed out in letters to two other papers, has a half life of over thirty years and, no matter how many fathoms deep it may be interred, it is still alive and kicking, radioactively, for three hundred years. Her indignation, though, and that of other opponents of the A.E.C.'s sea-dumping procedures did not sway the editorial page of the *Standard-Times,* which subsequently endorsed radioactive waste-dumping in the ocean as "a program vital to the national well-being."

And so it went on well into 1960, with the A.E.C.'s advocates periodically explaining how far the agency was bending over backward to be safe, out of deference toward unwarranted public apprehension, and with the Lower Cape Committee and its supporters periodically asserting that if the A.E.C. was taking as many precautions as it said it was, then the stuff it was getting off its hands must be hot potatoes indeed—conceivably hotter than anybody had conceded. In one sense, it was a standoff: The Lower Cape Committee could not prove that any human being, or any fish or clam, had yet suffered, or was ever bound to suffer, from Atlantic fallup ("fallup" is the oceanic cousin of fallout), and the A.E.C. could not prove that some man or fish or clam or microscopic speck of plankton would not someday be the worse for what it had done and could not now undo.

By the spring of 1960, most Cape Codders had begun to fret about less cosmic matters, such as whether the 1960 beach-plum crop would be good, like 1958's, or bad, like 1959's. (Bad, it turned out, but radioactivity was not to blame; it rained a lot while the beach-plum bushes were in spring flower, and the local bumblebees in charge of pollination stayed huddled in their hives.) Then, in April, nuclear energy suddenly reëntered the Cape's consciousness—again as a result of activities that had started years before.

Late in 1956, it developed, a Massachusetts commission had been set up to look into the possibility of putting the atomic-energy industry on the state map. The commission came up with a report that, after dwelling rhapsodically on Cape Cod's rose-covered cottages, tree-lined streets, and natural beauties, said the Cape would be a natural spot for a new nuclear installation, including a fuel-reprocessing plant. Such a plant revivifies the worn-out cores of old nuclear reactors, and this process generates radioactive wastes—not the low-level, fractional-curie, two-hundred-miles-

out, encased-in-steel-and-concrete-and-diluted-by-sea-water
kind that had been so much discussed, but wastes of the highest level, with a potency of thousands of curies, the kind that
the A.E.C. has been cautiously burying in stout underground
tanks in the sparsely settled West. In this case, that archfoe
the A.E.C. was not directly involved, except insofar as it
holds a checkrein on all national nuclear-energy work and
insofar as it would presumably have been invited to contribute a subsidy to the research phase of the operation. At
any rate, early in 1960, after some thirty months of investigation, a bill was introduced in the Massachusetts legislature
calling for a "nuclear park" to be constructed on a twenty-
thousand-acre abandoned Army base, Camp Edwards, on
the Upper Cape, near Falmouth.

As had been the case with oceanic waste-dumping, although the nuclear park had been publicly discussed, nobody
on the Cape—not even the little guys—seemed to have heard
anything about it. "Frankly, we were sound asleep," confessed a *Cape Codder* editorial afterward. When Grace
DesChamps, who had been nodding herself, came to and read
the commission's report, she burst out crying. She was
aroused, and so was the rest of the Cape, by the Falmouth *Enterprise*, a semi-weekly, which broke the story after being
jabbed into wakefulness itself by a subscriber's request for
enlightenment. Once awakened, Cape Codders, displayed
the vigor that often follows a long snooze. "It is becoming
increasingly clear that Cape Cod is facing some powerful
forces in its fight to escape ruination," cried the *Cape Codder*.

There were so many objections to a nuclear park that
Cape Codders hardly knew which to bring up first. Its very
name, perhaps; for three years they had been mulling over
a bona-fide national park, and now all at once here was the
word "park" with a startlingly different and far more un-
palatable connotation. "A rose by any other name . . ." be-

gan a letter that Miss DesChamps dashed off to the *Cape Codder*. Then, too, this masquerading park was to be cheek by jowl with the Otis Air Base, a very much *not* abandoned outpost of national defense. Suppose a stray plane should crash into a hot-waste storage tank, or a jet's supersonic boom should rupture a waste-carrying pipe? Or what if an underground tank should just plain leak? At no Western installation where high-level radioactive wastes are buried is the water table closer to ground level than two hundred feet; on the Cape it is nowhere farther from ground level than sixty feet.

The *Enterprise,* before sounding the alarm, had solicited and obtained a statement from one of its constituents, Dr. Albert Szent-Györgyi, who won the Nobel Prize for isolating Vitamin C and has lately been director of the Institute for Muscle Research at Woods Hole. Dr. Szent-Györgyi was already a member of the Lower Cape Committee, and on its behalf had signed, along with two other scientists, a letter published in the *Bulletin of the Atomic Scientists* inquiring tartly whether the A.E.C., in view of a pledge it had made to maintain a careful vigil over the drums dropped in the ocean, proposed to keep divers underwater round the clock to watch for signs of disintegration. (The A.E.C. had at least a hope of an answer to *that* one; it had begun experimenting, at the off-Boston dump site, with a sleepless monitor in the form of an underwater television camera.) Now the scientist, whose name means "Saint George" in Hungarian, took another thrust at the nuclear dragon. Referring to the shallowness of Cape Cod's water table, he said that if any high-level radioactive waste drifted from a tank at Camp Edwards into the Cape's sandy and porous soil, "we can wipe Cape Cod off the map as a place fit for human habitation."

Several other Woods Hole eminences, many of whom own property in or near Falmouth, rallied to the cause. Dr.

Ketchum, the oceanographer who had spoken up in favor of low-level dumping in the Atlantic, was moved to pay a call on State Senator Edward C. Stone, who, after talking with several more of the local scientists, concluded that a nuclear park had its drawbacks. In other parts of Massachusetts, there were people—particularly those in the atomic-energy industry, for whom a nearby fuel-reprocessing plant would be convenient—who considered the nuclear park a fine notion, but on the Cape itself the park's proponents were pretty well narrowed down to a few Chamber of Commerce executives and some businessmen from Buzzards Bay, a fried-clam-and-souvenir-shack enclave that calls itself part of the Cape but that lies on the mainland side of the Cape Cod Canal and is thus thought by some folk on the seaward side not to be an authentic part of the Cape at all. A pro-park electrical contractor, the president of the Buzzards Bay Chamber of Commerce, said, "We expected some of this opposition. We knew it would come from those who want always to keep Cape Cod as a vacation resort in the summer and a year-round nursing home for the elderly retired."

Senator Stone was eighty-two at the time of that remark, but he was not retired; in fact, he was just getting set to run successfully for reëlection. Nor was the opposition anywhere near as circumscribed as that. Its ranks were speedily swelled by a public-health doctor, who foresaw the Cape turning into "a huge atomic cesspool"; an outraged pathologist who specialized in the effects of radioactivity; an equally outraged marine biologist whose specialty was scallops; an almost splenetic biophysicist; a chapter of the D.A.R.; both the local Medical Society and the Health Association; the Portuguese-American Civic League; and, to no one's surprise, the Lower Cape Committee on Radioactive Waste Disposal. "Criminal negligence!" thundered Lehac. "Suicidal atomic amusement park!" He fired off a letter to the governor of Massachusetts, suggesting that if the nuclear park became a reality "we might as well change the Cape slogan of 'At the Beach' to 'On the Beach.' "

In May, at Senator Stone's request, the Massachusetts Legislative Joint Committee on Power and Light held two public hearings, at the upper end of the Cape, on the nuclear-park bill. "We have brought the government to the people," the committee chairman declared. The people responded with spirit. Scientist after scientist took the witness stand to assail the plan, one of them calling to the solons' attention an old Greek proverb that, in his translation, went, "Physician, before thou touchest thy patient, or before thou givest him thy herbs, make sure thy treatment will do him no harm." A former major general who had served as the Army's Deputy Director of Military Applications of Atomic Science said that the scientists not only had not exaggerated the hazards to Cape Cod of a fuel-reprocessing plant but had understated their case. "I could give some examples of things that can happen that would really create some panic in this audience," he said, creating a fair amount of panic with that teaser alone. Lehac, adopting what in other circumstances might have been considered a Chamber of Commerce viewpoint, reminded the legislators that the Cape Cod tourist business has been itself a hundred-million-dollar annual industry, and that for Massachusetts to jeopardize such a source of gravy by putting a nuclear plant right in the midst of the vacationers who ladle it out seemed to him preposterous. Shortly after the hearings were concluded, it was disclosed that the Commonwealth of Massachusetts was looking around for a less controversial nuclear-park site. "What has happened on Cape Cod reveals what an *alerted* public, willing to fight for its rights, can do to safeguard itself from the machinations of those in the atomic industry to whom public safety is not the primary consideration," Miss DesChamps exulted, and Muldoon rejoiced, "The Cape Cod decision is

historic. Public opinion, for the first time competently informed, for the first time has had a chance to make a moral
decision. What happened on Cape Cod is of countrywide
importance."

What happened may or may not have proved to have been
as consequential as all that, but the double dose of exposure
to radioactive affairs undoubtedly shook up Cape Codders
and prompted them to keep an eye quizzically cocked at the
meddling outside world. In June, 1960, they noted with due
interest an announcement by the A.E.C. that the Coast and
Geodetic Survey and the Public Health Service had jointly
checked its off-Boston dump site and had found no traces of
radioactivity in the water, the bottom sediments, or the sea
life. That same month, the International Atomic Energy
Agency published a statement by its director-general, Sterling Cole, who was formerly a co-chairman of the Joint Congressional Committee on Atomic Energy; Mr. Cole thought
that "waste" was a bad word for radioactive refuse, since
somebody might someday find a use for the stuff, and that
as long as that possibility existed, it seemed a shame to dis-
pose of it irrevocably, at any level of intensity. In August,
there was a small explosion and fire on the Boston wharf of
the original Atlantic dumper, and Lehac at once asked the
city's mayor to investigate the incident, adding, on behalf
of the Lower Cape Committee, "We hope this investigation
will lead to the conclusion that radioactive materials should
NEVER be stored anywhere near thickly settled communities."
At last report, he had heard nothing conclusive from the
mayor. Meanwhile, the Cape's Congressman Keith announced that he was trying to promote the increased use of
scallops in government dining rooms and in school lunches,
an executive of the Buzzards Bay Chamber of Commerce
wrote the *Standard-Times* that Communist agents had had
a hand in scotching the nuclear park, and Miss DesChamps,
who is a member of the Truro Republican Town Commit-

tee, replied with a lambasting rebuttal. ("I think I'm as intensely patriotic a person as you could find anywhere," she once said. "If loving your native heath and being willing almost to shed your skin for it isn't patriotic, I don't know what patriotism is.") The *Standard-Times* itself, which in June had editorially called a nuclear park "a means of endeavoring to bring better balance to the Cape's economy through additional industrial payroll," started off a later editorial crisply with "Litter is the bane of Cape Cod." This turned out, anticlimactically, to be a plea for non-radioactive tidiness at beaches and on roadsides. Truro had a special town meeting to discuss the safety and cleanliness of its beaches, and toward the end of the session Grace DesChamps took the floor and made a fervent and eloquent speech urging that somebody please do something about having a single rubbish barrel placed at the approach to a beach near her house. Prophets are not always honored at home, and no action was taken on her motion.

The
Infinite Variety
of
Customs

Before the war, I once met a ship carrying home to New York a lady who was trying, unsuccessfully, to smuggle in a fur coat she'd bought in Europe, and from which she had cannily, she thought, removed the telltale label. The dressing down she got when she was caught (let alone the penalties she subsequently had to pay) taught her a good lesson and made such a lasting impression on me, too, that ever since I have been apprehensive of, though never yet apprehended by, customs men everywhere.

Accordingly, as a person whose nerves have a consistency less like steel than like tapioca, I was perhaps the worst possible emissary who could have been entrusted, as I found myself entrusted in the summer of 1958, with spiriting out from behind the Iron Curtain an egregious symbol of Western culture. It was a tennis racket, the property of an American correspondent who'd been stationed in Moscow and, after being declared *persona non grata*, had had to de-

camp in haste. Hearing through a mutual friend that my
wife and I were going to the Soviet Union, he looked me up
and asked if I'd mind fetching his racket. So earnest was his
entreaty that I couldn't say no, though I also couldn't help
suspecting, from the apparent degree of his attachment to
the implement, that it was more than a mere plaything.

In any event, I said I'd see what I could do, and he instructed me to get in touch with an American radio-and-
television man at the Hotel Metropole in Moscow. Before
Jinny and I got there, we were having supper in Leningrad,
at the Hotel Astoria, a setting for big-time international in-
trigue if ever I saw one. We heard two men at an adjoining
table talking, in English, about some difficulties they were
having in connection with extraterritorial broadcasts. On a
hunch, I introduced myself to them and asked if either of
them happened to be the custodian of a certain tennis racket
I was seekng.

"Not here," said one of them quickly, in a low voice. "Call
me in Moscow." He then resumed his conversation, and
in a few moments, without a further glance of recognition,
left the room.

A few days later, we reached Moscow, and after some com-
plications in arranging a rendezvous—to go into the details
of which here might compromise that man's security, or
mine—we came face to face again in the lobby of the Metropole. He was clutching a tennis racket, and he handed it to
me quickly. I was glad to perceive that its handle, which in
my imagination had been thoroughly hollowed out, was in
fact of conventional heft, though the racket had two busted
strings, and from a tennis player's viewpoint hardly seemed
worth making much of a fuss over.

As I started off with it, its curator asked me where I was
staying. Thinking he probably wanted to get together for a
drink or something, I told him. "I'll have the keys sent
over," he said.

I looked puzzled.

"Aren't you supposed to pick up the trunk keys, too?" he asked.

"This is the first I ever heard about it," I said truthfully.

"You'll get them tomorrow," he said firmly. "Now wait here."

He boarded an ascending elevator, and, twenty minutes later, returned and thrust into my now sweating hand a tightly wrapped and stoutly sealed package, about the size of a soccer ball.

"That's the lot of it," he said, and then he disappeared.

I never heard from him again, and the keys never materialized. By the time Jinny and I left Moscow, we had so many last-minute chores to attend to that until we'd been waved through Soviet customs at the airport—many of the other tourists present carrying souvenir balalaikas, I carrying a tennis racket—we both forgot that the package, still wrapped as it was when I'd received it, was in my suitcase. For an instant, I felt panicky, but by the time we'd boarded our plane I felt as smug and debonair about the deception I'd pulled off as if my heels were full of heroin. I felt relieved, too, later on, that customs hadn't opened my bag. I'd have been terribly let down, had its contents been officially scrutinized, for customs to find, as Jinny and I found when we reached the sanctuary of the Western world, that the mysterious package merely contained a man's sport shirt, a pair of sneakers, and some dirty white tennis shorts.

The most upsetting experience I ever had with any nation's customs officials was with those of a friendly neighbor, Canada. The episode, however, did have one rewarding aspect. I had often thought, as I suppose others think who, like me, fritter away much of their time on crossword puzzles, that this avocation is profitless, inasmuch as so many of the words we wrestle with do not otherwise figure in our lives. The word "agio" had long seemed to me an excellent

example of this sorry state of affairs. Usually defined as
"premium on exchange" or simply "exchange premium,"
good old "agio" had time and again crept into the empty
squares of puzzles I had tackled, but until I made two round
trips, in fairly rapid succession, between New York and
Montreal one spring, I'd never had occasion to think of the
word in any other connection.

Each time, I travelled north by overnight train. Each time,
I took with me a small suitcase and a portable typewriter—
the latter because I planned to do some research while in
Canada and wanted to transcribe my notes on the spot.

On my first northbound journey, shortly after I got up in
the morning, there was a knock on the door of my roomette,
and I opened it to find a Canadian customs official standing
outside. He asked me· how much luggage I had, and I said
only two pieces.

"Personal effects, I suppose?" the customs man said.

"Yes," I replied. "That, and a typewriter."

He frowned. Might he inquire what I proposed to do with
the typewriter while a guest in his country?

I explained that I was on a business trip, and would be
transcribing notes on it. He said that in that event, he was
sorry to have to inform me, I'd be required to pay a deposit
on the machine, but he assured me I'd get back every last
penny of it when I left Canada. "Of course, it would be much
easier all around if you'd just let me take the typewriter and
put it in bond until you depart," he said. I pointed out that
if it was in bond, I couldn't type on it. The customs man
sighed, pulled out a sheaf of blank forms from a briefcase,
and began filling out one of them, in triplicate. It was something called a Temporary Admissions Report, inscribed with
a great deal of small print. Later on, I began to read some of
this, but I stopped upon reaching a warning, in print no less
frightening for being tiny, to the effect that under no circum-

stances was I to import into Canada an outboard motor for use in the operation of a commercial tourist camp.

The customs man asked me politely how much my typewriter, which he seemed pleased to see was a Royal, was worth. I had had it for eleven years, and I had no idea what it cost new, or how one would reckon depreciation on a typewriter even if the original cost was known. I told him his guess was as good as mine.

"Shall we say forty dollars?" he suggested.

That seemed fair enough to me, and presently, after some scribbled computation, the customs man declared that I owed him twelve dollars and eighty cents. I handed over thirteen dollars, in bills, and waited for my change.

"Oh, *American*," he said, looking at my money, and referring to it in the slightly patronizing tone that many Canadians began to employ as soon as their dollar became worth more than ours. "In *American*, that will come to thirteen dollars and twenty cents, sir. But don't fret; you'll get it all back."

I handed him twenty cents. He gave me the duplicate and the triplicate of the form he had made out, and he enjoined me not to fail to present these to Canadian customs on my way out of the country, so I'd get my money back. I thanked him, and he went on and knocked briskly at the door of the next roomette.

Several days later, I took a train south. Soon after I boarded it, a Canadian customs man came through my car. I stopped him, flourished my carefully preserved duplicate and triplicate, pointed to my typewriter, and said I believed I had a refund coming. He said that was quite correct, took my papers, and promised me that the Canadian government would be mailing me a check in a week or so.

I had to return to Canada before the check arrived, but I

told my wife to be on the lookout for it. I carried the type-writer with me on the second trip, too. This time, I was ready for Canadian customs, and when its agent duly came by in the morning, I greeted him cheerfully and told him at once that I had a portable typewriter. He bade me good morning and started to go on to the next roomette.

"Hey, don't I have to pay a deposit and get a Temporary Admissions Report?" I asked.

The customs man stopped, reflected for a moment, and then said that, by golly, maybe I was right. He dug into his briefcase, read a paragraph in what appeared to be a book of excise regulations, and nodded a couple of times. Then he brought forth the familiar form and asked me how much my typewriter was worth.

"Well, it was valued at forty dollars a fortnight ago," I said.

He accepted that valuation and said, "Let's see—that means you owe me twelve-eighty."

"Right you are," I said. "That's thirteen-twenty American, isn't it?"

He did some computing. "Thirteen-sixteen American," he said firmly.

I decided not to argue, and paid him thirteen-sixteen.

A few hours later, my wife telephoned me at my hotel, in a state of high elation, to report that a check had just arrived from the Customs and Excises Divisions of the National Revenue of Canada, by registered mail. I asked her if the check was for thirteen dollars and twenty cents.

"No," she said, "twelve dollars and ninety-six cents."

"Oh, of course," I said. "That's Canadian. When I cash it at the bank after I get home, I suppose I'll receive thirteen-twenty for it."

"But didn't you tell me that your deposit was the equivalent of twelve dollars and eighty cents Canadian?" asked Jinny. "Why should they give you back an additional sixteen cents?"

"Skip it," I said. "This call is costing us money."

On my second homeward trip, at the border, with my typewriter at my side and my duplicate and triplicate at the ready, I waited in vain for a Canadian customs man to turn up. Finally, I asked a passing United States customs man if his Canadian counterpart would be along soon. He said I didn't have to concern myself with Canadian customs, travelling in that direction. I explained that I had a Temporary Admissions Report to relinquish. The American customs man said he'd be glad to take it for me and pass it along. "We have an unwritten agreement," he explained.

I handed him my documents. But when he he looked at them and saw that a refund was involved, he handed them back hastily and told me to tell my porter to summon Canadian customs. I rang for the porter and gave him that message. He said authoritatively that there wasn't any Canadian customs man aboard.

"Nonsense. There must be," I said. "I make this ride all the time, and I know."

At that moment, the conductor entered the car, and the porter referred the problem to him.

"Don't you worry about customs," the conductor said. "If you're in a jam with them, they'll catch you. They always do."

"But I'm not in a jam and I want to catch *them*," I said.

"Why be so eager about giving them your money?" he said.

"I want *them* to give *me* money," I said, almost shouting.

The conductor was impatient to get moving. "Look, if you got anything to hide, buddy, hide it now, while you got a chance," he said, and off he went.

Eventually, a Canadian customs man did materialize, and I gave him my papers, and he told me a check would be forthcoming, and I retired for the night.

As soon as I could, I took the refund check for $12.96 Canadian to my bank, went to the foreign-exchange window, and presented it for payment. The teller examined it, did some calculating, and handed me $12.97 American. Two days later, refund check No. 2 arrived. It was for $13.14. I went back to the bank and presented it to the same teller, who handed me $13.17.

"There's fifteen cents Canadian clearing-house charge on this, you know," he said.

I nodded, but I certainly didn't know. I hadn't the foggiest notion why I should have been refunded $12.97 on a deposit of $13.20, and $13.17 on a deposit of $13.16. I had a hunch, though, that it all had to do with agio.

It is not often that one gets a chance to experience at first hand the inner workings of an arcane business, which is what the import-export trade had long been to me. My opportunity arose unexpectedly one morning when I fished a letter from the United States Bureau of Customs, down at Bowling Green, out of my suburban post-office box.

The letter was headed "ORIGINAL—Notification to Consignee (Addressee) of Mail Importation to Make Formal Entry (In Lieu of Bill of Lading)." It informed me that a shipment comprising one package of woollen wearing apparel with a declared value of over two hundred and fifty dollars had been sent to me by Davies & Son, London, W.1.

I knew what the shipment was. Now and then, I have had a suit made by that firm, and when its representative was in New York one winter, I went on a wild sartorial fling and ordered two suits at once. From the valuation put on my consignment, I concluded that both suits had been dispatched in a single box. What puzzled me was that on previous occasions I had been able to claim my clothes simply by paying my own postmaster the duty—usually around thirty-five dollars a suit. I had no idea what had happened this time, but I was anxious to get at, and into, my new apparel, and, being on my way to the city, I decided that when I got there

I would go straight down to Bowling Green and find out.

Once I had reached town, it occurred to me that customs might be less agreeable than my local postmaster about accepting personal checks, so I went first of all to my bank, and fortified myself with seventy-five dollars in cash. I was about to board a subway for Bowling Green when I took another look at my letter. "To meet customs requirements," it said, "this notice (in lieu of bill of lading) together with invoice and other related papers, should be presented at Entry Division, Custom House, Bowling Green, New York City (after arrival of the shipment) by the addressee (consignee) or his duly authorized agent or transferee. If you are not familiar with customs requirements, write or telephone the customs officer of the address indicated before proceeding to the Custom House. This may save time and expense on your part."

Eager to save both, I went into a phone booth, called the Custom House, and was connected with—I supposed—a customs officer, to whom I explained my situation. "You got your invoice?" he asked, and I said that, not yet having been billed by my tailor, I had no papers at all beyond my "Notification to Consignee (Addressee)." He sighed, not unsympathetically, and asked if my notice had "Morgan Annex" stamped on it. It had. "Then you got to go there," he said. "Ninth Avenue and Thirtieth Street." By this time, it was ten o'clock. I had a lunch date on the East Side at twelve-thirty. I set out hurriedly for the Morgan Annex.

At the Annex, which turned out to be an adjunct of the main post office, I was sent to Room 503, where a clerk at a desk turned me over to another man, who led me into an enormous, fenced-in storage area piled high with crates and packages. "Wait there," my escort said, pointing toward a stand-up desk with a ball of twine on top of it. I complied, the man went away, and in a jiffy he returned and handed me my parcel from London. He also handed me a wicked-looking knife. "Open the package and see if you can find an invoice," he commanded. I slashed the wrapping paper loose, reached under the box lid, and quickly found an invoice nestling on a sheet of tissue paper that covered my suits. I was about to pull one of the suits out and look at it when the man said, "O.K., tie her up again."

I tied her up, but in rather slipshod fashion. The man expressed dismay at my slovenliness, but I assured him it didn't matter; I'd be carrying the suits to my office in a cab, I explained, and the box would hold together. "You're not carrying them anywhere yet," he said. "I'll retie it myself. Go on back to the desk clerk."

I conveyed my invoice to the clerk, and took out my wallet. He asked what I was doing that for, and I said I wanted to pay the duty and get my suits. "Oh, you have to get an entry permit first," he said. "Go to Room 118 at Bowling Green." And as I backed off, he called cheerfully, "Better post bond while you're there. It'll save you time."

I left the Morgan Annex, hailed a cab, and accepted the driver's suggestion that we take the West Side Highway to save time. (I had already abandoned all hope of saving expense.) At Room 118, on the main floor of the massive Custom House, I presented my letter and invoice to a clerk. "You make entry over there," he said, pointing toward a desk where an official was seated, talking to a couple of men. I went there. As nearly as I could figure out, the official was telling the men that however tolerant the United States Customs might be of human frailty, it did not yet stand ready to go along with listing a boatload of umbrellas as chinaware.

Presently, his auditors slunk away, abashed, and he turned to me. "Sit down," he said. "You got a couple of hours of paperwork ahead of you." I asked how it could possibly take that long to redeem two suits. "Brother, it isn't a question of two suits any more," he said. "You might just as well have ordered a ton of jute. You get anything in one lot that's worth over two hundred and fifty dollars, you're in the import business. You're going to have four places to go upstairs after you finish here. Of course, if you don't want to bother, you can always engage a customs broker."

I sat down. I have enough brokers already—insurance, investment, real-estate, theatre-ticket, whatnot—and I decided that if I was going to have to be in the import business, I might as well learn it from the ground floor up.

For half an hour, while I waited, the man methodically filled out forms on my behalf, the principal ones being an "Entry Record Receipt Missing Documents" and a "Consumption Entry." I looked at my watch, and saw that it was nearly noon. He asked me if I was hungry, and I said I had a lunch date and perhaps had better postpone importing my suits. "Oh, don't do that," he said amiably. "You can fill out the rest of these forms yourself and bring them back this afternoon. Don't get here after four."

My lunch appointment was with a man who insisted on telling me, in detail, how he and some neighbors had formed a small combine to import their own French wines, and thus avoid the retailers' markup. He said that the ringleader of this vinous mob had told him there was really nothing to it. As soon as I could, I wished him Godspeed, excused myself, and repaired to my office, where I spent the next hour filling out forms, such as a declaration of consignee, or agent, for merchandise obtained in pursuance of a purchase or agreement to purchase. In the course of all this, I found myself airily referring to myself—following the example of my man in Room 118—as an Importer of Record, Commercial, who had a Single Entry consisting of eight pounds, net quantity, of Schedule A Units, under Paragraph 1115 (a). Commodity Number 3640.100.

At three o'clock, I was back in Room 118, Custom House, where my friend greeted me warmly and nodded approvingly as he read through my sheaf of papers and rubber-stamped each of them three or four times. "You should have bought only one suit," he said pleasantly. We both laughed, he somewhat less shrilly than I, and then, on the blank side of a square of scratch paper that had been cut from some mimeographed sheet, he scribbled a list of instructions for me:

(1) Mr. Brady or Mr. Sheridan for Bond in corridor outside Room 248, opposite Window 1.
(2) Bond Desk, Window 7, 8, or 9. Room 248.
(3) Window 1, Room 248. Wait for Papers.
(4) Cashier's Office, Room 217.
(5) Return to Room 118.

Clutching, among my other documents, a new form, "Immediate Delivery and Consumption Entry Bond (Single Entry)," I headed upstairs. In a crowded corridor, near a sign that said "Lodging Consumption and Warehouse Entries," I found both Mr. Brady *and* Mr. Sheridan, who, as representatives of the Seaboard Surety Company, issued me a four-hundred-dollar bond—conceivably the smallest sum they traffic in—on payment of a dollar and a half. (Certainly that sum was too puny for them, because they could not change a five-dollar bill. I got change by momentarily arresting the headlong flight of one of several dozen men, possibly customs brokers, who were running up and down the corridor in a kind of bureaucratic relay race, passing documents back and forth like batons.) Leaving Mr. Brady and Mr. Sheridan, I went on to Window 7, where a clerk took away all my papers and gave me a slip with a six-digit number written on it (I have since forgotten what it was), which he said would identify *my* number. I asked him what my number was, and he pointed pityingly to "927686," which

I then perceived, for the first time, had been profusely stamped on all my papers. I vowed never to forget it, and moved—or, rather, was shoved—out of line. Everybody seemed to be in a terrible hurry.

Window 1 reminded me of my post office back home—a tiny, grilled aperture surrounded by individual, locked boxes. As I approached it, men were rushing up, unlocking their boxes, scooping out papers, and dashing away—all time-savers, all, I surmised, customs brokers. I'd never seen such an agitated bunch. Feeling like a summer tenant who has to ask for his mail at the window because he doesn't have a box of his own, I stepped up and gave my identifying number.

A few minutes later, a voice behind the window cried out "E.J.!" and—pleased at this informal, if not downright intimate, touch—I grabbed the papers that the owner of the voice was thrusting at me through the bars, and strode briskly away toward the cashier's office. But I strode right back after a teller there had glanced at my papers and said scornfully, "You only have a permit. You haven't made entry." I got back to Window 1 in time to hear a voice calling out, "Six—eight—six!" This turned out to be another local nickname for me, and presently I got some more papers, signifying that I had now somehow made entry.

From there on, it was a relative cinch. Oh, I was held up for a while at the cashier's office because I didn't have in exact change the seventy-two dollars and thirty-three cents I owed in duty, but eventually (after filling out a depositor's ticket) I got it, and persuaded a teller to accept my money. Then I returned to Room 118, where I dropped all the papers I had on my mentor's desk. "Hey, you got *two* receipts for duty!" he said admiringly. "You're very lucky. Now you can go back to the Morgan Annex."

At the familiar old Annex, I turned in one of my receipts and asked if I could now have my suits. "No," said the man on duty. "They haven't been inspected by customs yet. Call us in two or three days."

Five days later, I got the suits. The box they were in had been stoutly trussed with copper wire, and I had to pay fifteen cents in postage due for "customs clearance and delivery." I could see that it was just as well I had finally managed to make entry; if I hadn't, there is no telling what might have happened. On the parcel were two printed labels, evidently the handiwork of British customs, one label saying that the merchandise therein should be returned to the sender if undeliverable, the other saying that once the merchandise had been mailed, it *may in no circumstances be returned to the sender.* (Italics theirs, or at any rate not mine.)

There you have it, and if anybody has a couple of carloads of dutiable merchandise en route and wants to dispense with the services of a broker, I know the importing routine. I think it only fair to point out, though, that I have no intention of getting mixed up in the export business as well. As I was leaving Room 118 at Bowling Green, my buddy there suggested jovially that I stop in someday and let him see how one of the suits looked on me. When I replied politely that I might, if I didn't have to return them to England for alterations, his mood sobered. "You better not have to," he said, "because if you do, it'll have to be done through here." Who cares if the shoulders ride high?

Some of our friends who had made similar jaunts had camped out along the way, and they denounced this accessory as not merely extravagant but effete; they urged us, if only to atone for our self-indulgence, to take along a tent and the accessories to go with *that*. One well-intentioned counsellor even gave my wife an apron and two pot holders as a bon-voyage gift. But we are not a field-and-stream family, and with a deliberateness in which I heartily concurred, Jinny left this gear behind, though she did buy a portable icebox out of which we could picnic on the road. (I wished later that she'd bought a fly swatter as an accessory for that.) The only other concession we made to the more or less rugged life was to carry, in case of emergency, three sleeping bags left over from a summer that the boys had spent in camp. We transported these on top of the car in a luggage rack that also held five large suitcases containing our dress-up clothes, in case of festivity.

My wife (who believes that one good custom-made frock, however costly, will outlast a closetful of ready-mades) commissioned a local craftsman to create a waterproof tarpaulin whose edges were supposed to snap snugly around the metal rails of the luggage rack. When I went to the fellow's atelier to pick the thing up, he assured me that the snaps would hold, no matter how far or how fast we drove; as an extra precaution, though, he added some grommets so that it could be tied on if need be. This was just as well. Our first day out, the snaps began popping loose, and the only tie lines we could find to keep the covering from floating away were our shoe-laces. Even after we had stopped at a hardware store and bought clothesline to replace these improvised bindings, the tarp kept flapping wildly. In Missouri, heading west on the celebrated U. S. 66, we halted to lash down one billowing corner, and a car that had been following ours pulled along-side. Its driver said he had seen a sleeping bag catapult off our roof twenty miles back. It was late in the day, and we were anxious to find a comfortable motel, so we didn't bother to turn around. In a way, it was a relief to have our capacity for roughing it thus providentially diminished.

Keeping our exterior luggage in place was such a nuisance that whenever we had it more or less firmly secured we were loath to tamper with it. So we found ourselves almost entirely confined to the skimpy wardrobes we had stowed inside the car. Informality is the keynote of most tourist stops these days anyway. To be sure, I was barred from the dining room of an Oklahoma City motel when I attempted to enter it in a pair of immaculate Bermuda shorts, but on changing into grease-spattered ankle-length khakis I was welcomed. We felt that we did have to unload the roof in La Jolla, California, when some friends invited us to dinner at a fancy restaurant. For the first time in a couple of weeks, my wife put on a dress, the boys put on socks, and I put on a jacket, a shirt, a necktie, and clean long pants. It came as a blow when, after dinner, the hat-check girl accosted me and asked for my tie; she was under the impression it was one she had lent me to make me presentable enough to enter the place.

In La Jolla, too, our water pump gave out, possibly because of the demands made on it, through day after day of near-hundred-degree temperature, by the air-conditioner. (The mechanic who made the repair said as he was finishing up that he was forever leaving his tools in engines. He rummaged through ours carefully, smiled, and bade us farewell. A few weeks later, in Waverly, Iowa, we found his screwdriver.) Frequently, our radiator would get so hot that service-station attendants only dared approach it behind the cooling splash of a hose, like firemen. An attendant in Texas, after spraying our radiator, sprayed his own feet. "These are the hottest boots I ever had on," he told us. "Coldest in winter, too." The boys had heard that Texas was a state partial to superlatives, and they were overjoyed to have

this confirmation of the theory—as they also were when they
read an item in the Dallas *Morning News* (the same issue
contained the headline "FISH HIDE FROM HEAT") about a
local oil man who had shot seven thousand jack rabbits since
the first of the year. Terry and Joey, voluntarily brushing up
off season on their arithmetic, calculated that this came to a
thousand jack rabbits a month, or about thirty a day—which,
they reflected, was something even for Texas. They were
equally impressed by an advertisement for a Texas drive-in
movie establishment that was showing three full-length
features, plus cartoons. Texas proved not to be pre-eminent
in all things, however. Near Chamberlain, South Dakota (a
state that proclaims itself a "land of infinite variety"), we
came upon a drive-in that boasted *four* full-length features,
running from dusk till dawn.

ACCIDENTALLY (also ACROSS, PROCEEDED, HURRIEDLY).
Americans are notoriously obsessed with speed, and since
our return home our friends, as American as anybody's, have
been asking us how fast we went. I have never exceeded
ninety miles an hour in an automobile and don't much care
to, but the nation's roads today are tempters, if not outright
seducers, and between Flagstaff and Holbrook, Arizona,
while Jinny was dozing, the boys cajoled me into accelerating
until the speedometer needle reached eighty-five. At that
point, another car overtook me with ease, and I was too
chagrined to play the game any longer. Later, Jinny confessed that in Nevada, while *I* was dozing, she had hit ninety.
We had our big chance to show off on the Bonneville Salt
Flats, in Utah, where cars were romping around at between
three and four hundred miles an hour all summer long, but
when we were in a position to let her rip, all three of the *boys*
were dozing, and their mother and I didn't want to risk jig-
gling them into wakefulness.

On the Bonneville Flats, though, by way of recompense,

my wife espied our fiftieth state license plate—Alaska. The
children had begun collecting plates, as I imagine most cross-
country motorists do, at the very start. Tony got discouraged
just half an hour out, on the George Washington Bridge,
when we zipped by an interstate trailer-truck so festooned
with plates that there wasn't time to identify them all. Without exerting ourselves, we had spotted all the states save
Alaska and Hawaii by our second day on the road. We captured Hawaii at Cody, Wyoming. The boys were proudest of
a rare Guam they bagged in Ely, Nevada, where I sought
to teach them a memorable lesson by losing two dollars in a
dime slot machine on our way into a hotel dining room.
Jinny undid some of the good by winning two jackpots after
dinner. (In the course of this demoralizing experience, she
got so excited she burned her good cashmere coat with a cigarette. One way or another, you can't beat the odds.) Also at
Cody—Buffalo Bill's home town—we saw our only double
rainbow. Our hunt for a pot of gold took us first to a miniature golf course, which we searched, vainly, in forty-five minutes and an average of fifty-five strokes. Our quest then led
us to a general store that offered for sale, in testimonial to
the Wild West love of violence, Indian Whackum Paddles
and matching tomahawks and sheath knives, and also, in
somewhat tamer vein, clip-on cowboy ties and Buffalo Bill
bookends. Terry bought a tomahawk set. He later discovered
that it was made in Germany, and, disgruntled, tossed it into
a leather purse that his mother had bought in Albuquerque
and had considered a delightful piece of Indian workman-
ship until she discovered that it was made in Italy.

The double rainbow was just one of the many colorful attractions of the journey. Not far from Meteor Crater, Arizona,
which is an impressive sight without any special embellish-
ments, Tony pointed out a freight train with seven cabooses.
The first blind hitchhiker any of us had ever seen was hopefully waving a white cane beside a Clabber Girl Baking

Powder billboard on an otherwise desolate stretch of highway near Nebraska, Indiana. We saw our first roundup (a
goat pursuing five cows) in Texas, and our first range-riding
cowboy in Oklahoma. Our first (and only) hillbilly was a
woman eating watermelon with her husband at a roadside
rest stop in New Mexico. She was wearing shoes, she was
very neat about spitting out the seeds, and her car had California plates, but she insisted to us, notwithstanding all this,
that she was a hillbilly. In New Mexico, too, we saw our first
elderly female Indian gas-station attendant.

We first saw a wrecked automobile on the road, in a nation known for its high incidence of accidents, on our first
day out, in Pennsylvania; we braced ourselves for repetitions
of the sight, but we didn't come upon another smashup until we had reached California, two weeks later. And we witnessed only three accidents *there,* which the natives told us
was far below normal. Actually, we didn't worry much about
the hazards of driving until the Labor Day weekend, when
we were on the home stretch. Then our car radio—previously
a transmitter of nothing much more disconcerting than hillbilly songs whined by authentic-sounding hillbillies, live-
stock-auction intelligence, and household hints for fluffing
up sagging pie crusts—began to hammer away ceaselessly
on the theme of how the mortality rate of us holiday drivers
was stacking up against the National Safety Council's traditionally pessimistic forecast. It was years since I'd been on
the road during a big summer weekend, and I became increasingly gloomy.

The previous spring, as it happened, I had met an executive of the Safety Council, and when I said I assumed he spent
his holiday weekends totting up fatality statistics, he said
why, no, he habitually holed up at a lakeside hideaway where
you couldn't see or hear even a scooter. He invited me to
join him at that retreat over the Fourth of July. I couldn't
make it, but I kept thinking wistfully of his invitation all

through the Labor Day period, and I remembered it with special poignancy when, as we were rolling along a two-lane road in eastern Iowa, a teen-ager barrelled past us, ignoring the double solid yellow line on a blind downhill curve where there wasn't any shoulder. If there had been anybody coming the other way, we would all have ended up as National Safety Council statistics. In Beverly Hills (where, unsurprisingly, we saw our first blonde talking into a cream-colored telephone while driving a lavender Cadillac), we had our one other close shave. Woman driver tried to pass on the right. I had to brake hard to avoid her, and I was pretty sore, until a long-time resident of the area who was riding with us identified the party of the second part as Simone Signoret. The boys were so proud I couldn't stay mad.

ACCOMMODATIONS (also DESIRABLE, STOPPED, CONVENIENCE). Like most Americans who tour by car these summers, we stayed overnight mainly at motels. They were astonishingly clean and comfortable; only once did we end up at a spot we wouldn't willingly have slept at again. (It was after dark, and we were tired, and there was no alternative within miles; and at that the place wasn't too bad.) Sometimes we made reservations a day ahead, but whether we did or not, it was rare that we found lodgings that failed to meet our sons' three minimum specifications: television, air-conditioning, and swimming pool. (We were almost too successful in finding the last of these. In California, Tony came down with an infection that a doctor diagnosed as pool fever. The ironic cure was for Tony to take nose drops while bent way over backward, as if making a back dive.) By now, so many motels have this trinity of essentials—or luxuries that travelling children think of as essentials—that their proprietors hold out as further lures to the prospecting motorist a glittering assortment of fringe benefits, among them alarm clocks, electric irons, soft water, rubber sheets, laundromats, wall-to-wall carpeting, ice machines, and Coke machines. At our motel in Oklahoma City, a settlement where mixed drinks may not be sold, there was even a draught-beer machine.

Oklahoma City also had Massage-a-Matic beds; if you put twenty-five cents in a slot near the headboard, your bed would pulsate gently for twenty-five minutes. St. Louis had temperature controls, colored telephones, a heated wading pool, and a dog kennel. (We had left our dog in a kennel at home, never suspecting that such roadside hospitality awaited him, too.) Amarillo had *free* vibrating beds, and the phones lit up, as well as rang, to signal incoming calls, not that there was anybody in Amarillo who was likely to call us. (A tract on our dresser advised us that Amarillo is the home of America's first Boys' Ranch, for boys who've never had an opportunity. Its slogan is "Give a boy a shirt tail he can hang onto." My wife, while our sons were enjoying an on-the-house workout on their Gyramatic Mattress, was moved to observe that an apt slogan for boys who *have* had an opportunity might be, "Give a boy a shirt tail he will tuck in.")

One motel in Phoenix had three swimming pools, and another (our sons ruefully learned after we were irrevocably checked in at a less richly endowed place) a comic-book bar. The latter establishment also published a house organ for its patrons. A San Diego motel had a house organist, and a La Jolla motel a swimming instructor. Cambria, California, had a hot-water heater for making instant coffee, while Gillette, Wyoming, had a percolator on our bureau, all ready to plug in, and at Cody free coffee was dispensed from a large urn on the patio. (I had left our car overnight at a garage there, to be serviced, and on my way to retrieve it, early in the morning, paused for a cup of coffee. "Why don't you take a cup to your wife, too?" urged the woman who ran the place. "She'll think you're a livin' doll.") Salt Lake City featured volleyball and fashion shows, and Jenny Lake, Wyoming,

featured educated dusting: "Your maid is Ann Walters, Colo-
rado State College," said a card in our room.

Perhaps the most bountiful of all the motels we stayed at
was one in South Dakota, where, before we had even registered, the proprietor pressed on each of the boys a fat plastic
packet with "Pepsi-Cola Vacation Tour Kit" stamped on it.
Inside each kit was a printed slip that said, "Packed by Students and Friends of Rocky Mountain College, Billings,
Montana." The contents of the kit were impressive indeed.
First, there were two comic books. One, sponsored by the
Greyhound Bus Company, was entitled "Driving Like a Pro"
and was full of tips about safe driving. The second, a Chrysler blurb, was called "Things That Even Dads Don't Know
About" and dwelt rhapsodically on various Chrysler products, concluding with a starry-eyed boy's breathless excla-
mation: "Now my dad knows what a terrific organization
the Chrysler Corporation is!" The largess that the Students
and Friends of Rocky Mountain College had assembled also
included a Bingo-type game, compliments of Humble Oil
Refining; a small package of Kleenex; one piece of Dubble
Bubble gum (sweet-spice flavor); two hard candies (lemon
and lime); a Chap Stick; an emery board; a guide to the Best
Western Motels system; four Bufferin tablets; two No Doz
tablets; two tablets of Nature's Remedy; and a package of
Tums. Here was the American dream, neatly wrapped up in
a plastic container that, if you stuck your head inside it, could
suffocate you.

INTERESTING (also DIFFERENT, VARIED, WEIRD). It was difficult, on a trip like ours, to decide how to reconcile the often
conflicting demands of sightseeing and ground-gaining.
There are those puristic tourists who argue that to travel by
turnpike, freeway, throughway, or thruway is downright
sacrilegious; you don't get to *see* anything, they wail. They
have something there, but if one stops to see everything, and,

between glances, travels via byway instead of highway, one needs far more time even than the month and a half we had allotted ourselves. At the start, Jinny and I were easygoing about mileage. We were hardly out of New York, for instance, when the boys said they would like to veer off the Pennsylvania Turnpike long enough to have a look at Philadelphia, which they had never visited. We accordingly set our course for Independence Hall, which I told our sons solemnly was an eminently symbolic jumping-off spot for sightseeing in the United States. (Also, "independence" was on our spelling list.) But next, en route to the Liberty Bell, we passed the Franklin Institute, and the boys begged us to go *there*. We did, and hung around until a guard shooed us out at closing time. As a result, we covered pitifully little distance that day, and my wife and I resolved to be firm about stops in the future.

The first real test of our restrictive policy came just west of St. Louis, where two caves vied for our patronage by means of alluring roadside signs. We rationed our sons to one cave —whichever they chose. It was a tough decision: Daniel Boone had discovered one of the grottoes; Frank and Jesse James had hidden out in the other. After deliberation so protracted that it almost took us past both places, our boys voted for the James boys. Presently, inside their lair—the Meramec Caverns—we were taken in hand by a guide who had one of those set spiels to which guides the world over (and cave guides especially, I have found) are partial. Meramec's speleological spieler was an irrepressible card. "Take your last look at the daylight behind you," he told the group we were assigned to as it started underground, "because if there's a cave-in it may be three or four days before we get you out." Two elderly women making the rounds with us tittered nervously. This is one of those caverns where every nook has a name—the Crystal Pool, the Wine Room, the Spaghetti Room, Lumbago Alley, and so forth. At a boulder called Loot Rock, where Frank and Jesse allegedly divided their spoils, and where wax effigies of the rascally pair now crouched, a wishing well had been rigged up. The old ladies dropped pennies into it, and while I looked on, horrified, our eight-year-old airily flung in a dime. (I asked him later what he'd wished for. "I wished I'd get my dime back," he said.) The climactic moment of our journey through this tourist Mecca came when we were all solemnly ushered into an underground theatre, called the Theatre. Colored lights were beamed on what our guide identified as a natural screen formed by stalactites and stalagmites, and from a loudspeaker the "Missouri Waltz" blared forth. Then came the main event. The music changed to a choral version of "God Bless America," fortissimo, and a fifty-star American flag was projected, in color, on the natural screen. The two women applauded. After a moment of silence, our guide, no longer the japer but a man so overcome with emotion that I feared he might need medical treatment, announced huskily that that was the end of our tour. We all tiptoed out to the strains of "In the Hall of the Mountain King."

The boys were a mite disenchanted about guided tours after that one, and they besought their mother and me to guard them against too many more such cut-and-dried presentations. We managed fairly successfully to keep faith with them, though in San Francisco, where we were able to spend only one day and wanted to see as much as possible, we splurged on a Gray Line limousine with a chauffeur-guide. This gambit proved to be not entirely prodigal. It would have cost us a quarter a head, for instance, to be admitted to the Dolores Mission as lone wolves, but as Gray Line lambs we got in for a dime. When we were ready to leave the shrine, Tony was missing. I found him out back in the graveyard. "I've never read tombstones before, and I'm just starting now," he told me. "Isn't this as good a time as ever?" With our limousine standing outside at I forget what hourly rate, it didn't seem a propitious time at all, so I dragged him away, though it gave me a twinge thus to have to stifle the spirit of independent inquiry.

We were all pleased with our San Francisco mentor's lack of parochialism. He candidly admitted, for example, that, among single-span bridges, the Golden Gate Bridge is eclipsed in length by the Mackinac Bridge, in Michigan. His information was admirably up to the minute, too; he told the boys that at the moment the suicides off the Golden Gate totalled a hundred and ninety-six. Also, he was commendably dedicated to his calling. He'd been doing some background reading, he said, and was disturbed because one reference book he'd consulted put the area of the Golden Gate Park at 1,013 acres, while another had it 1,017. Our man was not yet prepared to take sides. But he, too, had his pet vocational jokes. At one point, he said, "You see this big tall building? That's the one we usually drive past fast. It's the Internal Revenue Building." Jinny jabbed at a button that controlled the windows, and a smoothly ascending pane of glass pinned Terry's hand against the frame, with the result that our only articulated response to this jest was a howl of pain.

In San Francisco, we stayed overnight at a motel with a vending machine that dispensed not only coffee with or without sugar and/or cream but two consistencies of hot chocolate —rich and plain—and early the following morning we crossed the Golden Gate Bridge, safely, and went to see the redwood trees in the Muir Woods National Monument. The big trees were glorious, all the more so because when we got there we were practically the only tourists around. Terry told me—I am sure he was right; children usually are— that the tallest tree in Muir Woods was two hundred and and forty-six feet high and the tallest redwood anywhere was three hundred and something; he could hardly keep from snorting when a sightseeing bus hove to and its guide, assembling his flock under one giant redwood, told them it was *seven* hundred and forty-six feet high. They all gasped, impressed beyond words, and not a one of them questioned his astronomical figure. "Why can't they ever leave well enough alone?" muttered Joey.

GRANDEUR (also IRRESISTIBLE, SURPRISE, EXHAUSTED). Muir Woods is a National Park Service enclave, and within its boundaries, as in the other Park Service preserves we visited —among them the Petrified Forest, the Grand Canyon, the Grand Teton range, Yosemite, Yellowstone, and Mount Rushmore—we were impressed not merely by the natural wonders around us but by the spick-and-spanness of the area around *them*. We had read en route of a judge in Arizona or California who had given a woman convicted of throwing a beer can out of a moving car onto a state highway the harshest sentence he could think of: she was to police up a mile-long stretch of the road she had desecrated. The story added that she had filled something like five gunnysacks with refuse while paying the penalty. We saw no evidence that her punishment had had a deterrent effect on anybody outside of a National Park, but there is clearly something (national pride?) that stays the hands of litterers inside. Yellowstone remains amazingly tidy, even though it has to cope with bears who like to upset garbage cans. Our sons developed a fondness for Yellowstone, and so did I, for at an inn next to Old Faithful I succeeded, after half a dozen tries in as many states, in getting a club sandwich without mayonnaise. Just as I bit contentedly into it, Old Faithful erupted. The sandwich was delicious, and I hope Congress will always give the Park Service whatever it wants.

As we approached Yellowstone, Tony became more and more excited over bears. By then, we had gaped at the trained seals, dolphins, and whales at Marineland, outside Los Angeles, but apart from a few elk, buffalo, and deer, and a large number of prairie dogs, most of them flattened by automobiles, we had seen few creatures out of confinement. We will never know how close we may have come to seeing a footloose rattlesnake. In Arizona, I pulled to the side of the road one day so Joey could photograph a huge organ-pipe cactus, but just as he and I stepped out of the car, we heard a noise nearby. I said it was a cricket, and Joey and I began walking across the desert, but Terry said it sounded like a rattler to him, and Jinny insisted, over Joey's objections and mine, that we get back in the car at once, picture or no picture. We did. Two weeks later, we stopped at a Reptile Gardens, where an employee was prodding some captive rattlers with a stick. "You recognize the sound?" Jinny asked me. It sure did seem familiar, and there wasn't a cricket in sight.

We didn't want Tony to be disappointed at Yellowstone, so as soon as we were within its boundaries, we told him that because it was raining we might see no bears at all. He said that the record for one day's bear-spotting by a single family was twenty-three. We said bears don't like to get their paws wet. But suddenly a big black bear loomed up at the edge of the road, and then another, and soon after that a mother with two cubs. It proved to be quite an ursine day. Not a record-shattering one, perhaps, but we scored a very presentable nineteen. And what a splendid, varied assortment of bears they were! No. 8, a cub, tried to climb into our car. No. 12, a brown black bear, sat down next to us and tried to outstare us. (All Yellowstone bears are black bears, whether black or brown or cinnamon in hue, our No. 2 boy advised me; he had been reading up on them.) No. 17, a black black bear, lay down in the middle of the road, crossed its paws like a lounging Labrador retriever, and wagged its head indolently back and forth while holiday motorists piled up in both directions.

In another National Park—Yosemite—we spent our only night under canvas, though our tent had a wooden floor, beds,

and electric lights. "We call it 'roughing it—the easy way,' "
said a pamphlet put out by the operators of the camp. We
roughed it the easy way on a fine starlit night. On the floor
of Yosemite Valley, hemmed in by steep glacial cliffs, there
was an outdoor variety show, and just as a master of ceremonies was rendering a heart-tugging version of "I Believe,"
the satellite Echo I skimmed across the sky. He switched to
the "Indian Love Call," and some Park Service stagehands
spilled a cascade of flaming boughs down the face of a cliff—a
pyrotechnic display that, we gathered, went on nightly, regardless of Echo's orbit. The boys found the entertainment
singularly affecting. A filling dropped out of Joey's tooth,
and Tony went into a nearby store and spent fifty cents on
an Indian salt-and-pepper set—made, I seem to recall, in
Vermont.

The only Indian we saw in headdress and war paint, outside of a few captive braves in amusement parks, was a black-
pigtailed, bare-chested man climbing out of a pickup truck
at Mount Rushmore, but he had the self-conscious air of a
performer who was about to whoop it up for tourists, and
Jinny suspected that he was wearing a wig. In the Southwest,
of course, we had seen plenty of Indians in mufti and, in
Arizona, one group wearing steel helmets—Zuñis who had
been ferried in by helicopter to fight a forest fire near the
spot where we were picnicking. One day in New Mexico,
hoping to find some gaudily got-up Indians, the boys persuaded us to make a pilgrimage to the Old Town Plaza, in
Albuquerque, but after one glance Terry characterized the
spot with an adjective the boys had fastened on to—not always in disparagement—early in our travels and had clung
to throughout. "Touristy-trappy," he said. (I was glad to observe scattered evidence that some roadside purveyors themselves find embroidered - cactus - hankie - and - stuffed - baby -
rattlesnake meretriciousness distasteful; outside a truck stop
in South Dakota, for example, we saw the appealing legend

"No reptiles, no caves.") Terry's appraisal of the Old Town seemed to stand up under scrutiny. The Krazy Horse Gift Shop, which had in its window the encouraging placard "Don't take imitation Indian articles home from your vacation," was shut, but a neighboring emporium that was open and that stocked Indian handmade ties ($1.25; with beads, $1.95) had in its window the chilling words "Ask Grandma. She'll buy it for you."

We got the children out of there in a hurry and headed for the plains, in search of a bang-up rural Indian ceremonial rite that we could barge in on unobtrusively, or, when it came to that, obtrusively, and could photograph. Presently we saw a sign, "Laguna Pueblo," and headed for it. At the entrance to the pueblo, a modest-sized adobe village, the Department of the Interior had posted some orders. No liquor, no peddling, no soliciting within, these said; but there was nothing about no staring, so we pushed on, attracted to a central church building toward which a number of Indians —nary a one in feathers or beaded blankets—were purposefully walking. And then occurred one of the most astounding and, in a way, most exhilarating experiences of our journey. A truck swung in behind us, and the driver, a middle-aged Indian man in a Sunday-go-to-meeting suit, honked his horn. I pulled over, thinking he wanted to pass, but he drew abreast and stopped. "Awfully sorry, folks," he said, "but we're not allowing anyone in today. We're having our ceremony." Repulsed by this dignified defense of privacy, we drove sheepishly away, and reminded the boys never to drop in on folks without phoning first.

COURTESY (also PLEASANT, FRIEND, COURTEOUS). En route to Oklahoma City, toward the beginning of our trip, the boys saw a city-within-a-city advertisement for Frontier City, a local variation on the Disneyland theme; and as chance would have it, they guided me to a motel right at Frontier City's frontier. It was a blisteringly hot afternoon, and my wife and I let our sons step next door by themselves, while we sojourned at the motel's pool. On rejoining us, they reported that Frontier City had some cool diversions all right. "There was this guy with the dynamite and this woodchopper with this axe who just misses you," Tony said, ecstatically. His brothers, we were glad to perceive, had caught this beguiling chamber of horrors in a couple of spelling mistakes— "Pitchur" Gallery, for instance. I was relieved to have them tell me this, for earlier that day, while Jinny was at the wheel, I'd spotted some howlers on our own list of demon words. The word "misspell" was on it, orthographically, but in spite of that warning flag, whoever typed up the compilation had put "villian" for "villain," "cooly" for "coolly," and "gengeance" for, I presumed, "vengeance." I had told the boys you just couldn't trust anybody any more and urged them to keep a skeptical eye cocked on the most impeccably lettered print. Before our trip was over, I was to be amply rewarded: Terry said he wouldn't even set foot in one baited New Mexico tourist trap, because of a sign at its threshold saying "Souveniers"; Tony called to my attraction the cover of a Western Classics comic book he had bought in Arizona, using the dregs of his ebbing allowance, with the author's name spelled "Bret Hart"; and in California Joey, while giving Hollywood's Sunset Strip the nomadic eye, asked if he wasn't right in thinking that a neon "Burlesk" was wrong. I was proud of him, all the more so because "burlesque" wasn't on our list of demons and he must have picked up the word on his own.

While Jinny and I were poolside at Oklahoma City, a young woman joined us, identifying herself as the protagonist of a local morning television program. She said that her format was mostly interviews and calisthenics, all taking place on a living-room stage set—no wrestling mats for her; they were unladylike—but that to catch and pin down the young-mother audience, she supposed she'd have to compromise and use some animated cartoons, too; otherwise, she feared, her opposition would put on nothing but cartoons and murder her with the pre-schoolers. While we were trying to get in a sympathetic word, she asked where we were from and, on learning we were Easterners, reproached us for the uncommunicativeness and unfriendliness of our native habitat. Why, she said, she had once taken a train from Baltimore to Washington and the lady sitting next to her had been a regular old clam. Didn't we think that was a shame, and didn't we think that Americans, once you got away from the tight-lipped East Coast, were much warmer and more companionable?

Our acquaintance was well into another topic—as I recall, the superiority of Western to Eastern frozen Daiquiris—before we could answer, but Jinny and I thought a good deal about her question after we resumed our travels. We concluded that, on the whole, Americans are gracious and friendly to itinerants. In Pennsylvania, we had a foretaste of the courtliness we were regularly to encounter. At a miniature golf course there, Terry scored an ace on the last hole and was awarded a card entitling him to a free extra game. He declined it, explaining to the manager that he didn't expect to be around long enough to cash in on the bonus. "That's all right," said the manager. "Leave it at your motel, so somebody else can use it." The next day, we stopped for lunch at one of the myriad Howard Johnson restaurants that succor the East. A popcorn-vending machine was on the blink, and a mechanic tinkering with it let a spate of popcorn pour into a cardboard container and goodnaturedly handed this to Tony, who was watching him at work.

Friendly! There was the handyman at our Phoenix motel, who stopped by to put a full-length mirror on our door (we almost felt that we should run out and get our good clothes off the top of the car) and afterward began to reminisce about a trip *he'd* made to California. He had to go about his other duties after half an hour or so, but he said he'd be back to chat some more, and he was a man of his word; at nine-thirty that night, after we'd turned in, preparatory to an early-morning departure, there was a rap on our mirrored door and in he came, to inform me, in case I didn't know about it already, that I'd probably reach San Diego just in time to enter a local deep-sea fishing contest. There was also the waitress in Missouri who, even before we tipped her, scribbled on our check, "Thank you. Serving you has been a pleasure. Colleen." And there was the anonymous waitress in Texas who, when I asked my wife at dinner, "Are you tired tonight, honey?" immediately replied, "Oh, no. I feel fine." The next day, in New Mexico, a waitress called my wife "honey." "Come see us again soon, honey," she said. Everybody everywhere seemed to crave reunions with us. Except for "You can't miss it," there was no phrase we encountered as frequently as "Come see us again soon." (A friendly barber in Beverly Hills said to me one afternoon, "A little shorter than last time, sir?" and I replied "Why not?" before it occurred to me that I hadn't ever come see him before.) Several motels we stayed at had posted in their rooms a somewhat more elegant paraphrase of the ubiquitous leave-taking: "We wish you a pleasant and safe journey and should you by chance pass this way again we invite you to stay with us. Goodbye and Good Luck till we meet again." Equally touching was the amiable printed overture made to us on a wall of our Salt Lake City motel. "Greetings," it said. "We are honored to welcome you as a guest and sincerely hope our relationship will blossom into lasting friendship."

We came to feel that we'd never had so many friends. Whole communities voiced their amity. We were welcomed to Las Cruces, New Mexico, by, according to a highway sign, "37,000 Friendly People," and to Gila Bend, Arizona, by twenty-five hundred similarly self-proclaimed cronies. When we halted at a friendly Gila Bend supermarket, a friendly check-out girl insisted that we take our trading stamps, though we said we were really just passing through. "Oh, I hope not," she said. "You'll get a chance to use these some-day. I'm sure you'll come see us again soon." Camaraderie flourished on the highest levels of state government. At the Arizona-California state line, in the window of an agricul-tural inspection station, perched the cheery message "We are never too busy to be courteous," and the inspector who waved us through urged us to come and be seen by him again soon. (At the California-Nevada state line, an unofficial greeter, a short-order cook at a lunch counter, was so affable that he offered to cure a mild case of dyspepsia that was both-ering Tony by pouring a slug of whiskey into his eight-year-old stomach.) "HELL-O!" clamored huge painted letters on the pavement as we went from Utah into Idaho. "Hello—We're glad to see you," said a border sign as Iowa grabbed us out of the hospitable embrace of South Dakota.

PHENOMENON (also WONDERFUL, FICTITIOUS, REALLY). Throughout our trip, in part to keep up with the published news, in part to check on baseball schedules, we bought all the regional newspapers we could lay our hands on. In Williams, Arizona, we found that the local *Daily News* had a circulation stunt under way, a "Know Your Neighbor's Back Contest," the object of which was to identify photo-graphs of persons' backs. (It would never work in the East; we sometimes don't even recognize our neighbors' faces.) The boys, not to mention me, were fascinated by a series running in the *Nevada State Journal*, published in Reno, about the history of indigenous gambling. The first install-ment began, "There is a direct philosophical connection be-tween the gambling industry of today and the boom-or-bust thinking which impelled men to prospect in this region in the last century," and it went on to say that gambling "has always existed, virus-like, in the life-blood of the state to a greater extent than in any other commonwealth in the nation." A news story in the same issue disclosed that a Reno sightseeing company had just obtained delivery of a new bus, which not only had air-conditioning and piped music, but card tables, too. Somebody must have detected a trace of the virus in the life-blood of us tourists.

I had a newspaper in my pocket—a Los Angeles *Times* announcing the entrance into the 1960 Presidential race of a local dark-horse candidate who claimed to have the outer-space vote in *his* pocket—when we arrived at Disneyland early one morning. (The rides opened at 9:00 A.M., and the boys wanted to be waiting for them.) A Disneyland horseless-carriage driver saw me looking at the paper and laughed. "You'll never have a chance to read it *here*," he told me. "Anyway, why waste the time? You're ahead of thirty thousand people now. Take advantage of it." Abashed, I threw the paper into a metal trash container painted to simulate wood.

We visited Disneyland twice—once that morning, and once after dark, when we were well behind thirty thousand earlier-birds, or maybe three hundred and thirty thousand. That time, we took in the nightly fireworks display. We were coached in appreciating this by a canned and amplified voice that instructed us, as the skyrockets soared, to say "Eee" or "Aah" or to whistle. By day as well as by night, Disney-land mesmerized the boys. "This place has to be believed to be seen!" exclaimed Tony. It was one of the most pertinent malapropisms I'd ever heard, and it made me wonder if my own somewhat dim view of the institution stemmed from lack of faith. I couldn't get very worked up about a diorama of the Grand Canyon, even though it was billed as the largest diorama in the world, when, only a week before, I'd seen the original Grand Canyon. But my sons, on finally reaching the goal in pursuit of which they had scaled purple mountain majesties and crossed the fruited plain, would brook no criticism of it, and were, in fact, ready to endow it with qualities that Walt Disney himself may have overlooked. As we were finishing breakfast at the Red Wagon Inn there, Joey turned to me, his eyes shining like those of a footsore Trappist pilgrim at last arrived before Chartres, and murmured, "You know, Disneyland gives you more raisins in Raisin Bran than any other place in the world!"

Possibly because of television, the boys didn't seem much bothered by the commercialism that was appended to many of the rides. It was to be expected that there would be interminable tie-ins with Disney movies—rides, for instance, named after Peter Pan, Alice in Wonderland, and other creations of the Master. And who could quarrel with the Disneyland bookstore's selling nothing but Disney books and magazines, the Disneyland music store's trafficking exclusively in tunes from Disney shows, and the Disneyland Art Festival's exhibiting paintings of but a single subject—Disneyland? But I couldn't help suspecting that even my sons, though they never uttered a disloyal word, were taken aback by the aggressive commercialism of many of the concessions. The submarine ride was a plug for General Dynamics, the Moon Rocket a plug for Trans World Airlines, and the Picture Spots—scattered vantage points from which we were all enjoined to snap our shots, presumably because we needed advice—were plugs for Eastman Kodak. At each Picture Spot, we were further assisted by a display of color pictures that had been taken from the site, and by suitable exposure charts. "Bright sun" and "Cloudy bright" were the only exposures mentioned. At Disneyland, no other exposures—and, I guess, no other states of mind—are tolerated.

ATHLETIC (also PASTIME, PROFESSIONAL, AMATEUR). We rolled through Pittsburgh too late for an afternoon baseball game that was being played there that day, though on the outskirts of the city we did chance upon one oddly diverting spectacle: In the parking area of a shopping center, a bride and groom and their wedding party were parading around on a hay wagon towed by four farm horses. I thought for a moment we'd already reached California. We skirted Cincinnati, having heard that a big convention was on there and accommodations were hard to come by, but we stopped overnight at St. Louis, at the place with the heated wading pool for dogs. The next morning, Terry looked up from the *Globe-Democrat* and exclaimed, "Guess what! The Cards are playing the Braves here tonight!" Joey's eyes lit up for a second, and then he said resignedly, "We'll probably be in Joplin by then."

That turned out to be the case. Joplin itself, however, turned out to be a big baseball town, in a non-playing sense. We stayed there at Mickey Mantle's Holiday Inn Hotel, an establishment redolent with the aura of baseball, and, specifically, of its proprietor's team, the Yankees—American League, of course, but better than the minors, anyway. The cocktail lounge was called the Dugout, and shaped more or less like one; the dinner menu in the dining room was headed "Today's Lineup." There were suites named in honor of Yogi Berra and Whitey Ford, and the fanciest suite of all was named after the proprietor. While a waiter was carrying a trayful of drinks in to its occupants, our sons peeked through the door and reported that there was a large bar inside monogrammed "M.M." with a portrait of Mantle displayed over it.

Baseball men who run motels are strong for the elegant touch. We had dinner some days later at a motel belonging to Del Webb, who is a co-owner of the Yankees, and one of its customs, we learned, is to serve free champagne. At Mantle's, the only giveaways were autographed photos of the boniface. The boys thought this comparative state of affairs logical enough. Club-owners, they told their mother and me, are notoriously better-heeled than their field operatives. When Jinny and I complained ungratefully, after tasting the champagne, that it was almost undrinkably sweet, Joey wondered if that didn't perhaps explain why ball players, instead of swallowing the champagne their bosses dispense in the clubhouse during pennant-winning or World Series celebrations, pour it instead over one another's heads.

We arrived at Los Angeles without having taken in even a Little League game, and found there, to our dismay, that the Dodgers were on the road and wouldn't be back until the day we were scheduled to reach San Francisco, and that on *that* day, by cruel coincidence, the Giants would be meeting the Dodgers at the Los Angeles Coliseum. To soften this blow, I offered the boys a chance to see *something* at the Coliseum, and presently we were watching an annual rodeo put on for the benefit of the Los Angeles County Sheriffs' Relief Association. Then, as we were packing up to leave Los Angeles, Tony was laid low with the pool fever. Before he was hale enough to travel again, the Dodgers had come home and the Giants had come down to meet them, and the older boys found themselves back at the Coliseum, sitting contentedly behind first base while *both* ex-New York teams performed for their edification. The Dodgers won, 8-5, and Willie Mays hit a home run, and the following day Tony suggested that he deserved a present for getting sick enough to bring all this to pass. So his brothers went to the Farmers' Market and bought him an elegant gun-and-holster set of a type he had long coveted. It was made in Japan.

HINDRANCE (also AWKWARD, SENTINEL, ALL RIGHT). Our itinerary was reasonably elastic, and before we set out, my wife and I had urged the boys to let us know if there were any special places they'd like to see. In Indiana, Terry announced out of the blue that he'd like to visit a spot in a blistering section of Texas, called Cowboy Town, where he understood you could get a haircut for fifteen cents. But we were loath to go there, even with the air-conditioner.

At the Grand Canyon, Joey, in similarly impetuous fashion, put in a word for Phoenix. He had been looking at a map and had just remembered that he'd once done a paper on Phoenix for a social-studies class. He wanted to see how closely the city resembled his description of it. This seemed a reasonable enough, and laudably scholarly, request, and since we were already in Arizona, though a couple of hundred miles north of Phoenix, we headed for it. My wife's enthusiasm for this side trip was somewhat dampened when she saw in a newspaper that on the previous day only one city in the United States had had an official temperature reading of more than a hundred degrees—Phoenix, with a hundred and nine. Joey chuckled; that was Phoenix for you, all right, he said, and he added that the city's total annual rainfall was around seven inches. We pushed on nonetheless, and hit Phoenix only a couple of hours before a torrential downpour, accompanied by gale-force winds, hit it. The boys were enchanted, as, from our motel's dining room, they watched umbrellas and chairs fly through the air and into the swimming pool. "A table just went!" cried Joey, no longer the dispassionate sociologist.

Now that we were so far south, it seemed silly to Jinny and me not to dip down, however briefly, into Mexico, a country none of us had ever laid eyes on. The boys appeared strangely lukewarm about this prospect, and we presently learned why. It was the fireworks. Back in Missouri, we had stopped for lunch one day at a picnic table next to a roadside store, which our sons explored while Jinny and I were making sandwiches. They came back hugging three paper sacks filled with Roman candles, Chinese dragons, space missiles, and lesser rockets. It had never occurred to me that there was much of a retail market for such items except early in July, but evidently travelling boys whose home states' laws forbid their buying the stuff at all are avid customers no matter what the time of year. In any event, we let our sons keep these treasures after they'd convinced us that firecrackers were unlikely to go off spontaneously in an air-conditioned car. Now the boys were worried over how both Mexican and American customs would feel about our taking the fireworks in and out of Mexico.

The proprietor of a motel in Yuma, Arizona, solved that problem by recommending that we park our car in Calexico, California, and step across the line into Mexicali, Mexico. We did just that. "Fireworks!" said a sign at the first store across the border. (The first Mexican businessman we met up with, though, was a shoeshine boy, who begged me to avail myself of his services, despite the fact that I was wearing dirty white sneakers.) We didn't stay in Mexico long, but it was long enough for Jinny to learn that United States regulations permitted us to bring home ten dollars' worth of goods apiece, duty free. It wasn't mere friendliness, accordingly, that prompted a salesgirl in one shop we tarried in to say as we departed, "It's been *very* nice to have you in this country. Come see us again soon." While my wife and the boys strolled about, increasingly burdened with leather belts, metal belts, earrings, iced-tea spoons, straw hats, and bongo drums (many of these items, it developed, were at least Spanish, if not actually Mexican), I followed in their wake accumulating sales slips, on the assumption that United States customs would want them. When we strolled back over the border, these were ignored by the customs agent who dealt with us. He laughed when I presented them and said, "We don't go by what they charge you. We know more than they do about what this stuff's worth. We go by the foreign wholesale value, which is probably half of what you

paid." He merely wanted to know whether we had any fireworks on us. I said no, and the boys nodded in virtuous agreement.

The fireworks—aside from a few rockets that were ex-
perimentally launched, but failed to attain any altitude, on
the now scarred lawn of a southern California lady who had
asked us all over for a relaxed evening—caused us further
anxiety when we were nearly home. At Terry's behest, we
had called on a friend of his in Michigan, after which we decided to head for Westchester by way of Niagara Falls and
Buffalo. That meant driving across a stretch of Canada, and
that meant exposing the contents of our car to both Canadian
and American customs. Canadian customs was a breeze.
The inspector merely wanted to know if we had any fire*arms*
with us, and he may have been somewhat surprised at the
ringing and relieved fervor with which we chorused "No!"
But on observing that in Ontario, as in Mexico, fireworks
were freely on sale, I was afraid that on the American side
we'd be asked about this contraband, and I didn't relish the
prospect either of conspiring in a lie or of squealing on my
own flesh and blood. I never had to make the dreadful choice.
At Buffalo, customs merely inquired if we had bought anything in Canada, and, on receiving an honest negative answer, sent us cordially on our furtive way.

FINALLY (also GOVERNMENT, ATTENDANCE, PURSUING). Our
luck with state fairs was poor. On our way west, the nearest
thing to one that we came across was a county fair, at Olney,
Illinois, and there the emphasis seemed to be on swine research, Siamese twins, and a sideshow called "Beatniks of
1960." Outside the beats' tent were lurid posters of low-
class women smoking what was presumably marijuana; there
was no performance going on at that moment, but we
peered inside anyway, to be rewarded by nothing more sor-
did than a sleeping roustabout with an empty Mission

orange-soda bottle at his side. Heading back east, we were
still jinxed. Utah's state fair was scheduled a week too late
for us, and while South Dakota's was only a day too late—and
a spelling bee was on the agenda, in which I could have had
an entry running—we didn't have a day to spare on *our*
agenda by then. So Terry was dejected as we crossed the Canadian border and headed homeward on the New York
Thruway, without a single state fair to our credit. Near Syr-
acuse, though, we saw a sign that read, "Next Exit: State
Fair Grounds." And then another sign. The fair was on! We
hustled off the Thruway, and at the fairgrounds we were
greeted by still another sign: "Welcome Governor Rockefeller." The Governor was scheduled to make a speech in an
hour, and the boys were elated. A real state fair, with a real
state governor, in our very own favorite state, on the very
last day of our tour! It was almost too much.

While we waited for Mr. Rockefeller, the boys wandered
around the fairgrounds in what amounted to a nostalgic rev-
erie about their trip. Tony was reminded, by an agricultural
exhibit, of the Corn Palace, at Mitchell, South Dakota—a
huge landmark among exhibition halls, which has exterior
siding fashioned of corncobs, and which, at the time of our
dazed glimpse of it, was being refurbished, or, I guess, re-
cobbed. Joey was reminded, by a sideshow tortoise, of a turtle
he'd ridden at the incomparable children's zoo in San
Diego, and Terry, by a concession selling melon slices for a
quarter, of a Manteca, California, fruit stand where we'd
been offered two whole watermelons free if we'd buy a dollar's worth of fruit. When we got to the State Institutions
Building (the State Police had some English-setter puppies
on display, the State Department of Mental Hygiene some
apple cookies), it was evident that the Governor had arrived,
for a cluster of troopers was outside. I followed my sons as
they pursued him into, and out of, the exhibit hall and
finally bayed him, along with a blonde wearing a State Fair

Queen sash, beside a Nike missile. Once having got a close-up glimpse of their leader, the boys were content, and as the Governor headed toward a speaker's platform, they started to back off. But there is no getting out of a politician's path during an election year, and a moment later Tony was firmly patted on the head by the gubernatorial hand. Anything we might have tried to do or see after that would have been anticlimactic, so we forthwith bade farewell to the fair and returned to our car.

We drove home fast, because the boys were anxious to have a go at their Roman candles, and we hesitated only as we were approaching the Tappan Zee Bridge, where we were suddenly confronted by the stern warning "Explosives Not Permitted on Bridge." I deliberated for an instant, then took a deep, guilt-ridden breath, stepped on the gas, and followed a milk truck across. A few minutes later, we were home.

Recollections
from
Behind
a
Safety Belt

During the last couple of years, the airlines advertisements, in which "jet" is ever more frequently used as a verb, have been so obsessed with speed that it may not be long before they'll all be crowing about getting you to your destination—sorry, jetting you there—before your departure hour. Once the novelty of this magic-carpet form of travel has worn off, though, I have a hunch that some people (political candidates and stewardesses excepted) may sour on the whole accelerated business, if for no other reason than that they're at a loss to make use of the time they've saved. When my wife and I left the Soviet Union in 1958, we jetted out of Moscow at 8:00 A.M. Iron Curtain Time and, abetted by favorable time zones, jetted into Copenhagen at 8:00 A.M. Free World Time. As a result of having to start our morning all over again, we were exhausted and irritable by noon.

I took my first jet ride in Korea, in 1951. I had no particular wish or reason to fly in what was then, as far as civilians
were concerned, a new-fangled machine, but it seemed to
be the thing for a conscientious correspondent to do, and arrangements were duly made for me to take a reconnaissance
flight in a T-33, a dual-seater. The night before I was
scheduled to go aloft, I came down with a head cold, probably psychosomatic in origin. A flight surgeon looked me
over, and while—somewhat to my dismay—he would not
ground me, he instructed the pilot who was taking me up not
to indulge in any strenuous maneuvers. That might be bad
for my sinuses, the doctor said, and I could have hugged
him.

The most harrowing aerial adventure I ever had occurred
during the Second World War, but the armed forces were
blameless. I was taking basic Infantry training in South Carolina, and my contingent of recruits got weekend passes. One
of my fellow rookies was a chap who had a pilot's license but
had not disclosed this on being drafted. He had calculated
that his chances of surviving the war would be better if he
stayed on the ground. Actuarially, he was probably wrong,
but as a hunch player he was right: I met him, in blooming
health, after V-J Day. He was in life insurance, and was doing
fine.

This dissembler, eager to take fullest advantage of our
brief furlough, of independent means, and having a strong
off-duty affinity for aviation, hired a small plane to ferry him
to Newark and back. He had left his license at home, so he
also hired a pilot. He invited another soldier and me to go
along. After we'd taken off, it turned out that the other guest
had never flown before, and he got violently ill before we'd
reached an altitude of a hundred feet. Psychosomatic, perhaps, but none the less disagreeable for all that.

Our pilot, it also quickly developed, had never been to
Newark before, and had neglected to bring along any

navigational charts (he had no radio) that could be of use beyond Richmond. Fortunately, it was daylight, and presently we stumbled into, or rather above, Philadelphia, where we passengers spotted the familiar contours of U. S. Highway 1. We instructed the pilot to follow that road to Newark. It was getting dark as we neared the airport, so the pilot, who didn't know what Newark's landing procedures were anyway, fluttered down onto the first runway he came across.

Before our wheels had stopped rolling, we were surrounded by choleric airport officials, who declared we had violated every regulation on their books, and threatened to impound the plane, the pilot, and, near as we could ascertain from their spluttering remarks, the crew. But they finally let us proceed, by surface transportation, to New York City, and on Sunday afternoon even let us take off again. I sensed that they didn't care much what happened to us as long as we never showed up in Newark again.

In a way, they might have done us a better service by chopping the wings off the plane, for on our return flight the engine conked out over Virginia, and we had to make an emergency landing in a pasture. To reach our post by reveille, we were obliged to engage, at a horribly extortionate rate, a local taxi driver, who got us there by barrelling through the night at a speed very nearly the equal of our plane's. I have no idea what happened to the pilot. He may have stayed in Virginia and gone into tobacco.

From that day on, except when under military orders or on reportorial assignment, I have stuck pretty much to scheduled airlines. "Scheduled" is a word all airlines love. They fondle it and throw it around with all the ardor and energy a child lavishes on a new toy, although they often seem more surprised than their passengers when they accomplish anything on schedule. They also seem to find it hard to believe that they are no longer children themselves in the transportation world, and they often act, accordingly, with a hesitancy and gaucherie ill-befitting an industry so mature and powerful as to have all but driven the Pullman car off the rails.

This uncertainty often does grave damage to what I guess the airlines would call passenger relations. It took years for the airlines to stiffen their backs and start penalizing the irresponsible people known as "no-shows," who would make reservations on any number of flights and wouldn't bother to cancel out. And even after taking the blessedly adult step of inaugurating a reserved-seat policy on many flights, the airlines haven't been self-confident enough to reserve a reserved seat as long as they sensibly should—until just before a plane takes off. While they will reserve you a seat, they won't, out of lingering dread of those bugaboo no-shows, hold it for you later than ten or fifteen minutes before departure time. (Departure time, in commercial-aviation terminology, doesn't necessarily mean the time a plane departs, but then they have to put *something* on their timetables.)

It took me weeks to recover from an experience I once had in San Francisco. I was gratified at being allotted a reserved seat on a non-stop United Airlines night flight to New York reverently called, by United, the Red Carpet Special. I presented myself at the ticket counter, yielded my baggage, received my gate pass, and, feeling infinitely superior to the unreserved-seat rabble who were clustered supplicatingly around various clerks, strolled at a leisurely pace to the prescribed departure gate.

I was twenty minutes early, and nobody had said anything to me about when I should claim my seat, so I stood there watching approvingly as my bags were gently hoisted aboard and chuckling in anticipation as a big red carpet was rolled out from the gate to the plane. I noticed that many of my fellow-passengers seemed in a great hurry to board, but I couldn't imagine why, unless they were anxious to go to sleep. I found out why, all right, five minutes before scheduled departure time, when I presented my credentials at the gate and was summarily turned away. The plane was full, I was told, and I gathered that some standby had been ushered into the seat I thought was mine. Thoroughly deflated, I fought my way onto a carpetless, unreserved, non-non-stop flight east, got to New York four and a half hours later than I'd expected, and eventually caught up with my luggage.

I do not wish to single out United. I have enough spleen to share among all the airlines. Pan American once sweet-talked my wife and me into a theoretically non-stop, over-night flight from New York to London, but at midnight we landed at Gander and then, and only then, were advised we'd be laying over for three hours. Something about a change of equipment. It almost always seems to be midnight, and three hours, and a change of equipment. While we were hanging morosely around the airport lounge, we noticed a woman passenger from our flight furiously writing postcards. We couldn't imagine what in the world she'd already found to write about, unless she was dashing off a complaint to Pan American's Customer Relations Department, so Jinny peeked inquiringly over her shoulder. "We've stopped at Gander!" the woman had written. "Am I having a ball!" I mention this incident out of fairness, to indicate that I may be excessively churlish about airlines, and that what was not sauce for me at Gander evidently was for that silly scribbling goose.

Maybe that lady was in better spirits than I was because she was a better mixer. I am not an especially gregarious passenger, possibly because my luck is bad. Let Dag Hammarskjöld or Kim Novak be queued up to join me on a flight, I always find myself sitting alongside an ammunition sales-

man or a woman who doesn't think President Truman
should have relieved General MacArthur and wants to tell
me why.

My resulting standoffishness on planes, or sitoffishness,
suits me fine, but it once got me in trouble with my sons. I
happened to fly from Los Angeles to New York just after the
1959 World Series, which the Dodgers won, in no small
measure through some climactic heroics on the part of Carl
Furillo. I got to the airport well ahead of time and (San
Francisco was still green in my memory) planted myself
firmly in front of the appropriate departure gate.

While I was waiting to enplane, to use one more verb on
which the airlines dote, another early bird, who looked
vaguely familiar, strolled over and sought to engage me in
conversation. I'd been too busy during the Series to follow
them play-by-play, and had brought along a batch of newspapers I hoped to catch up on during the flight. I had no
wish to hold them unread in my lap for four or five hours
while this fellow, whoever he might be, told me all his troubles, so I somewhat brusquely rejected his overtures. He
shrugged and moved on, and a few minutes later I heard two
other passengers talking about him. "Isn't that Carl Furillo?"
one of them was saying. It was indeed, and soon they were
chatting merrily away with him about the great events just
concluded, while I sulked in a corner. My sons were incensed when I told them what had happened, and not without cause.

Scheduled airline flights figured importantly in one of
the most frustrating days of my life. I'd had a book published
early in 1960, and was invited to talk about it, along with
two other current writers, at a book-and-author lunch in
Chicago, sponsored by the *Sun-Times*. I was extremely busy
at the time, so I arranged to fly from La Guardia Field, in
New York, to Midway Airport, in Chicago, at 9:00 A.M.

that morning, and to fly back at 5:00 P.M. This seemed to give me ample leeway. My flight, an American Airlines concoction, would reach Midway at 10:30 A.M. Chicago time, and the lunch was from noon to 2:30.

Driving to La Guardia from Westchester, I was held up at the Triborough Bridge by an accident, and had to sprint the last lap to avoid losing my reservation to a standby. But I made it. I boarded the plane, and had been sitting on it for nearly half an hour, trying to restore my breathing to a nearly normal rate, when an announcement over a loudspeaker advised us passengers that our flight engineer had been in an accident on the Triborough Bridge (so that was it!) and we'd have to wait until a substitute materialized. Fortunately, the announcer said cheerfully, another engineer was at that instant winging toward La Guardia, and he would join our crew as soon as his plane landed.

Fifteen minutes later, we were told that La Guardia was closed to incoming flights, owing to fog, and although we could still take off, we'd have to wait for our original engineer to get his fenders unentangled. Half an hour after that, we were told that an inspection, conceivably by our engineer, had revealed a flaw in the fuel pump of one of our engines, and would we please all get off the plane and await further instructions.

I explained to an American official that I had to be in Chicago for lunch, and he told me not to worry, we'd be off in no time at all. I telephoned the master of ceremonies in Chicago and *he* told me not to worry, that if I reached the Ambassador West, where the lunch was being held, by 2:15, there'd still be time to speak my piece. He'd even try to have a car waiting for me at the arrival gate, he said, to rush me to the hotel. When I finished my call, I learned that our flight was rescheduled. We'd be taking off, at 11:50, with new equipment.

At 11:50, our departure time was changed to 12:10. At

12:15, we boarded the plane. It took off at 12:35. By this time, all we passengers who'd been hanging around were hungry, and it was distressing to find out that there was no lunch aboard. (I had long since abandoned hope of reaching the Chicago lunch in time to get any lunch.) It seemed that, according to the schedule, we were still technically on the 9:00 A.M. flight which was a no-lunch flight, even when it flew at lunch time.

We reached Midway at 2:10. I was the first passenger off, and there was no sign of a driver at the arrival gate. I hailed a cab and asked its driver to make all possible haste to the Ambassador West. He started off boldly, but then his engine began to miss, and just after we'd entered a tunnel that snakes underneath downtown Chicago, we ran out of gas. "Funny," said the driver. "I could of sworn I'd filled the tank this morning. That'll be three-eighty-five." He directed me to a dim-lit flight of stairs that he hoped would get me to ground level. It did, and I jumped into another cab.

I hustled into the hotel at 2:50. As I neared the banquet room where the lunch was being held, I noticed on a table in the foyer three stacks of books—one for each of the three authors on the program. Two of the stacks were ravaged, presumably by auditors who'd bought them on their way in to the literary affair. My stack was intact. No matter; the door to the banquet room was still closed; and I could hear the heartening hum of feminine voices on the other side of it. My audience was still there!

I reached for the door handle, and as I did the door swung open toward me, and six hundred women poured out through it. Before I could breast this tide and make my way to the speakers' table, the chamber was all but empty.

It took me an hour or so to compose myself sufficiently to apologize to my host, and when I'd finished I realized I'd better be heading back to Midway. I hopped into a cab, after first ascertaining its fuel pump was functioning, and

gave the driver my destination. He wanted to know what
time my plane was leaving, and when I told him he said we'd
never make it.

"But we have an hour," I said.

"Mister, this is Chicago," he said.

He knew the city better than I, and it was 5:20 when we
got to the airport. My plane had taken off on time. In the
next two and a half hours, as I tried to get myself booked on
one New York flight after another, I became ruefully aware
that the 5:00 P.M. must have been the only flight that day
that did leave on schedule. Oh, well, I thought, whatever
plane I catch I'll relax and have a big dinner, and that'll
make me feel better. I finally got on a scheduled 8:00 P.M.
flight that left at 8:45, or maybe it was a 7:00 P.M. flight.
Whatever it was, it turned out not to be a dinner flight. It
was 1:00 A.M., New York time, before I got home, and by
then I was really too hungry to eat.

The Three

I have rarely been sentimental about types of aircraft, with the exception of the DC-3—a plane to which I and many other passengers have been oddly attached, I because I set off for my honeymoon on a DC-3, they for their own doubtless equally compelling reasons. When the United Nations began emergency land and air operations in the Congo in the fall of 1960, it thus came as no surprise to me, nor to thousands of others in the United States and abroad, that among the planes used prominently was the DC-3—a venerable, if diminutive, twin-engine monoplane, which, unless it is souped up, has a cruising speed of only a hundred and eighty miles an hour.

Ever since the Douglas Aircraft Company, Inc., brought out this model, in 1936, it has been considered a uniquely serviceable creation. Its admirers point to the fact that although the last of these planes was assembled in 1946—an aeon ago, as aviation history is measured—five thousand DC-3s, or about half of all those ever turned out, are believed to be still flying. The DC-3's boosters concede that in the jet age there is no point in manufacturing more of their favorites, and they agree that some of the model's statistical achievements—such as having flown six hundred million passengers seven billion miles in less than a quarter of a century—can be attributed simply to Douglas's big-scale production of the plane, but they maintain that this hardly accounts for its astonishing tenacity. In support of their claim, they recall that in 1942 the Civil Aeronautics Board decreed that after 1947 it would no longer issue certificates of airworthiness to DC-3s as commercial passenger carriers, and that it repeatedly extended the deadline until, in 1953, it declared that the model would be rated airworthy indefinitely.

The D (for "Douglas") C (for "Commercial") -3 (for "Three")—sometimes referred to simply as "the Three"—is represented not once but twice in the collection of celebrated aircraft at the Smithsonian Institution, in Washington. Most of the planes there are enshrined because they participated in some single notable feat—Lindbergh's Spirit of St. Louis, for example, and one of the pair of DC-3s. This DC-3, known as an R4-D—the Navy's term for the model— was the first plane of any kind to land at the South Pole. (A so far unenshrined Army DC-3, or C-47, was the first plane to land at the North Pole.) However, the national museum's second DC-3, a retired Eastern Air Lines transport, is there not because of any historic event but merely because it is a run-of-the-mill example of what the United States government, in a citation to the Douglas Company, has solemnly proclaimed a "beloved aircraft" and, emotionalism aside, "the best single airplane ever built." That last has to be qualified, of course; it was the best single plane produced for its time. The surviving members of the species, though, have shown abundantly that they are still useful in our time.

For any museum piece to be in active service is unusual. The DC-3 has been likened to the Model T Ford, but Model Ts were hardly more of a factor in automotive travel a quarter of a century after their arrival on the scene than Edsels are now. The DC-3 is still very much a factor in contemporary air travel; indeed, at the end of 1960 far more DC-3s were engaged in scheduled airline service around the world than planes of any other type. The United States Air Force, for all its glittering stable of jets, had twelve hundred DC-3s in active service, and if they were not likely to make the Soviet Union throw in the towel, they were regularly called upon to perform important chores. One of them flew ahead of President Eisenhower's Boeing 707 during his 1959 tour of India and Pakistan and radioed back weather reports. A number of DC-3s have been assigned to Air Force ballistic-missile teams to take them, however prosaically, from factory to launching pad. Still others have been employed as flying laboratories to test new defense devices.

Similarly, the parent company, Douglas, relied on several DC-3s to try out many of the mechanisms it subsequently installed in its first passenger jet, the DC-8, which made its début in 1959. Douglas executives were taken aback when some aviation writers, after being given an introductory ride on the DC-8, seemed much less interested in telling their readers about the swift new giant than in reminiscing mistily about its lumbering old forebear. In their choice of emphasis, the writers were following an example set by American Airlines, which ordered the first DC-3s ever produced, and at one time had a fleet of eighty of them; American gave up the model in 1949, but with such reluctance that in one of its ads at the time, instead of crowing about the up-to-date planes it had just acquired, it dwelt on the DC-3s of its past.

Like American, the other major United States airlines

have pretty much outgrown the DC-3, save for scattered local flights—a Braniff run from Sioux City to Kansas City, Delta's Charleston-Atlanta run, and a few others. Nevertheless, approximately three hundred and fifty of the planes were still in domestic scheduled service twenty-five years after the DC-3 was born, not to mention scores of the planes operated by non-scheduled carriers. In 1959, a Dallas magazine called *Flight* made a survey of a dozen so-called feeder, or local, airlines—North Central ("America's Leading Local Airlines"), Central ("Serving the Ozarks Playground Area"), Ozark ("The Businessman's Airline"), Piedmont ("Route of the Pacemakers"), Allegheny, Frontier, Mohawk, Southern, Pacific, Trans-Texas, and West Coast. *Flight* found them using a total of two hundred and twelve DC-3s, many of which they had bought second-hand from the big airlines.

The survey was illustrated by a black-and-white map of the United States captioned "Local Service Airline Schedule Pattern Operated with Equipment Other Than DC-3." The routes on which other-thans were used were marked in red and blue, but the map was nearly bare of color. A similar map a year later would have been somewhat gaudier, because the feeders were beginning to switch to turbo-props, yet there were still many small lines that could not afford to buy, or operate, expensive new equipment. A few years before that, a couple of feeders that had been wholly dependent on DC-3s decided to order new planes. After using them for several months, at astronomically increased costs, both airlines sold them and went back to DC-3s. To many a local airline, a DC-3, puny and poky though it may seem by coast-to-coast standards, has been not only a comfortably familiar plane but a big one. Trans-Texas calls its DC-3s Super Starliners. Mohawk, which operates mostly in upstate New York, sought not long ago to turn the venerability of its DC-3s to nostalgic advantage, and it announced a for-men-only series of flights aboard them, called Gas Light Service. The passengers are served, according to a printed menu the airline got up in antique script, "mugs of cool, tasty, moustache-tickling Utica Club lager beer, heaps of crispy, salty, pre-stressed pretzels," and "tummy-patting" cheese.

Abroad, far more than here, the DC-3 has remained a ubiquitous work horse, being in faithful harness to a hundred and seventy-four scheduled airlines in seventy nations. (In the Netherlands, Hungary, and Chile, it has been depicted on airmail stamps—an honor that it never won at home.) A British magazine also called *Flight* calculated in 1959 that the DC-3s operated by scheduled airlines came to a thousand six hundred and seventy-two. "It is a sobering fact that numerically about thirty per cent of the world's total transport air fleet consists of DC-3s," this *Flight* said. Of eighty-six airlines, collectively using sixty-nine makes of aircraft, that subsequently reported on their comings and goings to the International Air Transport Association, a trade group with headquarters in Montreal, fifty-seven lines were flying some DC-3s, while two additional companies, in Poland and Czechoslovakia, were flying Russian-built copies of the DC-3. Air Ceylon's equipment consisted of one Super-Constellation and two DC-3s, Air Viet-Nam's of one DC-4 and six DC-3s. The Indian Airlines Corporation had eighty-three planes, sixty of them DC-3s. For Garuda Airlines, in Indonesia, it was twenty DC-3s out of a fleet of thirty-nine; for Iranian Airways, ten out of seventeen; for Jugoslovenski Aerotransport, thirteen out of twenty-two; and for Real Aerovias, in Brazil, sixty-nine out of a hundred and seven.

Quite a few airlines—Transportes Aéreos Salvador and Liberian National Airways among them—owned nothing but DC-3s at last reckoning. Well after the jet age became a reality, there was no machine other than a DC-3 on which one could take a scheduled flight between—to name just a few of countless routes—Great Whale and Montreal,

Tebessa and Bône, Amman and Jedda, Beirut and Aleppo, Asmara and Taiz, Abadan and Isfahan, Quito and Cuenca, Asunción and Curitiba, Tegucigalpa and La Ceiba, Vaasa and Turku, Blackpool and the Isle of Man, Jersey and Guernsey, Reykjavík and Egilsstadir, Granada and Tangier, Lourenço Marques and Quelimane, Nicosia and Tel Aviv, Vientiane and Luangprabang, Djakarta and Surabaja, Biak and Manokwari, Brewarrina and Coonamble, and Patna and Katmandu. An editor of a magazine called *Airlift* who made the Patna-Katmandu hop by Indian Airlines Corporation DC-3 wrote an account of the flight, rhapsodically headed, "DC-3 BUCKS HIMALAYA PEAKS TO SERVE SMILING NEPALESE," which said of the Katmandu landing facilities, significantly, "The airport isn't much to brag about, but it's adequate for DC-3s."

The DC-3's partisans are a fervent lot, as is clearly demonstrated by a sampling of the adjectives with which they have publicly hailed the plane of their choice—"stout-hearted," "indomitable," "irreplaceable," "incredible," and "sophisticated." Odes have been written to the DC-3 and songs composed about it, including "The Ballad of a Bush Pilot," which reaches its climax with the words "Before I die/ I want to fly/ A Douglas DC-3." A few years ago, a long-retired pilot in Santa Monica, California, where Douglas Aircraft has its headquarters, was granted the wish of an ebbing lifetime when finally, on his eightieth birthday, he got to fly a DC-3.

Some of the idolators of the plane tend to take an anthropomorphic view of it. An American pilot who was decorated during the Korean War for evacuating some trapped Marines said of the DC-3s he had used to accomplish the task, "Their countenances seemed to smile satisfaction" and "I wondered if they didn't deserve a Medal of Honor." He did not endow the planes with sex, but most laureates have viewed the DC-3—a squat craft weighing sixteen thousand five hundred pounds unloaded and unfuelled, and with a normal cargo capacity of sixty-five hundred more—as feminine. Two Air Force lieutenant colonels who in 1959 brought out a book-length eulogy of the plane entitled it "Grand Old Lady" and confessed they had been in love with her since their teens.

If the DC-3 has already become a grand old lady, it is nonetheless hazardous to guess at how long its, or her, life span may turn out to be. In 1950, the magazine *Aero Digest* asked rhetorically, "Who among us is emboldened to deny that the DC-3 will go on forever?" Just what constitutes an airplane is arguable. Some vintage DC-3s have had over fifty changes of engine, and, except for the fuselage, little is left of their other original parts, either. (In the DC-3's defense, of course, it can be pointed out that every living creature is constantly renewing its cells.) In 1959, Southern Airways detected a cracked wing bolt in one of its DC-3s, and sent the bolt to the Douglas Company, soliciting advice as to the cause of this defect. Careful examination revealed that the wing bolt had been part of the plane when it was assembled, twenty-two years earlier. By tracing the plane through its successive owners, the Douglas people established that the bolt, which, according to their engineers, had a theoretical life of sixteen thousand hours of flight, had actually stood up for sixty-four thousand eight hundred and seventy-nine hours and fifty-two minutes. "The only message we could think of to send Southern was 'Congratulations,'" a Douglas engineer told me. In 1960, North Central Airlines, the largest of the United States feeders, which operates out of Minneapolis, had two DC-3s that had flown fifty thousand hours each for Eastern Air Lines, for which they were built in 1939, and that racked up twenty thousand hours more each after being sold to their next owner. Together, they had flown a good twenty million miles, and both were still going strong.

The DC-3, of course, is not indestructible. Grace Moore was killed in a DC-3 crash, and so was Carole Lombard. In 1949, a Canadian Pacific DC-3 earned the unsought distinction of being the first airliner to be blown up in flight, when a man who hoped to collect insurance on one of its passengers —his wife—planted a bomb in it. Generally, though, the DC-3 has been both hardy and resourceful. In fact, one DC-3 foiled a would-be murderer when, flying across Mexico, it survived a bomb that ripped open one of its gas tanks; it landed forty-five minutes later, and no one aboard was scratched. (It was through Mexico's bracing skies, too, that a hitchhiker once travelled from Torreón to Mexico City, a three-hour ride, while clinging to a DC-3's tail.) The *second* plane to land at the South Pole was a fancy four-engine Navy craft; it got stuck there, and couldn't take off until a DC-3 settled alongside with some spare parts.

A few years ago, another DC-3 landed on a frozen Quebec lake. The ice was thin, and the plane broke through and sank. The owner despairingly sold what he assumed was its carcass to the first bidder, who fished the plane out, drained it, started the engines, and zoomed away. In England, a DC-3 once landed on the roof of a house without appreciably damaging either the house or itself. Many pilots regard the DC-3 as an exceptionally forgiving plane. They say it has the knack of somehow compensating for their errors. Indeed, some of them go so far as to insist that it can fly all by itself, citing as evidence an incident that took place in 1957 in Missouri. An Air Force DC-3 ran out of gas, and the pilot and crew parachuted. Presently, the plane landed gently in a field. The only damage it suffered came when, as it was rolling to a halt, one wing hit a bale of hay.

In the air, the DC-3 has weathered some remarkable

wrenches and tugs, including direct hits by lightning bolts, sixteen-inch naval shells, and kamikaze planes. During the war, one DC-3 pilot whose plane was riddled by anti-aircraft fire decided to ditch it in a Pacific lagoon. After hitting the water, the plane bounced fifty feet into the air. Spurred on by its resiliency, he changed his mind and flew on to his base. More recently, a DC-3 ferrying a cargo of monkeys from Pakistan to Morocco got to its destination even though several monkeys broke loose and swarmed all over the pilot's compartment, playfully pulling at the controls. When a DC-3 does crash, the reason is apt to be that the plane is not pressurized, which means that it cannot be flown comfortably over seventeen thousand feet and thus may bump into mountains. In 1957, however, a Frontier Airlines DC-3, in turbulent air over Arizona, plummeted four thousand feet and scraped a hill, which sheared twelve feet off one wing, yet the pilot was able to right the plane and get it safely home, where he laconically reported, "Aircraft settled uncontrollably, contacting west slope of mountain peak on my left wing."

The first Douglas commercial airliner, the DC-1, was an experimental twin-engine plane unveiled in the summer of 1933, when commercial air travel was more or less experimental itself. Only one DC-1 was made. (Howard Hughes bought it, and thought for a while of flying around the world in it; eventually, in other hands, it cracked up in Spain.) The DC-2, a 1934 modification of its predecessor, was reproduced a hundred and thirty-eight times. It was a fourteen-passenger plane with a wing span of eighty-five feet—ten feet less than that of the DC-3. (During the war, when a DC-3 lost a wing in India, a spare DC-2 wing was attached to it; this improvised but navigable hybrid became known, inevitably, as the DC-2½.) The DC-3 itself was designed originally as a sleeper plane for American Airlines, with fourteen berths in the main passenger section and a secluded honeymoon compartment forward. To accommodate all the berths, a longer fuselage than the DC-2's was required, and this increased the weight of the ship, necessitating a greater wing span and more powerful twin engines. (The DC-4, DC-6, and DC-7 were all four-engine planes, each larger than its predecessor. The DC-5, a 1939 model, was a two-engine, fourteen-passenger throwback, which flopped.)

Many air-minded observers believed that the DC-3 was too spacious to be economically practical. The Douglas Company more or less agreed, and prudently tooled up, at the outset, for a maximum production of twenty-five such planes, the first of which were launched early in 1936. It is difficult to state with assurance which DC-3 in operation a quarter of a century later was the oldest one around, not only because planes change numbers when they change hands but because some of the airlines that went on flying DC-3s have been reluctant to remind passengers that some of their equipment was almost twenty-five years old. But there was fairly good reason to believe in 1960 that the oldest then being flown commercially, which bore the Federal Aviation Agency number NC 16005, was an Ozark Air Lines plane, the second of the model ever built, and that the most ancient of all those taking to the air was the very first of the whole lot, NC 16004, a onetime American Airlines sleeper plane that came off the Douglas assembly line on June 28, 1936, and that in the next generation belonged to the Pacific Lumber Company, of San Francisco.

When the DC-3 was new, it was the behemoth of its day, and, despite its manufacturer's misgivings, it revolutionized air travel, though not as a sleeper, for it was quickly converted into a standard passenger plane. Before the DC-3 came along, airline passengers could not take out flight insurance at terminals, and airline pilots had to pay heavily for any kind of life insurance anywhere. The DC-3 was the first passenger plane to be equipped with an automatic pilot, a heated cabin, and soundproofing. Between 1936 and 1946, ninety-three per cent of all domestic-airline passenger service was via DC-3. In the fifties, the Douglas Company, hoping to put together a file of the plane's redoubtable early achievements, asked some owners and former owners to send in whatever recollections they might have of those days. American Airlines recalled that some of its DC-3s ferried nurses and medical supplies to Louisville during a 1937 flood, along with a posse of police to keep order. Eastern Air Lines reported that one of its DC-3s was the first commercial airliner to land at the Washington National Airport, and United reported that in 1939 one of *its* DC-3s was the first aircraft to receive television signals while in flight; beamed from New York, they were picked up as the plane was cruising at twenty thousand feet over Washington. Pan American proudly sent word that a DC-3 of its fleet had served as the first in-flight rostrum from which any President of Peru ever orated, by radio, to his constituents below. Braniff remembered that it had used a DC-3 to rush a Baylor University girl from Dallas to San Antonio, where a specialist was waiting to dislodge a bone from her throat, and Chicago & Southern remembered that it had used a DC-3 to rush an ailing robin from Chicago to New Orleans, where a bird-loving veterinarian performed emergency surgery. I remembered my honeymoon.

The standard capacity of a DC-3 is twenty-one passengers —fourteen in double seats on one side of the aisle, seven in single seats on the other. (Nowadays, though, in some parts of the world one side is reserved for freight.) But over the years, as the DC-3 continued to demonstrate its worth, some airlines began jamming more and more paying fares into it. Pacific Western, of Canada, has accommodations for thirty-two passengers on a DC-3 run between Vancouver and Powell River, and Philippine Air Lines has its DC-3s fixed up to carry forty passengers in as many rather small seats. Qantas, on its New Guinea runs, handles fifty tight-squeezed passengers at a clip, using canvas slings for perches. The all-time record is believed to have been set on a non-scheduled flight in Bolivia in 1949, when a town was imperilled by rising floods. A DC-3 carried out ninety-three refugees, together with a three-man crew; most of the passengers, however, were children.

In 1959, Aerolineas Argentinas disclosed that one of its DC-3s—a souped-up one, of course—had set a new DC-3 speed record for the three-hundred-and-sixty-mile run between Buenos Aires and Santa Rosa, making it in an hour and thirty-four minutes, for an average of two hundred and thirty miles an hour, or, in current parlance, Mach .31. Most of the airlines that rely on DC-3s don't give a hoot about speed records. It can be argued—and some of those airlines do argue—that an airliner's speed is a mystifying and often meaningless attribute. A DC-8 or a Boeing 707 can outfly a DC-3 by four hundred miles an hour, but considering what happens to a passenger before and after he gets up there—the long overland crawl to and from outlying airports, plus all the standing and waiting and walking and wilting and wailing—the big jets are often only a few minutes faster, if that, in terms of helping an individual move from the downtown area of City A to the downtown area of City B. Then, too, small planes can land at small airfields —like La Guardia and Midway—that are closer to town than the new giant installations for jets. The Federal Aviation Agency has announced, specifically, that a traveller from mid-Manhattan to mid-Chicago could save twenty-five minutes in total travel time by flying in a piston-engine plane instead of a jet. On short hauls—that is, between cities no more than a hundred miles apart—it is undeniable that the race is seldom to the swift, for the slower planes can land not only on smaller fields but with less fuss and delay. Faucett

Airlines, a Peruvian company, whose DC-3s on its Lima-Iquitos local run make eight stops in ten hours, couldn't use DC-8s for that trip even if it got them free. By the same token, MacRobertson Miller Airlines, in northwestern Australia, would find it awkward to supplant DC-3s with jets on one of its runs—a less-than-two-thousand-mile stretch in which its planes make about forty stops, some of them only eight miles apart.

When the United States went to war in December, 1941, three hundred and sixty DC-3s were in service on domestic airlines. The Air Transport Command swiftly commandeered nearly two hundred of these, and, at the behest of the armed forces, Douglas began turning out new ones as fast as it could. By 1945, it had produced over ten thousand, nearly half of them at a hastily constructed plant in Oklahoma City. A couple of thousand went to England and Canada. The Soviet Union got seven hundred, and, with plans and tools provided by Douglas, built around two thousand more for itself, calling them Lissunov-2s and neglecting to pay any royalties. (My wife and I rode what I took for one of these from Leningrad to Kiev, during the cold war. We paid royalties, or, at any rate, our fare.) In 1959, when the celebrated Soviet plane designer Andrei Tupolev was in the United States, Donald W. Douglas, who founded the Douglas Company and is now its chairman, invited him and some travelling companions to lunch at Santa Monica. During the toasts, Tupolev made a flowery speech about the DC-3. Mr. Douglas, when his turn came, responded handsomely that he'd heard the Russians had done a magnificent job building DC-3s. At this, Tupolev and his compatriots all looked stonily blank, and Douglas, deducing that they had no intention of admitting that they owed him anything, tactfully changed the subject.

While the war was on, the Douglas Company built a total of over twenty-nine thousand planes. The majority were battle weapons, but Mr. Douglas has said that the DC-3s he made gave him the most satisfaction. "It was kind of nice to be making something that you didn't drop bombs out of or shoot bullets out of but that could still do a good job," he once told me. By mid-1944, his company was churning out DC-3s at the rate of nearly two an hour, following an urgent personal appeal to its factory workers at the start of that year by General H. H. Arnold, the Air Force chief of staff, who said he desperately needed four hundred more of the transports than the production schedule called for. He got his extra four hundred in time for D Day, when the greatest fleet of DC-3s ever assembled—twelve hundred of them, flying in a column two hundred miles long—delivered parachutists and glider troops to Normandy.

Meanwhile, DC-3s had been active in other theatres. They were used for flying tank parts to Montgomery's forces at El Alamein, and, in the South Pacific, for flying troops of the 32nd Infantry Division across the Owen Stanley Mountains of New Guinea—the first United States combat ground forces ever airlifted to battle. They also flew in fuel to the fighter planes based on Guadalcanal during the fighting there. Stilwell, Mountbatten, and Chiang Kai-shek had DC-3s equipped as command posts, and another DC-3 that participated in the war against Japan was equipped as a travelling laundry. In the course of the war, DC-3s toted disassembled fighter planes and heavy trucks to this or that destination, to be welded together again on arrival, while to the snow-shrouded Battle of the Bulge they ferried two dozen dog sleds, a hundred and fifty Huskies, and twenty-five dog-handling soldiers. In all theatres of war combined, they carried a total of seven hundred and fifty thousand sick and wounded servicemen to hospitals.

Notwithstanding Douglas's pleasure in the thought that the DC-3 was a noncombatant plane, it was used in both Europe and Asia as a bomber (the bombs were kicked out of

open doors) and as a fighter, too (machine guns were
mounted in the doorways) . One peripatetic American inter-
ceptor pilot, who had already earned the right to paint German, Italian, and Japanese flags on the fuselage of his P-51,
added the Stars and Stripes to his collection by bringing
down a DC-3 when its navigator became confused and
started to land, with an important cargo, on a Japanese-
held island. To prevent the DC-3, its crew, and its freight
from being captured, the P-51 man fired at it, forcing it to
make a crash landing on friendly territory.

Right after V-J Day, DC-3s were a glut on the airplane
market. Many of them were abandoned—and still stand
rusting—on remote Pacific bases. DC-3s in good shape were
sold as surplus for as little as twelve hundred dollars, and
incapacitated ones for as little as two hundred and fifty.
(Some of the latter were trucked off and converted into
homes.) At the time, nearly everybody in aviation assumed
that the DC-3 was all but washed up as a passenger plane,
and it was then that Douglas stopped manufacturing it. The
company tried to make the best of what seemed like a bad
situation by introducing the Super DC-3—a plane two and a
half feet longer than the original model, and incorporating
various improvements, which increased the cruising speed
to around two hundred and forty miles an hour with a load
of over thirty passengers. The company promotionally acclaimed its new offering as a plane "capable of carrying on
indefatigably in the noble tradition of its famous ancestor,"
but despite this hoopla, and a transcontinental sales tour
that Donald Douglas himself made in a Super DC-3, it never
proved to be all that capable. The Navy bought a hundred
of the planes, but all other customers together ordered a
mere ten.
    In the meantime, the famous ancestor found itself in grad-
ually mounting demand. Its relatively low purchase price

made it extremely attractive to shoestring entrepreneurs offering modest non-scheduled air-coach transportation. Cargo carriers found it appealing, too—notably in the Antipodes. Before long, DC-3s were trundling emigrants from Italy and Cyprus to Australia, beef from inland Australian abattoirs to coastal ports, and sheep from Australia to grazing lands in New Guinea, and were being used to spread fertilizer in New Zealand. DC-3s were also being used to harass browntail moths in the United States, while DC-3s on skis were patrolling the DEW line, and DC-3s on floats were wafting fishermen to remote trout-packed lakes.

DC-3s were doing everything, and quite a few of them kept on doing that. In 1959, former Governor Earl Long, of Louisiana, commuted between mental hospitals by DC-3, and a while later a DC-3 carried the leaflets that so outraged Fidel Castro when they showered down on Havana. Early in 1960, when a new one-and-a-half-million-dollar control tower was opened at the Newark Airport, the first plane to be waved aloft from it was a DC-3, the property of the Federal Aviation Agency. That same day, the electrical system of a DC-3 carrying a professional basketball team over Iowa went on the blink, but the plane made a smooth emergency landing in a snow-covered cornfield. Douglas Aircraft employees shuttle back and forth between plants at Santa Monica and Long Beach in four DC-3s; the company, which no longer owns even one, charters these from an airline called the Stewart Air Service, and at night the four planes—Stewart's whole fleet—keep in trim by hauling gamblers to Las Vegas and back.

Fifteen years after the Douglas Company turned out its last DC-3, it was making and selling a million dollars' worth of spare parts for the plane annually. Almost every day, the Douglas offices would receive an order for parts from some DC-3 owner—Malayan Airways, perhaps, or the Royal Nepal Airline, or an American business firm that maintained a private plane. The larger corporations, like the larger airlines, have lately been turning to larger planes, but the executives of close to four hundred companies that could scarcely be called small—among them Campbell Soup, Abitibi Power & Paper, Freeport Nickel, Webb & Knapp, Rockwell Spring & Axle, Fort Worth Pipe & Supply, and North American Life and Casualty—hung onto DC-3s. Some of these have been elegantly fitted out. Houston Lumber had one with mink-covered doorknobs. The furniture in Alcoa's was all of gleaming aluminum. A rancher in Texas, one of dozens of individuals with a DC-3 at his beck, upholstered the interior of his in unborn calfskin. It has been not uncommon for such private craft to be fitted out with divans and dressing rooms and picture windows and hi-fi and tape recorders and air-to-ground phones and cedar closets and the latest electronic equipment and fogproof, iceproof, birdproof windshields and, of course, bars, which in the aircraft-trade press are called refreshment consoles. Pillsbury Mills equipped its DC-3 as a laboratory to test the quick-rising properties of biscuit mix at varying heights, and a number of other firms have used the planes as travelling showrooms, in which new products are demonstrated aloft to customers consoling themselves with refreshments.

The first twenty DC-3s built cost American Airlines a hundred and ten thousand dollars each. In 1960, used DC-3s were selling for as much as two hundred and sixty thousand, and one that was fit and fitted for corporate use was not likely to fetch less than a hundred and fifty thousand. As for the DC-3s owned by a few Middle East sheiks, who fancy studding the panelling with precious jewels, their value has been impossible to compute. Even the dowdiest old cargo-carrying DC-3 cannot be bought anywhere in the world for much under twenty-five thousand, and in this country the minimum market price at last report was fifty thousand—a substantial appreciation since the end of the war. W. S. Shackleton, of London, a leading international dealer in used planes, who has shipped old Aer Lingus DC-3s from Ireland to Tanganyika and who has sold a couple of DC-3s to the Sydney *Morning Herald* to deliver papers, observed long after the DC-3 was supposed to be out of the picture that it "still plays the most significant role of all in the used-plane market."

Ever since the war, an American DC-3 has nestled high on Mount Fujiyama, but although the United States government announced its willingness to consider offers, no one came forward to bid on it. Used-plane dealers have competed eagerly, however, for more accessible DC-3s, or fragments of them, and have converted the more or less whole planes into polished executive-style aircraft, relying on the bits for spare parts. A South African Air Force DC-3 that crashed in the Transvaal, in 1944, was sold for eighty pounds to a local man, who transformed it into a roadhouse, its wings ablaze with neon. Twelve years later, a travelling salesman of airplane parts came upon the odd-shaped café, bought it on the spot, shipped it to California, and had it reconditioned as an airplane.

Of the several domestic companies that have made a good thing out of this kind of salvage work, the most prominent has been Remmert-Werner, in St. Louis, which after the war revivified more than two hundred DC-3s, and which a while ago sold one that it had pieced together out of a fuselage picked up in Minnesota, a wing from California, another wing from Florida, and odds and ends from other states. The fuselage of a plush DC-3 that Remmert-Werner sold to a large and sedate corporation for its officials to gad about in was, when the company first spotted it, a chicken house in the backwoods of Alabama. The DC-3 bought by another corporation from AiResearch Aviation Service Company, a

Los Angeles salvaging firm, had previously been used in Hawaii to haul fish. The main problem AiResearch had in fixing that one up was to get the smell out of it.

What is perhaps the most harrowing pursuit of old DC-3s
on record began in 1955, when Remmert-Werner heard that
Turkish State Airlines wanted to sell seven such planes that
were laid up in the inland city of Ankara. Inquiry revealed
that they had been stripped of engines, radios, instruments,
panels, interiors, floors, windows, and fuel and hydraulic
systems, but so short was the supply of available DC-3s at
the time that this seemed no serious drawback. Remmert-
Werner sent an agent to Turkey, where he learned that he
would have to compete in the bidding against agents from
England, Egypt, Israel, Brazil, Italy, Germany, and Canada.
After many complicated negotiations, he got the nod from
the seller, and then discovered that the sale would have to be
sanctioned by several echelons of Turkish officialdom, including the Cabinet and the Prime Minister. Before the appropriate papers could be signed, a pistol-brandishing debate was staged on the floor of the Turkish legislature, and
the government fell. Dazed, the Remmert-Werner man re-
negotiated successfully with the new government, but it
wouldn't issue an import license for the parts that would
be needed to fly the planes out, so they had to be shipped
by rail and sea. En route, four wings were destroyed when
a freight car overturned on a mountain curve. Three and
a half years after the start of the dickering, the seven plane
skeletons arrived in St. Louis, with the Remmert-Werner
people looking on, as pleased as they were punchy.

The many DC-3 zealots who have never trafficked in the
planes but merely ridden in them are likely to have singularly retentive memories. In England, the members of an
organization called Air-Britain and subtitled the National
Association of Aviation Enthusiasts can rattle off the serial
numbers of long-gone DC-3s, whose peregrinations from one

owner to another the enthusiasts have faithfully charted. In the columns of British aviation magazines, for instance, spirited arguments are regularly waged over whether the Nazis did or did not capture and sneakily avail themselves of certain Allied DC-3s during the war. One of the Queen's subjects, who operates out of Nairobi, wrote the following cryptic passage in a lengthy and astonishingly learned letter to a buffs' magazine called *Air Pictorial:* "Regarding Mr. Bateson's comments on K.L.M. DC-3s, c/n. 1935 was PH-ALH, later becoming PC-EA in the Luftwaffe. Its earlier acquisition by D.L.H. as D-ABUG is probably accounted for by the fact that it was in Germany on the day Holland was invaded by the Nazis. His other DC-3 listed, c/n. 2036, which he claims to be another ex-K.L.M. aircraft, I cannot find listed in the 1939/40 K.L.M. fleet list in my possession. It might therefore be an ex-C.L.S. DC-3 or even one of the two Sabena DC-3s referred to in my letter." While the Berlin airlift was on, a newly arrived United States Air Force colonel, who had been flying DC-3s over the Hump to China five years before, was walking across a West German runway when he stopped short, arrested by the sight of a DC-3 that to most mortals would have been indistinguishable from ten thousand others. To him, though, it evoked poignant recollections. "I'll be damned!" he exclaimed. "Unless I'm having hallucinations, that's old 316051!" It was.

There can be no doubt that the DC-3 has exerted a powerful pull on man's emotions. A few years ago, Donald Douglas got a nine-page, single-spaced letter from a Canadian banker who had been a wartime wing commander in the R.A.F. At the age of twenty, he wrote Douglas, he had travelled from Halifax to Montreal merely to gape at a DC-3—"a beautiful mechanical beast," he called it. He had at once fallen for the beast, and on flying aboard it as a passenger had found the experience "smooth and firm and straight and level." During the war, he had flown a DC-3 himself, and when the Japanese destroyed it on the ground, he was heartsick. "I missed her—as a person, not a piece of machinery," he wrote. "And that, to a driver who gets a 'right' plane in his hands, is the spell of the DC-3. . . . If ever an inanimate object earned, deserved, and received the love of a man, your DC-3 was that object. In fact, I, and probably thousands of others, consider it callous to refer to her as 'inanimate.'" Douglas was touched by this testimonial, since he, too, is fonder of the DC-3 than of any other inanimate object his company has manufactured. "The Three is certainly the best and best-loved airplane we've ever produced," he told me, speaking like a father. "But the circumstances that made it great just happened. They were not of our making. I doubt whether any airplane will have the same impact, or the same opportunity, again."

THERE

A Little
Knowledgeability
Is
a Dangerous
Thing

I took my first long trip, a voyage to Europe, when I was ten years old. I at once fell in love with ocean liners, not to mention with a sixteen-year-old girl whose name I forget but whose scorn I remember. For me, the only acceptable replacement for the old-fashioned, luxury-ridden ocean liner would be an airplane the size, the shape, and, equally important, the speed, of the *Ile de France*. It would need open decks, too, for the smell and feel of fresh salt air. I do not expect this to come to pass, but we can always dream, just as I once dreamed the sixteen-year-old would play deck tennis with me.

I am so much an ocean-liner buff that in 1949, when my wife and I had a holiday trip abroad planned, I wouldn't let Jinny join me in Europe, where I happened to be, but instead flew back to the United States in order to be able to share with her the fun of crossing the Atlantic at sea level. We were to land at Liverpool, to tour England and Scotland for a couple of weeks by car, and then to spend a fortnight in London and Paris.

My wife had never been to Europe before, but because I wasn't available it fell to her to make our preliminary arrangements. I suggested that for our motor tour she pick up *Baedeker's Great Britain,* and for further possible guidance I dug up for her a diary I'd kept, but hadn't glanced at for years, in the course of a similar journey I'd made as a teen-ager, under the aegis of a high-school English teacher, an elderly man in his thirties.

I left the packing in Jinny's hands, too, as I would even if I had all the time in the world. I stipulated merely that she take along some bottles of Scotch, as gifts for the natives, and evening clothes for us both, since we had first-class accommodations on shipboard. I warned her, though, not to overburden us with daytime wear, for the rented car that we were to pick up at Liverpool was a small English make with limited luggage space.

It wasn't until our second day out that I got around to inquiring how she'd fared. Then she said that in addition to a tweed suit I'd embarked in, and my dinner jacket, she'd packed one other suit, which she calculated was the minimum I could get by with. She added that Brentano's had been out of the Baedeker I wanted, but that she'd been lucky enough to find a second-hand copy. Proudly, she showed it to me. It was a frayed and brittle volume, and no wonder, for the title page revealed that it was the 1887 edition of the work.

I observed, after scanning the book, that most of the major sight-seeing attractions in Great Britain were far older than sixty years anyway, and that we would doubtless make out fine with the Baedeker if we were careful to ignore certain of its archaic travel tips—such as a warning to tourists to avoid monetary confusion by keeping their gold and silver coins in separate pockets. Besides, I said cheerfully, for relatively up-to-date counsel, we could always fall back on my own 1933 notes.

Jinny expressed some misgivings. "Mostly you seemed just to jot down things like 'Bill the Conq' and 'Second fender gone,' " she said. "Except in Edinburgh, where you really got carried away." She plucked my diary from one of her suitcases and read aloud, " 'Edinburgh. Castle. Went to four bars. Had four drinks. Gin, whiskey, ale, gin. Wonderful evening. Wonderful city.' That's the entire entry for Edinburgh. And here's what you had to say about Warwick Castle: 'Two-thousand-year-old Grecian cup. Once used for wine. Big enough for a man to stand in.' You must have been mixing your drinks *that* day, too. Who ever heard of a wine cup you could stand in? Anyway, Baedeker says it's a vase. Now let's dress for dinner."

Our cabin steward stopped by while I was knotting my tie, and said that begging my pardon it really wasn't necessary for me to get all dolled up; that while we were indeed first-class, that was a euphemism of sorts. The ship had no other class, and as a result evening clothes were optional. (Naturally, we hadn't dressed the first night out; even I knew better than that.) So I switched to my second informal suit, a dark-blue one, and I wore it every night—even the penultimate night, when the Captain's Dinner was held and practically all the other men on board, perhaps counselled by their cabin stewards, turned up resplendent in black tie.

On docking at Liverpool, we discovered that we had with us one more bottle of Scotch than British customs permitted. But a kindly customs agent said we could keep it if we'd unseal it. I uncapped it, recapped it, and stuffed it into my suitcase. We were delighted to find in the glove compartment of our car a Royal Automobile Club hotel directory, and, heartened by having this up-to-date crutch to lean on, I got behind the wheel and asked Jinny to name a destination. "Edinburgh," she said. "It should be a novel experience for both of us."

We headed northeast. I must have been overanxious to persuade Jinny of my knowledgeability, for we were hardly out of Liverpool before I was telling her to be on the look-out for thatched-roof cottages, which I remembered with affection and thought she would find delightfully quaint. When, two days later, we pulled into Edinburgh, we hadn't yet seen one of them, and I decided I had better demon-strate quickly that I wasn't afflicted with total non-recall. (Southwest would have been a better course to set for thatch, I later realized.) A good opportunity seemed to present itself when we got to Edinburgh Castle. Jinny had our Bae-deker with her, but its binding was so loose and its type so small that she couldn't read it easily while on the move. She proposed accordingly that we join up with a group of tourists being shown around by a uniformed guide.

I demurred. To pay for information that I was perfectly capable of giving myself would, I told her, be a foolish ex-travagance. I soon regretted my rashness; the place didn't seem anywhere near as familiar as I'd hoped it would. To cover up, I eavesdropped on an official guide, and then pre-tended to Jinny that what I had covertly gleaned from him was the fruit of my own recollection.

As we entered one chamber, for instance, identified by a sign outside it as "Queen Mary's Room," I heard a guide say that King James I had been born there. Inside, on the far wall hung a large tapestry, and prominent among the figures woven into it were a maternal-looking woman and an infant. "The historical importance of this particular chamber is pretty well covered by that tapestry," I told my wife with studied casualness. "It shows Mary and her son, who was born right here and who of course became James the First." An instant later I perceived that the tapestry had its own identifying legend, which revealed its subject matter to be the Judgment of Solomon. I got Jinny out of there before she could notice that herself, but it was a near thing.

A few hours afterward, with the Castle safely behind us, I urged that we climb to the top of Calton Hill, from the summit of which, I said confidently, we could enjoy a fine panorama of the city. We had put in a long day, and Jinny was tired, but she agreed sportingly to this proposal, even after I had dredged from my memory the warning that the Hill could be ascended only by foot. We parked our car at the bottom and trudged up, reaching the top at the same time as a charabanc-load of tourists who had been driven there along a paved road that curled up the other flank of the slope.

After that Queen-Mary's-Room episode, I resolved never to go on record about an exhibit without first reading its label, if any. Thus, at Hampton Court Palace, a week or so later, as we came upon an old and, it appeared to me from a distance, finely carved timber that had been dislodged from some ancient ceiling, I espied a placard, sneaked a look at it, and saw enough, I thought, to describe the relic.

"That's a carving of some of the action in Death Watch Battle," I told Jinny, who this time had her Baedeker open and was boning up on Hampton Court.

"I never heard of any such battle," she said, "and Baedeker doesn't mention it."

"Oh, *Baedeker*," I said. "I imagine the battle took place in one of the early Wars of the Roses."

I stepped aside to let her examine the chewed-up timber from close up.

"Look at those so-called carvings of yours again," she said, "and next time don't read the sign so hastily."

I looked, and read again. "A timber from the great hall," the sign said, "showing action of Death Watch Beetle."

I did most of the driving, so my wife could concentrate on differentiating between my accounts of the scenery around the next bend and the scenery itself. Each afternoon, as we approached the town we'd decided to stop at, she'd select a likely hostel from our R.A.C. guide. One day, though, she chanced to be at the wheel toward sunset, and it was up to me to choose our lodgings. The guidebook I consulted described one hotel as "a first-class establishment, old-fashioned but well-equipped and comfortable," and we elected to go there.

The place seemed a trifle run-down, and we had no trouble getting a room. While I was registering, Jinny inspected the lobby, a dimly lit and somewhat dank enclosure, and in the dining room later, while we were ordering from a menu so antiquarian that its newest-fangled dessert appeared to be chicken livers on toast, she told me the lobby boasted a wall plaque naming some of the more illustrious guests who had preceded us there, among them Queen Victoria.

"Well, I told you the place was old-fashioned," I said.

"More so than you think," said Jinny, distastefully eyeing a stained and shabby tablecloth. "Victoria's last visit to this joint seems to have been when she was a girl in her teens and came here with her mother. I don't mind staying here, for one night, but I must say I'm surprised that the guide book recommended it."

It was then that it dawned on me that I'd picked the spot out of our Baedeker.

When we were within a day or two of Warwick, Jinny began to reproach me, not unreasonably, for my adolescent ranting about the man inside the wine goblet. On arriving at the Castle there, she insisted right off that we attach ourselves to a professional guide, who she hoped could set me straight. I yielded, and soon our mentor was pointing to a conservatory on the grounds.

"If you'll kindly stroll over that way," he said, "you will find a huge cup dating back to the pre-Christian era. It is being cleaned at the moment, but I am sure you will be interested to see it anyway. I understand that in the old days they used to drink wine out of it."

As we headed toward the conservatory, my head was higher and my step springier than at any moment since I'd reached the semi-finals of a mid-ocean shuffleboard tournament. Then we were at the cup. It was big, all right, and while we were gazing at its massive girth, above its lip suddenly materialized the head and shoulders of a workman who was standing inside it.

Moments of victory like that linger in the traveller's memory long after he has forgotten which road he took from Ghent to Aix. Moments of defeat hang on, too. I recall with equal vividness the afternoon I took my wife for a stroll through Piccadilly, and my embarrassment at being unable to point out to her with assurance, despite all she had read of the gamy carrying-ons there, a single indisputable prostitute. After that setback, we repaired for tea to Brown's Hotel, an establishment of unshakeable propriety. While we were sitting in the lobby, we heard, from behind a pillar that hid our view of the speaker, a man's voice brashly state, "I'll have that little tart in the corner."

"My God, not in Brown's!" Jinny gasped.

"They've probably been driven off the streets," I suggested.

We both peeked around the pillar, just in time to watch a waitress with a pastry tray serve a stately-looking gentleman.

On the road, my spare suit was stowed in our most inaccessible suitcase, and I didn't bother to drag it out at night,

figuring that I'd rely on the tweed and send it out to be
cleaned when we reached London. It needed cleaning.
One sleeve had a nasty grease spot, traceable to my grazing a
stanchion while trying to apply body English during the
shuffleboard semi-finals. And at Oxford, while we were punt-
ing on the Cherwell River with some friends, I had inadvertently sat on a companion's picnic lunch, a cold veal-and-
ham pie.

Arriving at our London hotel, we found a chit from an
Englishwoman, inviting us to her flat that night. She was
giving a small dinner, she said, for a Nawob in from India
and his Begum. Jinny rang for the valet and chambermaid
and asked for a rush pressing job on our evening clothes. We
got them back just about the moment our hostess phoned to
tell us dinner would be informal. I pulled out my dark-blue
suit, but it smelled awful. Our uncorked bottle of Scotch
had been nestling inside it, and there'd been some leakage.
I had no other recourse but to crawl back into my woebegone
tweeds.

Dinner was pleasant, but the Nawob seemed to be ill at
ease. Afterward, the Begum and my wife got to chatting,
and the Begum confessed that the occasion represented a
milestone in her husband's social life. He had never before
attended a dinner party without dressing, it seemed, and he
was having some difficulty adjusting to the unconventional
informality of it all. My wife tried to say that we, too, felt
embarrassingly tacky, but before she could get a word in, the
Begum went on to relate how, a few hours earlier, our hostess had called and said some Americans were coming who
probably didn't have any evening clothes with them, and
would the royal couple mind terribly if, just this once, they
roughed it?

When my wife and I returned from our 1949 trip, we
found with our mail a tantalizing remnant of a newspaper

clipping, half destroyed by our oldest son. It read, "And skipping from the Aga Khan to E. J. Kahn, Jr., the latter . . ." We were all the more fascinated by this inconclusive hop-step-and-jump because, while abroad, we had on more than one occasion got involved, if for the most part subjectively, with the Khans.

I had long had a vicarious interest in the dashing pursuits of the late Aga's son, the late Aly, because my first name is Ely; and every so often, after he had scored some notable triumph in a horse race or a night club, a friend would make a tiresome joke about the similarity, or dissimilarity, between Aly Khan and Ely Kahn. It was in the summer of 1949 that Aly married Rita Hayworth, and they were honeymooning in Europe concurrently with our visit. Their courtship had been fully reported—almost too fully, my wife thought, when she read in a *Time* account of their wedding that the bride's red-dyed hair was showing brown at the roots. Jinny's reaction to this intimate disclosure was perhaps oversensitive, for she had not long before dyed her hair red, too.

Notwithstanding all these coincidental links between Rita and Aly and Jinny and me, it never seriously occurred to either of us that we'd be taken for the newlyweds until an Immigration man at Liverpool, looking first at the name on my passport and then at the color of my wife's hair, asked if by any chance we were the bride and groom. The same thing happened when we checked into a couple of rural British inns. Each time, I laughed off the whole absurd proposition, but Jinny seemed to find the misidentification increasingly beguiling, until I began to fancy that she fancied herself Miss Hayworth. How else, I mused, could I account for her odd and nearly petulant remark, as we were returning to our London hotel from dinner with the Nawob and the Begum, "You know, her jewels were bigger than mine."

In Paris, a few days afterward, between the acts of a ballet at the Théâtre Marigny, we found ourselves standing shoulder to shoulder with the old Aga and *his* Begum. I feared for an instant that Jinny was going to address some daughterly remark to the patriarch, but she held her tongue and merely stared at him affectionately. I, alas, could not hold mine. Overhearing a remark of a woman nearby who was also ogling the Aga, I could hardly wait to convey it to my wife.

"There was a dame in the lobby who took you for Rita!" I whispered excitedly as we were returning to our seats.

"Nonsense," said Jinny, without conviction. "What'd she say?"

"She told the man with her, 'If you don't believe me, look at that red hair. It's turning brown at the roots.' "

At this, to my surprise, Jinny went into a frightful sulk, and the first thing the next morning she cancelled our plans to go to the Louvre and instead went to a hairdresser's. But within a few days she had bounced back, and when we subsequently were introduced to an American living in Paris who said, "I believe I know a relative of yours," I was astonished to hear her reply, "We bumped into the Aga just the other night. He was looking very well, I thought." Our companion blinked. He'd been referring, it came out anticlimactically, to a female cousin of Jinny's mother. We never saw any of the Khans again.

Die
Luftbrücke

In the pre-Hitler days, I made a couple of trips to Germany, where I learned to like beer and had my picture taken outside the house at Eschwege where my grandfather was born. Over twenty years passed before I revisited Germany. I had missed the European Theatre of Operations during the war, and didn't get to my ancestral land until the spring of 1949. My return was anything but sentimental. I can't imagine ever getting sentimental about Germany again. I went there specifically to look into and make a fairly comprehensive report on the Berlin airlift, perhaps the greatest logistical triumph in the annals of freedom.

Nothing quite like the airlift had ever happened before. For the first time in history, a community of a couple of million people, cut off from its sources of supply, as far as land and water transport are concerned, was kept alive for nearly a year with supplies brought in by air. Specifically, the nearly two and a quarter million residents of the three Western-

power sectors of Berlin were sustained by the lift economically, and perhaps ideologically, from June 26, 1948 to May
15, 1949. (Officially, the airlift continued until September 30.) One of the propaganda lines about this extraordinary delivery service that was thrown hopefully toward
West Berliners by the fourth occupying power went, in effect: "Don't let those Americans, British, and French kid you
into thinking that they're exerting themselves on your behalf. Have you forgotten so quickly that during the war,
when they bombed your homes and killed your children,
they never seemed to have any trouble sending four or five
hundred planes to Berlin at once? So why should you get
excited over this vaunted airlift of theirs? What does it con-
sist of, anyway? Just one measly plane at a time." Arithmeti-
cally, such an argument was unassailable. Unlike a fleet of
bombers, the airlift did not fill the sky, either visually or
aurally. However, the argument ignored both the obvious
fact that the wartime bombers did not have to land inside
Berlin to deliver their cargoes and the fact that while during
the blockade there were never many aircraft over the city at
any one time, there was almost always at least one. Twenty-
four hours a day, as a rule, and seven days a week, no matter
where a person happened to be in the three hundred and
forty-four square miles that comprise the shattered city of
Berlin—an area twenty-two square miles larger than that of
the five boroughs of New York—he could hear the steady,
patient drone of an airlift plane overhead. An instant after
the sound of its engines ebbed away, the purposeful hum of
another plane would come within earshot. Just as a trickle of
water can, if sufficiently prolonged, wear down the stoutest
rock, so the airlift, with its unostentatious but ceaseless
trickle of flights, carved a large hole in the Soviet blockade
of Berlin, if, indeed, it was not in large measure responsible
for the Russians' decision to lift the blockade.

The airlift was unimpressive to the Berlin eye and its

planes averaged only seven or eight short tons apiece per trip, but it provided the inhabitants of West Berlin with a million and a half short tons of supplies. The French played only a modest, earth-bound role in the airlift operation. The Americans and the British did all the flying and between them worked out so precise and smooth a procedure that, unless hampered by weather, they were able matter-of-factly to deliver to West Berlin, from eight outlying airbases, around eight thousand short tons of airborne cargo every twenty-four hours. One day in mid-April, when ideal flying conditions prevailed and everybody worked extra hard, the airlift ferried in 12,940.9 tons of cargo. Just ten days after that performance, by what may have been pure coincidence, the American State Department announced that the Soviet Union seemed disposed to sit down with the Western powers and discuss doing away with the Russian blockade, the Western counter-blockade, and the muddled dual-currency situation that had prompted an admirer of Samuel L. Clemens to declare that the main intention of the occupying powers in Berlin seemed to be that never the twain marks should meet. Or again it may not have been coincidence, but rather an eye-opening revelation of how the Russians react to a show of strength.

The American and British personnel engaged in the operation called it the airlift, the literal German version of which is *"Luftversorgung,"* but the Germans themselves, uncharacteristically, preferred the shorter word *"Luftbrücke,"* which means "air-bridge." To its direct beneficiaries, the lift was almost invariably *"die Luftbrücke."* During the summer of 1948, the Americans and the British worked independently. In mid-October, they set up a joint organization, called the Combined Airlift Task Force, with headquarters at Wiesbaden, in the United States Occupation Zone, two hundred and eighty miles southwest of Berlin. The United States Air Force and the Royal Air Force had separate titles for their respective assignments. The Americans called theirs Operation Vittles. The British called theirs Operation Plainfare. They had decided on "Planefare," to stress the manner of transport of Berlin's supplies rather than their austerity. Shortly after the airlift began, however, an R.A.F. man inadvertently used "Plainfare" in an official document, and that spelling became official. There is no evidence that any American airman thought of switching to "Operation Victuals."

The names "Vittles" and "Plainfare" were invented when the airlift was starting and when its sole objective was to keep West Berlin from running short of food. Both names, once the airlift was an apparently permanent phenomenon, became metonymical misnomers. Only thirty per cent of the tonnage ferried to Berlin was edible; such is the complexity of modern urban civilization that in Berlin coal, not bread, proved to be the staff of municipal life. It took only fifteen hundred tons of foodstuffs a day, or a little more than a pound per person, to provide West Berliners with an adequately nourishing, if not notably fancy, diet. But it took two two pounds of coal per person per day to provide even the subnormal quantities of heat, electric power, gas, and other utility services needed for the blockaded community. Three out of every five tons of cargo carried on the airlift consisted of coal. Quite a bit of this was for Berlin's manufacturing industries, which also received a small but steady flow of raw materials, for without industrial activity there would have been even more unemployment in the Western sectors than there was, and unemployed residents of those sectors had trouble, naturally, buying their daily allotment of food. (The Americans and British weren't giving the food away; they just fetched it in.) Some of the industrial plants that received airlift coal were below the flight paths that all airlift planes had to follow, and now and then the smoke from the flown-in coal, as it billowed from the factories' stacks, would obscure the vision of the airlift pilots. Among the products manufactured by the West sectors' struggling factories were small locomotives, which were exported, in airlift planes, to the coal mines of the Ruhr, where they expedited the production of coal to be airlifted to the plants in Berlin that created the smoke that annoyed the pilots who flew in the coal. The Berlin airlift was a complicated business, as I realized soon after I checked in at the Wiesbaden headquarters and got set to fly the lift and, what interested me even more, try to find out how it worked.

At the Potsdam Conference, in July, 1945, Germany was cut up into four zones of occupation, and Berlin, deep within the Soviet Zone, into four sectors. A belt of Russian-occupied territory, nowhere less than seventy-five miles wide and at some points twice that wide, separated the Western zones of Germany from the Western sectors of Berlin. In November, 1945, the members of the Allied Control Council, the four-power agency then supervising the Occupation, wrote down a set of rules covering air traffic to and from the quadripartite city. Straight lines were drawn, on a map, from the Allied Control Authority building, in the heart of Berlin, to three westerly cities—Frankfurt am Main, in the American Zone, and Bückeburg and Hamburg, in the British. Each line represented a twenty-mile-wide corridor, through which all non-Russian air traffic from the Western zones to Berlin would thereafter have to be routed—as it still is routed. The Bückeburg corridor, crossing a hundred miles of Russian-occupied Germany, is the central one. The Hamburg corridor, to the north, also crossing a hundred Russian-occupied miles, and the Frankfurt corridor, to the south, crossing a hundred and eighty, converge on the Bückeburg corridor as it nears Berlin, like the outer edges of an enormous arrowhead. Each of the occupying powers, including the Soviet Union, has the right to send planes along all three corridors at any time. In 1945, there were four landing fields inside Berlin. The sectors assigned at the Potsdam Conference to the United States and Great Britain included two of them—Tempelhof, the city's most elegant airdrome before the war, and Gatow, which had been a training center for Luftwaffe fighter pilots. The Soviet Union got the other two. It also had eight fields in its own zone, just beyond the city limits. When, on June 24, 1948, the Russians stopped all land traffic to Berlin from the west (water traffic was not halted until two days later), the Western powers had good reason to be grateful for that formal agreement about the corridors. Without them, and without the two fields in Berlin, there couldn't have been any airlift.

On June 25th, two B-17s, based in Wiesbaden and ordinarily used on passenger runs, each delivered five tons of food and medical supplies to West Berlin. The day after that, General Lucius D. Clay, the American military governor in Germany, telephoned from his headquarters in Berlin to the headquarters of the U. S. Air Forces in Europe, in Wiesbaden, an order that an all-out cargo airlift to Berlin be created immediately. (The British hurriedly took similar steps.) Before the day was over, twenty-five C-47s—the military name for the DC-3—had ferried eighty tons of food and medicine to Tempelhof. The airlift was under way. It was estimated that forty-five hundred tons was the minimum amount of supplies required daily—once the reserve supplies on hand were exhausted—to keep the inhabitants of that area alive, reasonably healthy, and unreceptive to whatever advances might be made to them from the east. That minimum was attained in a little over six weeks.

Veterans of the airlift were fond of reminiscing about the early days, telling such stories as the possibly apocryphal one about an American pilot who arrived from the States one morning at the principal airbase in the United States Zone, at Rhein-Main, near Frankfurt, for what he thought would be a fairly relaxed tour of ground duty in Europe. He dragged his luggage over to an Air Force colonel and asked him where he should report in. The colonel responded by asking him if he was qualified to handle a C-47. The newcomer, puzzled, replied that he was, and ten minutes later was flying to Berlin. He made two round trips before he got a chance to unpack his bags. The incident may not have happened just that way, but it certainly could have, such was the extreme shortage of flying personnel. Commercial-airline pilots in the United States are forbidden by Civil Aeronautics Board regulations to fly more than eighty-five hours a month; in July and August of 1948, some airlift pilots logged a hundred and fifty a month. Staff officers left their desks—in most instances gratefully—and took to the air.

Planes were as scarce as pilots. The Americans had around a hundred C-47s and two four-engine C-54s—the equivalent of the DC-4. The C-47s were considered obsolete (this was a bad guess, as we have already seen), and there were few spare parts for them in Europe. A C-47 could theoretically carry only three and a half tons. The C-54, a later-model plane, could carry ten. Washington was asked urgently to send as many C-54s as possible to Germany. Almost at once, world communications being what they are, C-54s en masse headed for Germany from the United States, the Canal Zone, Alaska, and Japan, loaded with flight crews and maintenance men and as many spare parts as they could carry. A squadron of ten C-54s based at Ladd Field, in Alaska, received orders the night of June 27th to leave for Europe without delay. Half the squadron took off twelve hours later and reached Wiesbaden, five thousand miles away, in four days. Twelve hours after that, one of these planes was over Berlin with ten tons of freight.

Around that time, planes were so few, the need for haste was so great, and the operating procedure was so haphazard that when the crew of a C-47 carrying a diplomat around the Continent landed at Wiesbaden one day and left their plane unattended for half an hour while they and their eminent passenger grabbed a bite, they returned to find it loaded with sixty hundred-pound bags of flour. And from up in the British Zone came a story about an airlift pilot who landed at Berlin in a C-47 (or, as the British chose to call it, a Dakota) and complained that there was something dreadfully wrong with his plane. He had barely managed to take off, he reported, and had fluttered along the corridor at five hundred feet, unable to get higher, and, when he had set down in Berlin, both his main-landing-gear tires had blown out. It was presently discovered—or so the story went—that an overenthusiastic and underinstructed loading crew of Germans had stuffed his three-and-a-half-ton-capacity ship with seven and a half tons of cargo.

It is impossible to calculate the total number of people who were involved in the airlift. Inestimable numbers were occupied moving supplies and equipment by air, land, and sea from the United States, the British Isles, and other points to airlift bases. Hundreds of mechanics, stationed in the United States, completely overhauled every American airlift plane after it had flown a thousand hours—or, roughly, once every four and a half months; five thousand United States Air Force maintenance men were stationed at Burtonwood, just outside Liverpool, in England, to give each plane sent there a somewhat less thorough checkup every two hundred flying hours; and hundreds more men were employed at an Air Force training installation in Great Falls, Montana, where pilots about to be assigned to airlift duty were given a course in precision flying in a narrow corridor. On the Continent, seventy-five thousand people had a hand in the operation, including forty-five thousand Germans engaged in airfield construction, cargo-handling, and a few minor clerical and maintenance functions. (It was not true, as was rumored from time to time, that, owing to the shortage of pilots, Luftwaffe veterans were recruited for the airlift. Some of them applied, but all were turned down.) Three thousand displaced persons, largely from the Baltic region, were employed on loading details and as guards. Among others directly concerned, there were eight thousand British Army and Air Force personnel, including fliers from Australia, New Zealand, and South Africa; two thousand members of the United States Army Airlift Support Command, most of them Transportation Corps men, who supervised the movement of cargoes to and from planes; a few dozen French soldiers, engaged in the same kind of work; several hundred American, British, and French civilians in military-government agencies; eight hundred men from the air arm of the United States Navy, which dispatched two squadrons of C-54s to the airlift, from Hawaii and Guam, early in November; and twelve thousand members of the United States Air Force, which ferried in three-fourths of all the supplies carried.

Since the venture cost United States taxpayers considerable money, it could be argued that they, too, were involved, but it could also be argued—and frequently was by Air Force spokesmen—that this money was really being invested in Air Force training and that a considerable fraction of it would have been spent for this purpose anyhow. The cost of the airlift was impossible to compute (who could say how much, if any, of the pay of a pilot who would have been flying for the Air Force anyway should have been charged against it?), but General Clay, whose estimate was undoubtedly not extravagant, told me at the time that the American share alone came to nearly half a million dollars a day, or a total of a hundred and fifty million dollars. (The British probably spent an additional fifty thousand to one hundred thousand a day.)

To our Air Force, the airlift was not a brand-new idea. A similar operation was carried on, for three wartime years, between India and China, across the Hump. A month after Operation Vittles got going, the command of it was given, logically, to an alumnus of the Hump, Major General William H. Tunner. When the Americans and British pooled their efforts, he became head of the Combined Airlift Task Force. The India-China run, too, was a twenty-four-hour-a-day, seven-day-a-week, all-weather air-freight service between two otherwise unconnected points. Across the Himalayas, however, there were twenty-five routes, along any one of which—depending on the weather, the Japanese, and other variable factors—traffic could proceed. For the Berlin traffic, there were only the three corridors. At the India end of the Hump line, there were thirteen airfields, and at the China end ten, no two of them less than sixteen miles apart. At the western end of the airlift, there were plenty of airfields— the British had half a dozen in their zone, near Hamburg and Bückeburg, and the Americans two big ones, at Rhein-Main and Wiesbaden—but in West Berlin there were at first just Tempelhof and Gatow, only twelve miles apart and with but a single runway at each.

From the start, it was agreed that eastbound traffic would use the outside corridors and westbound traffic the middle one. Additional runways were constructed at Tempelhof and Gatow, and another airfield was built at a place called Tegel, in the French sector, on the site of a Nazi ground-force training area. By December, West Berlin had five runways, and by that time, too, the Airlift Task Force had amassed an imposing fleet of airplanes, substantially, in volume and types, what it ended up with. The regular fleet was composed of a hundred and forty British planes— a third of them C-47s and the rest four-engine ships, which could carry an average of eight tons—and two hundred and thirty American planes. Of these, all but five were ten-ton C-54s, which flocked to Germany in such gratifying numbers in the summer of 1948 that the American C-47s were taken off the job entirely on October 1st. The C-54s proved to be the work horses of the airlift; they carried two-thirds of the tonnage delivered. The five other American planes were of the type designated C-82, a twin-boomed ship known as the "flying boxcar," because it looked vaguely like a boxcar and because its spacious cargo compartment could accommodate objects that wouldn't fit inside the more streamlined C-54s —ambulances, dump trucks, rock-crushers, steam rollers, cement mixers, and other bulky items. Except for a dozen or so British freighters, the C-82 was the only type of plane used on the airlift that was designed to carry cargo. All the others were converted bombers or passenger transports.

The people running the airlift frequently compared it to a commercial airline, and sometimes even *called* it an airline. Quite a few of its pilots and staff officers—men with reserve commissions—were recruited from airline jobs, and their work was characterized more by businesslike efficiency than by the dashing, romantic spirit that was so rampant in the Air Force during the war. Hardly any of the airlift planes were adorned with the gaudy illustrations and lively names that combat fliers went in for. One reason was that airlift pilots, like airline pilots, were not often assigned to the same plane two days in a row. Toward the end of the airlift, enough fliers were available to make businesslike hours possible; no pilot was allowed to put in more than a hundred flying hours a month, and few did much above eighty-five. Some of the old-time pilots who made close to two hundred and fifty round trips to Berlin got bored with travelling the same course day in and day out, or night in and night out. Others professed to be delighted with the routine, because they were able to get far more practice than they could have got elsewhere in instrument flying, which the weather forced them to resort to during the winter seventy per cent of the time.

The North Sea was the principal source of airlift weather

trouble, and a most inhibiting source, too. Cold, wet air masses would swirl down from it and settle in hollows. Then warm air masses would drift up from the Mediterranean and settle on top of the cold masses, producing fog. The air-lift people couldn't change this state of affairs, but the Air Force's weather-service personnel in Europe made am-bitious efforts to keep abreast of the variations. Every day, a couple of B-17s based in Bavaria would fly to Luxembourg or Paris or Bremen and radio their observations to the American traffic-control center at Frankfurt. Every day, also, a couple of B-29s, based in England and fitted out as em-pyrean meteorological laboratories, would cruise over the North Sea and radio their observations, usually gloomy. In the airlift region, the weather fluctuated so rapidly that fre-quently one airfield would enjoy perfect weather while one less than twenty miles away—a pin-point distance on a stand-ard weather map—was closed down. Airlift operations of-ficers wanted to be advised, every minute or two, of even hundred-foot variations in ceilings and eighth-of-a-mile variations in visibility. From time to time, the weathermen would station observers at each end of every runway at every airlift base.

During December and February, Berlin had twice as many foggy days as it had averaged for the same period in the pre-ceding thirty years. At some of the Western zones' bases, fog conditions were even worse. At Wiesbaden and Rhein-Main, all air traffic, and all ground traffic as well, was sometimes halted. A pilot who had flown the lift from the Wiesbaden airbase for two and a half winter months was surprised to hear a fellow-flier remark that he regarded a large gravel pit beside one end of the Wiesbaden field as a mental haz-ard; the first pilot had never seen the pit.

The hours the pilots put in, and the tons of cargo they de-livered, were in large part determined by the weather in

Berlin. Ordinarily, each plane in operation could average four round trips a day. When the weather was clear throughout West Berlin, a plane landed at each of the three fields every three minutes. This was the fastest rate regarded as consistent with safety, but on occasion a two-minute interval was in effect. When ceiling and visibility were somewhat limited, the period between landings would be extended to four or five minutes. When ceiling and visibility were very limited, one or more of the Berlin fields would have to shut down, but there wasn't a single day that at least some freight wasn't airborne to the city. The all-time low was on November 30th, when the British made seven trips, totalling sixty-two tons, and the Americans got in just one ten-ton load. If one plane had landed at each field every three minutes for twenty-four hours, the landings would have totalled fourteen hundred and forty (with, of course, a corresponding number of takeoffs). The day before Easter, when the Task Force set its thirteen-thousand-ton record, thirteen hundred and ninety-eight round trips were made—only forty-two under the theoretical maximum.

At most civil airports, it is not unusual for planes to be stacked up for some time when traffic is heavy or weather discouraging. On the airlift, such dawdling was forbidden. Airlift planes were allowed just one approach. If a pilot misjudged his landing and had to pull up, he had to head for the central corridor and fly all the way back to his home base. Otherwise, dozens of planes might have been held up while he was having a second chance. The same fierce dedication to an even, orderly flow of traffic prevailed, of course, at the airlift bases in the Western zones. There, as in Berlin, the airlift planes had priority; a non-airlift plane wishing to land at an airlift base was obliged, except in an emergency, to circle around high above the field until a break in the airlift flight pattern enabled him to come in. General Clay's wife was once kept in the air over Rhein-Main for an hour and a half. That sort of thing rarely happens to a commanding general's wife.

All the planes using the southern corridor—a hundred and nineteen C-54s, based at Rhein-Main and Wiesbaden, and the five C-82s, based at Wiesbaden—normally landed in Berlin at Tempelhof. Takeoff times from the bases were staggered, so that, in accordance with the assigned time interval, a Wiesbaden or a Rhein-Main transport would pass a radio beacon at Darmstadt, a few miles from Frankfurt, every three, four, or five minutes. The planes, which were expected to maintain the stipulated interval, as well as a stipulated altitude, all the way to Tempelhof, travelled at exactly a hundred and seventy miles an hour. To make sure that the air-speed indicators on the planes were reliable, every so often an F-47 fighter plane, its air-speed indicator carefully checked, would cruise alongside one transport after another, at exactly a hundred and seventy. Up north, the British worked out a slightly different procedure. The planes using the Hamburg corridor also had set altitudes, but they didn't have to fly at a definite speed, and instead of being fitted into a time pattern upon leaving its base, each fitted itself into one by regulating its progress so as to reach a certain radio beacon in Berlin at a prescribed instant. Of the six airlift bases in the British Zone, three fed into Gatow and three into Tegel.

Outgoing traffic from Berlin didn't have to be controlled quite so meticulously, because of the large number of regular landing fields in the Western zones, not to mention a string of emergency fields, extending from Ireland to Marseille. The westbound British Zone planes flew through the middle corridor at the same altitudes they kept to on the way in. The outbound American Zone planes flew above the British Zone traffic. A system was worked out so that preparations for reloading a plane could begin a long time—by Air

Force standards—before it had completed its round trip. For example, a C-54 pilot might call in by radio to the operations tower at his home base when he was fourteen minutes out, give an identifying number, and report succinctly that his plane was either "positive-positive," "positive-negative," "negative-positive," or "negative-negative." The first adjective would refer to the condition of the plane (if positive, it was ready for another trip immediately, and if negative, it required maintenance work) and the second to its load (if negative, the plane was empty, and if positive, it had something that must be unloaded—even if only a bunch of empty coal sacks or a visiting congressman—before a new load could be taken on).

The plane's number was identical with the number of a bay, or hardstand, off the edge of one of the taxi strips at the field; that particular plane always berthed at the particular hardstand. If the pilot indicated that his plane could set out again right away, the operations tower telephoned its hardstand number to a dispatching office beside a huge parking lot filled with loaded trailers. In the office, a card file showed its capacity. A C-54 is theoretically a ten-ton ship, but aircraft of that type vary in capacity; one may be able to carry only as little as 18,600 pounds, another as much as 21,400. The file card also showed the number of pounds that the plane could accommodate in each of the eleven sections into which its cargo space was divided. Every one of the trailers in the parking lot was filled with twenty-two thousand pounds of freight, or slightly more than the maximum load a C-54 can take aboard. A representative of the Army Transportation Corps in the dispatching office decided what kind of cargo—flour, coal, dehydrated potatoes, cheese, or whatever—should be put on the approaching plane. An Air Force representative told the Army man how much could go in each section. A loading crew of ten or twelve Germans or displaced persons climbed aboard the trailer. Its driver was told which hardstand to head for, and if everything worked out right, he arrived there—along with gas and oil trucks, which had also been alerted, and, if the pilot had radioed that his ship required some minor maintenance work, a specialist capable of handling *that*—at almost the instant the plane taxied to a halt at its berth. In no more than fifty minutes, it was refuelled, reloaded, and ready to taxi again —with the same crew or a new one—toward the takeoff runway.

If the plane hadn't begun to move within precisely fifty-one minutes, and the operations tower hadn't received an acceptable excuse for this sluggish behavior, a radio-equipped jeep, manned by an officer known as an expediter, raced up to the hardstand to find out what was causing the delay. At Tempelhof, twenty minutes was the maximum time allowed for unloading. When the airlift was young, flight crews would sometimes wander off while their planes were being emptied, to check on the weather or get a cup of coffee, and wouldn't return on time. After a while, to speed things up further, the crews were required to stay by their planes, at the home base as well as in Berlin. They continued to receive their weather information and refreshments, however. Both were brought to them, the former by a mobile navigation-and-briefing office, the latter by a mobile snack bar. Attached to the side of the mobile snack bar was a mobile trash receptacle. It was another triumph for American know-how.

A little less than two-thirds of the freight delivered by the airlift was coal, and a little less than one-third food; the rest, amounting to seven per cent of the total, was industrial raw materials, liquid fuel, and whatnot—all intended to help, in one way or another, to convince the people of West Berlin that, considering their peculiarly isolated position, they were faring quite handsomely, and to give the million-odd folk in East Berlin something to think about, too. The Combined Airlift Task Force brought West Berlin, among other things, pig iron, X-ray film, vitamin tablets, newsprint, pencils, stationery, snowplows, hand tools, machine tools, surgical instruments, combs, window glass, cement, nails, chemicals, police uniforms, matches, candles, ladies' underwear, TNT, and detonators, the last two (for removing rubble) in separate shipments. Berlin is a big radio-manufacturing center, and the radio industry had to have magnets for loudspeakers; the airlift furnished them, but because magnetized magnets throw airplane compasses out of whack, the magnets had to be demagnetized before they were shipped and remagnetized afterward. The list also included bicycle parts, sheet steel, needles, thread, typewriter keys, asbestos, buttons, quicksilver, insulating tape, paints, lacquers, medicine bottles, roofing felt, and a thousand other items, among them five and a half pounds of dried-banana flakes that the airlift ferried in every week for each of three German infants who had a rare digestive ailment and were unable to assimilate any other food.

Once a month, the Task Force's planning experts would get together at their headquarters, in Wiesbaden, and, with frequent recourse to the slide rules that invariably decorated their desks, make an informed guess at the amount of tonnage they expected to be able to fly to Berlin the following month. Their estimate would be passed along to the Bipartite Economic Commission, a mammoth agency in Frankfurt, generally known as Bico; the information would then be sent on to a Bico subsidiary called the Berlin Airlift Coördinating Committee, or Bealcom. Meanwhile, Bealcom would have obtained from German and Western officials in Berlin an estimate of the Western sectors' requirements for the month. Bealcom then had to decide how much of what kind of commodities would be shipped to Berlin from each base in the Western zones. It had established priorities among commodities, so that if the Task Force should prove unable to do as well as it hoped to, the most essential items could be carried in—newsprint, say, on the eve of an election. The Task Force nearly always did better than its announced expectations, and this made people in some small-minded non-aviation circles suspect that the air people set their quotas a mite low, so that they could point with pride to the regularity with which they exceeded them. Whenever there was space to handle more than the assigned cargo, it was given over to coal. The procedure of assembling cargoes was little different from what it was before the blockade. Food, coal, and other commodities were simply sent by the dealers who handled them to airbases, instead of to railway freight houses, barge piers, or truck depots. When the commodities reached Berlin, they were turned over to the German distributors who handled supplies before the blockade.

Tempelhof, the airfield in the United States sector, was among the Nazis' most splendid ornaments before the war. Its hangars and administrative offices—quite a few of them later damaged by bombs and Russian artillery—formed a continuous, curving, half-mile-long structure, with only twenty per cent less floor space than the Pentagon. Surmounting the edifice was a twenty-foot eagle, clutching the earth in its talons. In the customary Nazi fashion, a swastika shield was once appended to the globe. Soon after the Americans took over the premises, they denazified the bird with a speed and ingenuity they were accused of not always applying to livelier holdovers from the old regime. They slapped some white paint on the eagle's head and some gold paint on its beak and then superimposed the Stars and Stripes on the swastika. They ended up with a very presentable American eagle. Tempelhof was poorly situated, for an airlift airport, or any other kind of airport. A seven-story apartment house stood near the approach to the field, and a number of industrial plants, some with tall smokestacks, were nearby. One of the plants, a brewery, had a chimney almost five hundred feet high. After the owner had ignored a few oral complaints by the pilots, some American engineers came around one day and made a few exploratory nicks at the base of the offending tower—the kind of nicks designed for the insertion of charges of dynamite. The brewer soon clipped a couple of hundred feet off his chimney. The French were more forthright in dealing with navigational hazards. A couple of hundred yards from Tegel, the airfield in their sector, there stood the two towers of Radio Berlin, a station under Soviet control. Some French engineers blew them up one day, and not only didn't give the Russians a hint of their intentions but didn't even tell the Americans, who were in charge of airlift flight operations at the field.

The principal drawback of Tempelhof, when the airlift began, in June, was that it had only the one runway, and that was in indifferent shape. Two weeks later, engineers began to repair the runway and construct a second one there. By mid-September, it was finished, and in October a third was completed. Meanwhile, the British improved the runway at Gatow, and meanwhile, too, the Americans were building the field at Tegel, with one runway. Bulldozers, graders, rock-crushers, dump trucks, asphalt, and steel matting were flown in for the work; several of the larger pieces of machinery had to be cut apart with acetylene torches in the Western zones, and then welded together in Berlin. The engineers had nowhere near as much equipment as they wanted, however, and they were obliged to follow the example set by other engineers during the Hump operation. At that time, Indians and Chinese built airfields practically by hand. Almost the same thing happened in Berlin. Six hundred thousand cubic yards of brick rubble were con-

verted into runway foundations by Germans working with
hand tools and wheelbarrows. At Tegel, twenty thousand
Germans were employed, in round-the-clock shifts. Women
made up forty per cent of this labor force. A Hearst man
took a photograph of some of them on the job and sent it to
the United States, where a Hearst paper tacked on a caption
identifying the subjects as slave laborers toiling under the
lash of the Reds. The runway at the Tegel airfield was completed in just under three months, and the field was officially
dedicated in November, when an American airlift plane
flew in with twenty thousand pounds of cheese and two Air
Force generals.

The Germans in West Berlin at first reacted to *die Luftbrücke* with a mixture of enthusiasm and skepticism. Most
of them were certain that the venture was ill-starred, but
many of them felt that it nonetheless deserved a thumping
round of applause, for effort. Accordingly, they turned up
at the airfields in large numbers and showered pilots, along
with a few passersby in uniform, with tokens of their grati-
tude and esteem—bouquets, old coins and stamps, books,
stickpins, souvenir plaques, songs about the airlift, and, in
one instance, a pair of dogs. The Germans also spent a lot
of time looking up, wide-eyed and open-mouthed, at the
sky, even though there wasn't much to see. During October,
to commemorate the completion of the airlift's first hundred
days of operations, the West Berlin post offices cancelled all
outgoing mail with a *Luftbrücke* postmark. In subsequent
months, the airlift got to be taken as a matter of course,
and a freight-carrying plane would attract no more attention
in Berlin than a United Parcel Service truck does in Westchester. West Berliners would gaze at the sky only when there
wasn't an airplane in sight. In three years, they switched from
being apprehensive at hearing an alien plane to being apprehensive at not hearing one.

Before the blockade, the American, British, and French sectors got a total of some fifteen thousand tons of cargo a day, by railroad, barge, truck, and plane. The eight thousand tons a day that were delivered by the airlift had a somewhat greater utility per ton. In the pre-blockade days, West Berliners got fresh potatoes. During the blockade, they got dehydrated ones, which weigh and bulk less but which, though inferior in taste, provide equal nourishment. In addition to potatoes, their airborne bounty included frozen and canned beef, frozen and canned pork, frozen and smoked fish, flour, processed and natural cheeses, dehydrated vegetables (mostly carrots, onions, and cabbage), lard, suet, margarine, butter, sugar, honey, salt, rolled oats, rice, grits, macaroni, spaghetti, noodles, pudding powder, yeast, cake flour, coffee, tea, cocoa, powdered eggs, soup powder, dried skim and dried whole milk, dried fruits, chocolate, and assorted baby foods. A little more than half of this was produced in West Germany and the rest was imported—vegetables and potatoes from England, the Netherlands, Italy, and Hungary; cheese from Switzerland and Denmark; wheat and flour, oats, dried peas and beans, meat, powdered eggs, and dehydrated potatoes from the United States. The frozen meat, the cheese, and the chocolate had the highest shipping priority. They were regarded as the most perishable of the foods and also the most pilferable, and the longer it took to get them on a plane, the more tempting they became to the occasional weak-willed German or displaced person doing the loading.

No loader had a chance to be tempted for very long. The usual elapsed time between removing meat from refrigerated freight cars at a siding at the Rhein-Main airbase, trucking it to a plane, loading it, flying it two hundred and eighty miles to Berlin, unloading it, and trucking it to a cold-storage warehouse came down to four hours. Salt, a com-

modity carried exclusively by the British, was a problem of
another sort, early in the airlift, because it corrodes the
metal parts of aircraft. The British got around that for a
while by moving it in flying boats that commuted between
a lake in Hamburg and a lake in Berlin and that had already
been treated to make them impervious to salt water. During
the winter, it was feared that the lakes would freeze over,
and the flying boats were grounded—or, rather, docked. By
then, though, somebody had come up with one of the many
ingenious ideas that the airlift inspired. Noncorrodible copper panniers were suspended from the bomb bays of several
old British bombers, and the delivery of salt without harm
to the delivery wagons was thus triumphantly assured.

The American, British, and French colonies in Berlin
then added up to less than one per cent of the population of
the West sectors, and it wasn't difficult to keep them reasonably well provided with delicacies peculiar to their tastes
—kippered herring for British breakfasts, wines for French
lunches, and olives for American Martinis. (The wives of
some United States military-government officials in Berlin
put out a cookbook entitled "Operation Vittles," the proceeds
going to charity. The recipes dealt with such unaustere con-
coctions as beef Stroganoff, cherries *à l'eau de vie,* eggnog
chiffon pie, and crêpes Suzette. Only one entry, a punch called
Block-ade, seemed at all indigenous. Its ingredients are two
cans fruit cocktail, one cup sugar, two bottles cognac, six
bottles red wine, six bottles white wine, six bottles champagne. Serves seventy-five.) All the food brought in for the
Germans in the Western sectors was rationed. The amount
allotted was varied according to how strenuous the recipi-
ent's occupation was. The average German was authorized
to buy enough food in each of a dozen major food categories
—meat, potatoes, bread, sugar, salt, and so on—to give him
about two thousand calories a day, which, though slightly
below the amount recommended by our National Research

Council for a sedentary man (twenty-four hundred), was more than enough to sustain life. Many Berliners amplified their food allotment by growing produce, and then there was always the black market, for those who could afford it. The Western occupation authorities, eager to stimulate husbandry, brought in, via the airlift, garden implements, vegetable seeds, and fertilizer, and, on one occasion, a three-ton shipment of young fruit trees. West Berliners occasionally complained, as soon as the success of the airlift made them feel secure enough to complain, that they didn't care for the taste of dehydrated potatoes, but from a strictly medical point of view, it was believed that they thrived during the blockade.

Before the war, Berlin manufactured more than half the electrical products used in Germany, and it was a flourishing industrial center generally. Not long after the blockade began, when it became evident to the Western military governors that unless the city was to become a giant poorhouse, its economic life would have to be kept functioning, they began to permit manufacturers to import raw materials. (German manufacturers were required to pay delivery charges, at the pre-blockade rail rate, for whatever goods they received by airlift.) Toward the end of the airlift, two hundred and sixty tons of raw materials were being flown in daily, and—what was equally important—a hundred tons of manufactured goods were being flown out. The value of the radio tubes, light bulbs, lathes, milling machines, telephone and telegraph equipment, and other precision instruments shipped out was a quarter of a million dollars a day. In addition, the airlift flew fifty thousand Germans out of Berlin. The British, who took care of nearly all the native passenger traffic (though there were several American Overseas Airlines flights between Berlin and Frankfurt every week, and the United States Army ran still another passenger service for its own people), decided at one point, in order to demonstrate that blockaded Berlin was getting along all right not only economically but also culturally, to fly the Berlin Symphony Orchestra, seventy strong, to London for a concert. Two handsomely outfitted passenger planes, dispatched from London to pick up the musicians, stopped en route at Wunstorf, one of the airlift bases in the British Zone. To the R.A.F. men it was unthinkable that any plane should fly into Berlin without adding its mite to the airlift's daily tonnage, so they had a hundred-pound sack of flour deposited on every seat in both ships. Each sack was tied down with a safety belt. It was undoubtedly the most stylish delivery of flour ever made.

There were remarkably few accidents on the airlift. In the first hundred and eighty thousand round trips, fifty-one fatalities occurred, or one for each 1,750,000 miles. And only once—in the early days, before the traffic pattern had been so carefully worked out—did two planes collide in flight. The fact that so many aircraft were able to fly in that congested area in all kinds of weather with almost perfect safety was attributable largely to the airlift's reliance upon radio and radar. Every airlift plane was constantly in touch with at least one radio-control point, and nowhere else, up to then, had radar been used so intensively as a guide for landings. The airlift used both the short-range American system, Ground Controlled Approach, or G.C.A., and a somewhat similar British setup, called the Blind Approach Beacon System, or B.A.B.S. It also had in operation in Berlin an especially magical long-range radar device never used anywhere before then for transport operations. This new one picked up only moving objects, and its maximum range was a hundred and fifty miles, as opposed to G.C.A.'s mere twenty-eight. When it was first installed, many airlift pilots were unaware of its existence. One of them, who was familiar with the limitations of G.C.A., was amazed on landing at Tempelhof one day to be told that he had strayed momentarily, and naughtily, from his corridor at a point seventy-five miles out of Berlin.

The radar scopes on which such discoveries were made are about a foot in diameter. Two planes flying at a three-minute interval at a hundred and seventy miles an hour are eight and a half miles apart. On the long-range radar scopes, the planes in the airlift showed up as tiny blobs of light in close proximity, some moving toward Berlin, in two ragged, ant-like columns, some moving away, in a third column. At times, almost a hundred planes could be seen simultaneously. On these instruments, the three corridors fanning out from Berlin really looked like corridors.

The Task Force communications people were as fond of statistics as any of their colleagues, and when the record-breaking tonnage was flown in on April 16th, they announced that they had also established a new mark in their special department that day—39,640 radio contacts with airborne planes over the twenty-four-hour period, or 1,651⅔ contacts per hour, or .91759 contacts every two seconds. The harmless preoccupation with speed and achievement that has long been typical of Air Force officers inspired one of them, after nearly a year of airlift operations, to calculate that the American planes serving Berlin had flown the equivalent of a hundred and thirty-three round trips to the moon.

Some non-flying folk also became record-conscious. The Germans who handled cargoes kept trying to set new marks, and every so often they had a contest to decide which of the crews at a certain airfield could load or unload a plane the fastest. At Tempelhof, four unloading crews held a competition, and, according to the report of a correspondent for a Task Force newspaper, it must have been something like a Yale-Harvard boat race. "Surplus German workers formed a cheering section and chanted encouragement to the unloaders," the reporter wrote, "then shouted loudly as the anchor man was tossed into the truck by two of his co-workers at the conclusion of the performance." A few such well-intentioned time-saving efforts were a headache to the men responsible for keeping the airlift planes in spare parts. The cargo doors of a C-54, for example, are supposed to be fairly sturdy. During a two-week stretch, when overzealous truck drivers were backing loaded trailers up to planes at full tilt and overzealous pilots were taxiing off with ladders still attached to their doors, ninety-five doors were so badly damaged that they had to be replaced.

Just as in the summer of 1948 the airlift people were bothered by a shortage of C-47 parts in Germany, they were bothered by a corresponding shortage when the C-54s became the principal cargo carrier. Early in November, more than thirteen per cent of the C-54s were out of commission for lack of spare parts. But factories in the United States stepped up production, and the rate went down eventually to below one per cent. The job of maintaining the aircraft used in the operation was immense. For every hour that a C-54 was flown, twenty man-hours of maintenance work had to be put in on it. Furthermore, the work differed notably from the kind that C-54s required in the pre-airlift era. These planes have a normal cruising range of from fifteen to twenty hours; on the airlift, they took off and landed every couple of hours. The result was an unusually high consumption of parts not designed for short, frequent hops. Every day, two dozen main-landing-gear tires were ripped to shreds. The United States Air Force, with its usual resourcefulness, took steps to profit from this particular adversity. In the spring of 1949, not long before the airlift was concluded—or, in the view of some of its admirers, temporarily abated until such time, however many years afterward, as the Soviet Union might make its resumption necessary once again—a motion-picture-camera crew camped for several weeks beside a runway at Tempelhof. They had been sent from the United States, with over a ton of special equipment, for the sole purpose of photographing airlift planes as they landed, the idea being that the pictures would help engineers design better landing gear. Never before, the head of this research team told me elatedly one afternoon, as plane after plane threw dust in our faces, had there been an opportunity to stand in one spot and observe so many heavily loaded air transports touching their wheels to earth. I had to agree that the airlift was quite a sight, and I'm glad I had a chance to see it.

No One
but
the Glosters

In the spring of 1951, I went to Korea for three months, to cover the war. I was in the neighborhood of, though not actively involved in, a two-and-a-half-day engagement, the Battle of the Imjin, that was characterized as "epic" by the supreme command in Korea less than a week after it ended; and while the memories of its survivors were still fresh, vivid, and unencumbered by the frills that retrospection sometimes adds to reality, I talked to a good many of these men and tried to piece together some of the details of this epical action.

The battle began, just south of the Imjin River and some twenty-five miles northwest of Seoul, on the night of April 22nd, as the Chinese were launching their spring offensive all across the front, and it continued, without letup, until midafternoon of April 25th. The great majority of the United Nations troops who participated in it were British, of the 29th Brigade, but it was nonetheless a fittingly multi-

national affair, involving Belgians, South Koreans, and Fili-
pinos, as well as Americans from both the continental United
States and Puerto Rico. The 29th Brigade, with a total
strength of sixty-six hundred and a front-line fighting
strength of four thousand, suffered more than a thousand
casualties during that bloody span of time. In return, it in-
flicted a vastly larger number of casualties on the enemy; the
exact count was indefinite, inasmuch as the British traditionally decline to assume credit for killing anybody unless they
have actually seen him dead. They saw a great many dead
Chinese those two and a half days, being frequently in hand-
to-hand contention with the enemy, and on occasion, to conserve ammunition, being under orders to hold their fire until
their attackers were only fifteen yards away.

Out of something like sixty thousand Chinese who as-
saulted the seventeen-thousand-yard sector the brigade was
holding when the battle started, it was widely, if unofficially,
believed that between ten and fifteen thousand were dispatched. And what was perhaps more important—since
hordes of dead Chinese were almost as commonplace as
hordes of live ones in Korea that particular week—was that
the steadfast resistance of the British to this massive assault
was very likely the most influential single factor in the dashing of the Communists' probable hope of celebrating that
May Day in the capital city of the Republic of Korea.

The entire 29th Brigade saw action in the Battle of
the Imjin, but the worst assault fell upon one unit, the 1st
Battalion of the Gloucestershire Regiment, informally called
the Glosters. Of the six hundred and twenty-two Glosters
who were in the most advanced of the brigade's three echelons when the fight got under way, just five officers and thirty-
four other ranks were available for duty three days afterward,
and they only because they had made a near-miraculous
withdrawal through enemy fire so intense and enveloping
that they subsequently said they felt like human targets in a

shooting gallery. Their commanding officer, a tall, taciturn, pipe-smoking lieutenant colonel named J. P. Carne, who had served with the Glosters since 1925, and who was taken prisoner during the action, was later awarded the Victoria Cross for his heroism in it.

When, on the morning of the twenty-fifth, the Glosters were so hard pressed and so inextricably cut off from all other friendly troops that they could no longer function as an effective fighting force, every man was authorized to break through the encircling Chinese as best he could. The Colonel and his Sergeant Major, E. J. Hobbs, elected to stay with the wounded, along with the Glosters' medical officer and chaplain. The handful of Glosters who did get out brought back several versions of Colonel Carne's last words to them. The one most generally accepted was that as they took leave of him, and as he stood there among the sad and suffering remnants of the organization to which practically his entire adult life up to then had been devoted, he said, with the perfect discipline for which his soldiering countrymen have long been noted, "Any of you chaps happen to have a spare twist of tobacco?"

The 29th Brigade, which arrived in Korea early in November, 1950, was composed of a number of units with ancient traditions, among them the 1st Battalion, Royal Ulster Rifles; the 1st Battalion, Royal Northumberland Fusiliers; the 45th Field Regiment, Royal Artillery; and the 8th King's Royal Irish Hussars, this last a cavalry outfit that was formed in 1693 and took part in the Charge of the Light Brigade at Balaklava, but in Korea was mechanized and equipped with fifty-two-ton tanks called Centurions. The Ulster Rifles, who wear as a device the harp of Ireland and the crown of Britain, had a rough time early in January in the brigade's previous costly action in Korea; two hundred and thirty of them were killed. This loss happened to occur in the very area assigned to the 29th Brigade in mid-April, and on their return to the unhappily familiar scene, the Rifles reburied some of their dead who had fallen there, and commissioned a stonemason in Seoul to cut an obelisk to mark the spot. Dedication of the monument was scheduled for April 23rd, but the ceremonies were, perforce, postponed.

April 23rd is a big day for the British. Not only is it Shakespeare's birthday but it is also the day consecrated to their patron saint, Saint George. To the Northumberland Fusiliers, who trace their martial lineage back to 1674, the holiday is especially precious, for Saint George and his dragon are represented on the badge they wear on their berets. They had planned a turkey dinner for the twenty-third, and had fitted themselves out with the red and white roses (made of cloth, on this occasion) that are the traditional cap ornaments for the day. The banquet had to be cancelled, but the Fusiliers wore their roses anyway. Some of the gunners of the Royal Artillery joined the battle sporting real roses, which they had had flown in from Japan for the holiday. But they, too, were unable to pay any further tribute to Saint George. While the battle was on, they were busy firing more rounds per weapon—the average was a thousand—than had been hurled even at El Alamein, theretofore considered the biggest show ever put on by British artillerymen.

The Royal Artillery motto is *"Ubique,"* and its guns in this case were twenty-five-pounders, mounted to permit a traverse of three hundred and sixty degrees, and during the Battle of the Imjin, with Chinese assaulting some of the gun emplacements from the rear, they had to be traversed full circle. The guns had a range of thirteen miles; they were fired point-blank, over open sights, at enemy riflemen fifty yards off. Toward the end of the battle, every round of twenty-five-pound ammunition in Korea had been delivered to the British gun positions, and lorries were waiting at two airstrips for a fresh supply that had been urgently ordered from Japan. But the battle was over before the ammunition ran out.

As for the Glosters, they dated back to 1694 and had acquired forty-four battle honors—more than any other British regiment. The men of the 1st Battalion—the only element of the regiment in Korea—earned a forty-fifth at the Imjin, and they were also awarded an American citation for their stand there. The Glosters have streamers on their regimental colors for Waterloo, Sevastopol, and Gallipoli, among other legendary arenas, and General Wolfe is said to have died in the arms of a Gloster during the Battle of Quebec. On March 21, 1801, while arrayed against the French at Alexandria, the Glosters, who then fought in geometric rows, were surrounded, and received the order "Rear rank, rightabout face and fire!" They battled back-to-back until the French were driven off, and ever since then the members of the regiment have been entitled to wear two cap badges, one in front and one in back. They are the only British troops who enjoy this privilege.

The men who were to fight virtually back-to-back again, just a month after the hundred-and-fiftieth anniversary of their most cherished day, were for the most part experienced soldiers, many of them reservists, with wives and children, who were recalled to service when the Korean War began. Their average age was over thirty. At five minutes to eight on the morning of April 25th, when, after fighting almost without food or water or sleep for nearly sixty hours, these Glosters reported to brigade headquarters that their radio was about to run out of power and that they would appreciate having some air and artillery missiles dropped thirty yards from their own position, the brigade commander, a normally unbending brigadier, had a special message relayed to them. "No one but the Glosters could have done it," it said.

During the daytime of April 22nd, there were no particular signs of trouble to come. All along the front, to be sure, the United Nations had for several days been awaiting the Chinese offensive, but no one could anticipate precisely when it would be launched, nor did the British seem more or less likely to bear the brunt of the attack than any other troops in the line. The American 25th Infantry Division, at whose headquarters I was then staying, might just as easily have been hit, and indeed the British had good cause for believing they were not a primary enemy target. On the twenty-first, the British, who had the 1st Republic of Korea Division on their left and the American 3rd Infantry Division on their right, had sent an exploratory patrol across the Imjin. It had travelled ten thousand yards beyond the river and had encountered only a scattering of enemy troops. A British intelligence report took note of a "large undetermined number of enemy north of the river," but concluded that nothing more worrisome than strong enemy probing patrols could be expected on the twenty-third and twenty-fourth. The brigade troops in the line were getting hot meals and, assuming that they would continue to get them, had no combat rations along. That turned out to be unfortunate, for the most any one of them had to eat during the battle was one hard-boiled egg and a slice of bread.

As it soon developed, not only were the Chinese ready to undertake far more than probing patrols but the ones on the Glosters' front were an exceptionally well-outfitted bunch of Chinese. They had new uniforms, ample rations, new Russian weapons in prime condition, and new shoes. One enemy soldier who was taken prisoner even had a spare pair of new shoes, made in Shanghai, a most unusual luxury for a Chinese infantryman—or, for that matter, a British or American infantryman—in combat. But it was to be doubted whether all the soldiers facing the brigade were as sharp as their equipment. During the battle, for instance, one Gloster rifleman saw two Chinese sitting in plain view on a ridge six hundred yards distant, eating lunch. He shot one of them, and the man toppled over. The other, scarcely a foot away, didn't even glance at the victim, but placidly went on eating.

In any event, the brigade's orders from above committed it to holding its positions, no matter what opposition might be forthcoming. On the eve of the battle, a battalion of Belgians attached to the British was deployed just north of the Imjin, on the brigade's right. Behind the river were the Fusiliers. On the left were the Glosters, in an especially rugged area, four miles broad, dotted with sheer rock cliffs rising to a height of two hundred and fifty feet. The Ulster Rifles were in reserve.

The weather was clear on the twenty-second, as it was to be throughout the battle, but things were so quiet during the day that only one supporting air strike was asked of the United States Air Force and Navy fliers backing up the brigade. At six o'clock in the evening, the Belgians were attacked and almost immediately cut off; four hours later, the Fusiliers were hit. A patrol from the Rifles set off to aid the Belgians but couldn't reach them, and for most of that first night the Belgians were the main objects of concern. They stayed in their ticklish situation for another twenty-four hours, in the course of which a tank column tried, and failed, to get to them; on the night of the twenty-third, they managed to slide over to the right flank and sneak out, with relatively few casualties.

Shortly after midnight of the twenty-second, when Saint George's Day was only half an hour old, Able Company of the Glosters was attacked. By four o'clock, the whole battalion was engaged, and by six the whole brigade. The enemy came in three waves. In the first rush, Able Company lost its commander and two other officers. One walkie-talkie operator, running out of ammunition, used his rifle as a

club, swinging it at the Chinese as they came into his foxhole
and shouting, "*Banzai,* you bastards! *Banzai!*" A few minutes later, the radioman regained his hereditary reserve and
called into his transmitter, with finality, "We're overrun.
We've had it. Cheerio."

By midmorning, the Glosters had at least a regiment in
front of them and, because the South Koreans on their left
had been driven back several thousand yards, an indefinite
number on the hills behind them. By midday, the Glosters
hadn't been budged from the high points they had instructions to hold, but they were completely separated from the
rest of the brigade, and the Chinese had penetrated so far
back that the battalion's supply echelon was overrun, too,
and nine of its men were taken prisoner. Quantities of the
things the Glosters needed most desperately—machine guns,
ammunition, and medical supplies—were packed into straw-
lined bags and dropped to them by six light observation
planes.

A larger-scale airdrop was set up for the following morning. At dawn on the twenty-fourth, three Flying Boxcars were
poised high over the Glosters' positions, waiting for the
morning mist to lift so they could descend close enough to
drop their cargo accurately. But when the mist rose, the
pilots found the Glosters, and not a few Chinese, fighting lit-
erally inside a curtain of falling shells that the brigade's gunners and mortarmen were throwing around them. The
planes couldn't dip down unless the shelling was halted, and
the decision was up to the Glosters. The Glosters waved the
hovering Boxcars away.

There had been three air strikes on Saint George's Day.
On the twenty-fourth, there were so many that at noon a
young American Air Force lieutenant who was serving as
liaison between the brigade and its tactical air support
stopped keeping track of individual strikes, as he had been

conscientiously doing up to then. Probably some fifty planes gave the brigade a hand that morning. There were plenty of targets available to them. So many Chinese had infiltrated around the Glosters' flanks, both of which were by then exposed, that one air observer spotted some seven hundred of them standing around nonchalantly in a single group, in the open. One dive-bomber seared a Chinese-held hill with napalm. The nine Glosters captured the day before were on it, along with their guards. Several of the guards caught fire, and while they were frantically trying to beat out the flames, seven of the Glosters, who had somehow contrived to avoid being more than uncomfortably warmed, ran down the hill and escaped into the lines held by the Fusiliers and the Rifles. This was a particular relief to one of them, who had spent five years in a Nazi prisoner-of-war enclosure.

The Fusiliers and the Rifles were better off than the Glosters, but they were having no picnic, either. There were Chinese behind them, too, and brigade headquarters organized a makeshift reinforcement party to help them out. It was composed of what little could then be mustered for the purpose: eight tanks from the Hussars, some Royal Engineers acting as infantry, a few Royal Army Service Corps lorries—which under normal circumstances wouldn't be sent too near the enemy but whose drivers in this instance volunteered to lumber along behind the tanks right to the front—and forty green replacements who had reported to the brigade that day and had been assigned to the Fusiliers. Some of them never got to report to the Fusiliers. There were so many enemy wandering around the countryside by then that the headquarters was under small-arms fire, and mortars were being lobbed out at the enemy from behind brigade headquarters—which, as a major in charge of the mortars later remarked, was a most ungentlemanly way to wage war.

The Glosters were in pretty bad shape on the morning of the twenty-fourth. The enemy had been at them all night long. Baker Company, which, like the three other rifle companies in the battalion, had a normal strength of a hundred and fifty men, was down to one officer and fifteen other ranks. It was nearly impossible to move out of a foxhole anywhere along the battalion line without drawing machine-gun fire. The Glosters nevertheless reassembled around a hill on which the battalion command post had been established. The line had shrunk from four miles to six hundred yards, but it still hadn't been breached. The Glosters begged several times that day for a helicopter to come and evacuate their more seriously wounded. The enemy, however, was so close on all sides that no helicopter could be sent out with any real hope of accomplishing this mission.

That morning, Colonel Carne was asked if he thought a relief column could get through to him. He said no. (Communications with him had been spotty for some hours; artillery fire had knocked out all the telephone wires, and only two gradually fading radios linked the Glosters with the rest of the brigade.) That afternoon, in disregard of the Colonel's opinion, the first of three attempts to rescue the Glosters was made. A battalion of Filipino infantrymen and some supporting tanks got to within fifteen hundred yards of them, and then, in a defile, the lead tank was set afire, and the entire column was blocked and had to withdraw. Neither of the two subsequent relief columns—one composed of Belgian, Filipino, and Puerto Rican infantrymen and elements of the 8th Hussars, and the other of tanks and infantrymen from the American 3rd Division—got even that close. When the third try had failed, the Glosters, by that time seven miles deep in Chinese, were on their own.

Early on the morning of the twenty-fifth, the brigade was finally instructed to pull back to new defensive positions. It had held up the Chinese long enough to disrupt their timetable all across the front. Those of the Fusiliers and Rifles who could walk managed to withdraw in fairly good order. The non-walking wounded from these units were worse off. Some two hundred of them were loaded onto the backs and sides of eight Centurions, which started off toward the rear through a narrow mountain pass. They were ambushed by the Chinese. The wounded, lying exposed on the tanks, couldn't do anything about it, and the tank crews were almost as impotent. Their vehicles were so slippery with blood and so jammed with sprawled bodies that it was impossible to traverse the gun turrets.

On the way out, two tank commanders were wounded. Both remained standing in their hatchways, one fainting there and reassuming command when he came to. An officer riding on the outside of one Centurion, who while aboard ship en route to Korea had memorably entertained at a troop show by putting on a fake mental-telepathy act, was startled when one of the wounded men raised his head and said, "Beg pardon, sir, but there's something I've been wanting to ask you. How'd you do that bloody trick?" The driver of another Centurion, one that had no wounded on it and was, accordingly, buttoned up tight, was surprised to hear a thumping noise overhead. Looking up through his periscope, he saw a Chinese soldier perched above him, pounding on the hatch cover in an effort to open it. Without slowing down, the driver swerved to one side, drove the tank clean through a Korean house, brushing the interloper off, and then resumed his course.

Before daylight each morning during the battle, the Chinese had been sounding the bugle calls with which they customarily heralded their armed approach. Before dawn on the twenty-fifth, the three hundred or so Glosters who were still fit to fight counterattacked in just about the only manner left to them: their bugler blew a long reveille. It rang out, clear and astonishing, and it was followed by a series of other calls—short reveille, half-hour dress, quarter-hour dress, cookhouse, and, just for the hell of it, the American variation of reveille. It was an amazing concert. For the few minutes it lasted, both sides stopped firing. Then the Glosters cheered, and the fighting started up again.

At five minutes past six, shortly after daybreak, the Glosters were advised by brigade headquarters that they had permission to break out. At six-twenty, the Glosters reported that they were surrounded and couldn't break out. But they still wanted air support, and they got it. By almost split-second coördination between air and artillery, a flight of dive-bombers swooped on the enemy just one and a half minutes after the artillery lifted a barrage it had been laying in. The Glosters by then were down to one small yellow air-ground recognition panel, and it was hard for the diving aircraft to know exactly where to strafe and bomb. But the Glosters threw a couple of smoke grenades out from their perimeter —thirty-five yards is a fair throw with a smoke grenade— and the planes aimed their machine guns where the grenades landed. Then bombs were dropped, at a somewhat, but not terribly much, more circumspect distance. The Chinese were hurt, and momentarily relaxed their pressure.

Colonel Carne summoned his company commanders to a hollow near his headquarters, where fifty or sixty stretcher cases were lying on the ground. He told them that all hope of carrying on as a unit was gone. He said he was going to stay where he was, and he gave them the option of surrendering or fighting their way out in separate groups. The commanders of Able, Baker, and Charlie Companies and their remaining men headed south, toward the United Nations line.

It was the commander of Dog Company, Captain Mike Harvey, a twenty-eight-year-old officer from Portsmouth, who led out the group of thirty-nine that got back. He was in charge of Dog Company only by chance; its regular commander, a major, had gone to Japan on April 22nd for a rest.

When the major arrived there, he heard that the spring offensive had started and caught the first plane back to Korea.
Despite several tries, he was never able to make his way far
enough forward to reach his unit. Harvey, a pink-cheeked
man with horn-rimmed glasses and an unkempt mustache,
was a Reserve officer who was in the Hampshire Regiment
during the Second World War; up to April 22nd, he had
thought of himself as a Hampshire man on loan to the Gloucestershire Regiment. He subsequently came to think of
himself, without reservation, as a Gloster. He was unusually
abstemious for a soldier, forgoing both tobacco and alcohol,
principally because he had been interested in judo since the
age of twelve and held one of the highest ratings in the art.
After he had assembled his withdrawal party, consisting then
of twelve officers and ninety-two other ranks, he let the remnants of the three other companies start off ahead. "I stood on
a hill watching them to see if they were really going," he
told me afterward. "It was unbelievable that things had come
to this pass." He decided not to go south himself but instead
to try the unexpected and proceed due north for a mile,
straight toward the Chinese rear, and then swing west a couple of miles, in an outflanking movement, before turning
south. He warned his group that they would have to travel
fast, exhausted though they were, and that there could be
no stopping to aid anybody who might be wounded.

Proceeding cautiously, Harvey and his men didn't see a
single Chinese for the first three miles. His scheme was working fine. Then, just as they were veering south, they ran into
a few Chinese. The Glosters shot them and moved on. When
only a few miles from a point where they thought friendly
troops would be, they were heartened by the appearance
overhead of a Mosquito plane, generally used as liaison between ground forces and fighter aircraft. The Mosquito cir-
cled above them and wagged its wings encouragingly, and

they waved back. The Mosquito began to guide them homeward through the hills.

Harvey was keeping his men on low ground whenever possible, knowing that the Chinese habitually congregated on ridges. Ultimately, they came into one valley, two miles long, that was almost a canyon, with precipitous walls on both sides and a floor about a quarter-mile wide. A stream flowed through it, and they waded along this for a mile or so, until it dwindled away. As they came out on dry ground, thirty or forty machine guns opened up on them, from both flanks. The Glosters made for a ditch about a foot deep and dived into it. By then, the Mosquito had radioed for fighter planes, and they had come buzzing along and were working over the slopes as energetically as they could. But the machine guns didn't let up. The Glosters crawled forward, keeping their heads below the level of the ditch, since raising them as much as an inch above it had already proved fatal to several. The ditch, like the river bed before it, was full of stones, and the soldiers' arms and legs were lacerated. One man's shoes had fallen apart in the river, but he kept going, first in his socks and then, as those disintegrated, barefoot. Every so often, the men came to a four- or five-yard stretch where the ditch petered out, and in the stumbling race for the next ditch more were hit and dropped.

Finally, rounding a bend, they saw some American tanks down the valley, just half a mile away. They crawled ahead eagerly, and got to within five hundred yards of them. The tanks opened up with machine guns and 76-mm. cannon, and the six Glosters in the lead fell. The Mosquito pilot, horrified by this case of mistaken identity—the tank men had no idea any friendly troops were still that far north—flew frantically toward the tanks, diving almost on top of them, but they kept on firing.

Harvey's single file of men, on their bellies in the ditch,

were receiving fire from the front and both sides, and the
men at the rear of the column, most of whom had exhausted
their ammunition, were being stabbed by Chinese who had
rushed down the valley behind them. Harvey tied his hand-
kerchief and scarf to a stick, put his cap on it, and waved it
at the tanks. Simultaneously, the Mosquito made another
pass at the tanks and dropped them a note. The tanks, suddenly aware of their error, ceased firing. The remaining Glosters reached the tanks and crouched behind them. Using
them as a partial shield against the continuing enemy fire,
they withdrew another five hundred yards, to the reverse
slope of a small hill. There they climbed on the tanks and
rode out, for three more miles under steady enemy fire.

The tank men were heartsick over their mistake. One of
them took off his shoes and gave them to the Gloster who'd
lost his. The lieutenant in command of the tanks kept asking
how many of the Glosters his people had wounded. The
Glosters, not wanting to make him feel any worse, wouldn't
tell him; indeed, they didn't know for sure. The lieutenant
was wounded himself getting them out.

As soon as Harvey got to a telephone, he called brigade
headquarters. "I thought we had better get back, in case
they wanted us again," he explained to me. "Then I learned
that we were the only survivors and that everyone else was
missing. And everyone else is still missing." A week after the
battle, the Glosters he had led out invited him to stop by for
a beer. He hadn't touched the stuff in over three years, but to
please them he drank a glass. "It tasted pretty awful," he
said. "Being a judo man, it didn't suit me."

The 1st Battalion of the Gloucestershire Regiment began reorganizing the day after the Battle of the Imjin ended.
A few days after that, the handful of men from the old battalion and the new replacements lined up in a green Korean
field for a simple memorial service. A handful of outsiders,
like myself, joined them. Massed around a table covered

with a white cloth and bearing a cross and two candles, they stood with heads bared as their new battalion chaplain walked toward them in a white robe. Captain Harvey, now the battalion's new adjutant, distributed hymnals. The Glosters sang two hymns and, snapping to attention, a stanza of "God Save the King." After a few words from the battalion's new commander, who himself had been shot in the wrist during the Battle of the Imjin, the chaplain recited the names of the known dead, and the names of Colonel Carne and Sergeant Major Hobbs, as symbolic of, respectively, the officers and other ranks listed as missing.

Then the chaplain told a story from Ecclesiastes about a city under siege, and how, after all hope was seemingly gone, a good and wise man had saved it. And yet, in spite of that, the chaplain said, the poor wise man was very soon forgotten. "In England, they'll remember for a little while," he went on. "The soldier does have his day. I want to remind you this afternoon that it is not enough to remember now. We've got to show what we think of their sacrifice in the way we conduct ourselves in the days ahead. We are, as it were, a link between our past and the future, and if we are to be faithful to our past, we must hand on to future generations some of the heritage of the past. Having handed it on, we will be in some measure worthy of those who died that we might live."

A

Bon Voyage

In the summer of 1957, my wife and I took our three sons on their first voyage to Europe. Terry was ten at the time, Joey eight, and Tony five. Our itinerary called for us to sail to Le Havre on the *paquebot Flandre,* to stay at the Hotel Vendôme in Paris for a week or so; to pick up a rented Volkswagen Microbus and drive to Ciboure, just outside Saint-Jean-de-Luz in the Pays Basque, whence we could make side trips through the Pyrenees and down into Spain; and then to drive back north through the Loire Valley, relinquish our car in Paris, and take the boat train for London, where a friend had offered us her house for ten days prior to our sailing homeward on the *Ile de France.* It was a fairly extensive, and fairly expensive, journey, but I did manage to economize to a degree by persuading Jinny and the children to share a passport. This meant, of course, that they had to have their passport photograph taken en masse. Most people resemble somebody else in their passport photos, but there

can be few travellers who, like my wife, have ended up re-
sembling Laocoön.

As we boarded the *Flandre,* the boys were understandably
curious about life on the high seas, and they asked me if there
were any special precautions, or rules, they should observe.
"Just don't fall overboard," I said, plagiarizing the sage counsel my grandfather had given me when I was ten and a shipboard tyro. One of the wonderful things about an ocean
liner is that any other advice is really superfluous.

I also enjoined them not to fail to read faithfully the daily
shipboard newspaper. I have a strong affection for these papers, in part because I once edited one. To be sure, this was
a rather special maritime journal, since it was published, in
mimeographed form, on a wartime troopship crossing the
Pacific. The radio operator was stingy about passing along
news of the outside world, so I found it necessary to concentrate on shipboard intelligence. The voyage lasted more
than three weeks, and before it was anywhere near over, I
ran out of legitimate stories. At that point, my commanding
officer suggested that, to pad out the sheet, and maybe even
liven it up, I invent some local news. His suggestion was my
command, and in the next issue I put in a front-page bulletin to the effect that a San Francisco-society-girl stowaway
had been discovered on D Deck and taken to the brig
in irons. My commanding officer's commanding officer found
no amusement in the piece, and I was deposed.

It was with great interest, then, that I picked up, outside
my stateroom door on the *Flandre,* a copy of *L'Atlantique,*
whose cover bore, along with a photograph of a hunk of coral,
the promising legend *"Nouvelles de Dernière Heure."* A notice in English on page 4 advised the passengers that they
would receive *L'Atlantique* every morning and that its editorial policy was "to tell them, in a very modest and abbre-
viated way, about what is going on in France and to give them

world news as received by the ship's wireless. It will also give them news of life aboard ship."

A quick glance through the paper revealed that our daily ration of last-hour news would indeed be modest; of its dozen pages, all but two appeared to have been printed some time before, most likely in Paris, and were largely given over to essays on contemporary French literature, undersea life, and so on. Some of them were in English and some in French, and scattered among them were cartoons, *bons mots,* a crossword puzzle in French (the one next day was in English), and a great deal of advertising. The first item was a selection from *Selections from the Reader's Digest,* which began, "The airplane has become indispensable to private enterprise." The choice of this triply digested nugget for the lead-off spot surprised me almost as much as if it had read "Go Cunard," and I sensed that the editor of *L'Atlantique* must be a fellow of a beguilingly independent turn of mind.

As a matter of fact, I soon concluded that *L'Atlantique* must have two editors—one on land, to deal with the pre-printed matter (while I was aboard, this included treatises on folk costumes, Angkor Vat, French music, French perfume, French art, French couture, and French Line cuisine), and the other stationed somewhere on the *Flandre,* for the *dernières nouvelles.* It struck me that the second chap must have to make some thorny editorial decisions, since he had only two pages at his disposal for actual news, and one of them was filled with bilingual announcements of shipboard events —ping-pong tournaments, clay-pigeon shoots, the day's movie, and the rest of it. The other page was all world news, about a thousand words of it, and the editor split the space fairly between the two languages, the English text on the starboard side of the page and the French aport. Since there simply wasn't room for a duplication of stories, the editor had to decide which should go in French and which in English. As far as I noticed, he touched on the same theme in both

languages only once during the whole trip, and in that instance the details were entirely different. The story was
about a nuclear explosion in Nevada; in the English-text
version the editor played up the fact that the flash was seen
as far off as San Francisco, while in the French-text version
he said (unless my limited reading knowledge of French led
me astray) that a light radioactive fallout had obliged the
scientists and technicians on the scene to abandon their
control center. Clearly, to be as *au courant* as it was possible
to be on the *Flandre,* one needed two languages, and I wondered how people who, like my sons, didn't have them were
making out. (The boys may have made out better than some
of their fellow passengers; they pressed their cabin steward
into service to interpret the cartoon captions for them.) For
my part, I accepted the situation as a stimulating challenge,
and felt flattered that the editor seemed to think we passengers were up to it. I fear I wasn't, though. For several hours
one day, I was happy in the thought that the stock market
had gone up sharply, but then, with the aid of a French-Eng-
lish dictionary I found in the ship's library, I realized that
it had actually moved in the opposite direction.

For some reason, all financial news, regardless of its national origin, was printed in French. I deduced from this
that our editor believed the French passengers were more
prosperous, or at any rate more money-minded, than the
American passengers, and that seemed to me a refreshingly
new slant on *le tourisme.* However, market quotations in
English were posted every morning on a bulletin board outside the purser's office. The figures were typed on a form
that had the names of certain stocks already printed on it. It
must have been an old form, for Socony Mobil was still carried on it as Socony Vacuum, a name the firm had forsaken
the year before, and the North American Company, which
was dissolved in 1954, was also listed. Whoever filled in the
figures wrote "Unquoted" next to North American every

morning. For the first couple of days out, the major-league baseball scores, which on most ships occupy a prominent spot in the paper, were also posted outside the purser's office, next to the market quotations, but thereafter, to my sons' dismay, we had no baseball intelligence whatever, either on the bulletin board or in the paper. Maybe it was raining at home. A few sports stories were sandwiched in among the *dernières nouvelles*, but they always turned up in French, and had to do with cycling, Rugby, and the like. The only American athlete who rated a plug in the paper while I was dependent on it was someone called Gutowski, who broke the world's record *"de saut à la perche."* My wife told the boys at first that this was a competition for cooking fish, but as we all got deeper into the story we realized it must have been pole vaulting, since Gutowski cleared the bar—if that is what he did—at 4 m. 819.

The passengers who read only English were informed, among other things, that a new Canadian government contemplated no changes in foreign policy; that the mayor of Roghudi, Italy, hadn't really kidnapped a young school-teacher but had just eloped with her; that Haiti had had what *L'Atlantique* called a "bloodbat"; that Senator Wayne Morse had warned liberal senators to be careful about something or other; and that New York City had been in the throes of a terrible heat wave. How we snickered at that one as we churned along through a cooling fog! We were a bit puzzled, though, by one more or less English-language story that went, "New Yorkers have been hot for four days, but hopeful glances North for an import of Canadian air see little change for relief." Apparently Canada's determination to maintain the status quo covered air as well as foreign policy.

The French news diet, like all French diets, was a little richer. The passengers aboard who could make no sense whatever out of French presumably did not know, for ex-

ample, that the United States Senate had approved a foreign-
aid program of $3,637,000,000, or that the world's highest
dam (two hundred and twenty-six metres) had been—or
perhaps it was "would be"—built in Italy (just where,
L'Atlantique did not divulge), or that *le Japonais* Ishimoto,
comme l'Américain Gutowski, had broken a world's record
—this one for the butterfly breast stroke—or that an un-
named Nationalist Chinese officer on the island of Matsu
thought that his base and Quemoy were under threat of in-
vasion from the Communists.

For all his journalistic enterprise, though, the *dernières
nouvelles* editor of *L'Atlantique* was curiously remiss in
keeping us posted on one newsworthy event that might well
have rated a mention in at least one language, if not in both.
The day before we were due at Le Havre, and a couple of
hours after that morning's *L'Atlantique* hit the deck, we were
astonished to hear, over the ship's loudspeaker, that we
wouldn't be landing in France after all. It seemed that there
was a strike of French Line engineers at Le Havre, although
L'Atlantique had never even hinted a strike was in the wind.

The result was that we Le Havre passengers had to disembark at Southampton early one morning, take a hastily
coupled boat train to Newhaven, make a three-hour turbulent crossing of the Channel to Dieppe, and take another
train to Paris, where we pulled in at around nine-thirty at
night. The boys were all still conscious, which quelled whatever doubts my wife and I had entertained about their capacity to withstand the rigors of foreign travel; but I didn't
want to test their elasticity any further, so I sent them ahead
to our hotel with their mother, while I stayed behind to shepherd our luggage—nineteen pieces, Jinny told me—through
customs.

It was a Sunday night, and customs either hadn't been
alerted to the unscheduled arrival of a few hundred weary
tourists, or just didn't care. At any rate, only a handful of

customs men turned up at the Gare Saint Lazare, and to make matters even more chaotic, our baggage was dumped on the station platform in widespread disregard of the posted initials under which travellers normally can find their gear if they can remember their surnames. It took me nearly two hours to round up our belongings, count them, find an inspector to pass them through, and commandeer a taxi whose driver would agree to transport them to the hotel. When I finally staggered into our rooms at the Vendôme, I felt not unlike Hercules, though much weaker.

I was slumped in a chair when Jinny, who had just finished tucking the boys in bed, joined me, swept her gaze over the pile of suitcases that were strewn about, and asked quietly where Tony's big bag was—the one containing every stitch of his clothing save what he'd worn that day. Feverishly, I counted again. Eighteen. I rushed to the lobby, thinking I'd probably left the suitcase there. No bag. The night concierge and I jointly searched the sidewalk outside. No bag. The concierge and I went back to my room, and we counted together, in two languages. Same total.

The next morning, before the children were awake, Jinny and I mapped out our strategy. Tony, we knew, would be upset at losing all his clothing, to some items of which he was devoted. When he awoke, accordingly, we at once congratulated him on his good fortune. His poor brothers, we said, would have to travel through Europe in the same dowdy, unimaginatively American clothes they habitually wore at home. But he, Tony—oh, what a treat there lay ahead for him! As the result of certain circumstances beyond his father's control, he and he alone would have a brand new, authentically Parisian wardrobe. He, in vivid contrast to his unlucky brothers, would be the cynosure of all eyes, foreign and domestic. First thing after breakfast, while his brothers and their father were engaged in some such lacklustre activity as ascending the Eiffel Tower, he and his mother would head straight for the Galeries Lafayette and buy a whole new suitcase full of clothes, and a suitcase, too.

We laid it on as thick as we could, and although it isn't easy to pull the wool over a five-year-old's eyes, we finally succeeded, in part because his eyes weren't yet fully open anyway. Jinny and I had barely scored this triumph, and convinced Tony that the clothing he had lost was so much dross, when there was a rap at the door and in marched the concierge, who at dawn had slipped off to the railroad station, found the missing bag, and was now proudly returning it to us. I don't recall exactly how we squared things with Tony; I think we promised to give him the Eiffel Tower.

On the previous trips I'd made to Europe, as man or boy, I had taken no account of golf, though as far back as I can remember, a cozy intimacy has prevailed between the game and travel. A perennial sports-page feature of my childhood was an interview with some golf nut who had ranged the world collecting out-of-the-way courses much as an ordinary gadabout might collect baggage labels, and who, having returned to his home club, was now holding forth rhapsodically on the subject of the fourth hole at Singapore or the fourteenth at Tierra del Fuego—each to him as heady a discovery as a rare wine might be to an oenophilist touring the *domaines* of his dreams.

I had never even paid much heed to conventional golf at home, but, thanks to pressure put on me by the boys, I had begun to take some notice of golf's own irrepressible offspring, miniature golf. My excursions in this obstacle-ridden field, however, had been relatively confined, and if a while before our European trip *Sports Illustrated* had asked me to write a reminiscent account of my golfing experiences, I should have been limited to such far from far-flung courses as the one at the drive-in theatre at Harmon, which—except, perhaps, for its tricky asphalt greens—is not the sort of place a travelling golfer would burble over.

Playing miniature golf in the fierce, competitive, no-strokes-conceded fashion prescribed by my sons can be fairly harrowing if one does it regularly, and I had anticipated a welcome respite from the grind while we were in Europe. But we hadn't spent even one night on the Continent before I began to have misgivings. Jinny and I had instructed the boys to make the most of their opportunity and to look at everything, and, gazing out the windows of the boat train en route to Paris, they spotted three or four miniature-golf courses. Their squeals of delight were so shrill that a French customs official passing along the corridor paused to express his appreciation of their appreciation of the glory of his native Norman countryside.

In Paris, Terry and Joey hardly had their land legs back before they got wind of a miniature-golf course tucked into a corner of the Bois de Boulogne. They and I spent two entire afternoons there (the fifth hole, I must confess, is rather a beaut), and we were thus obliged to eliminate a visit to Montmartre from the uplifting itinerary I had mapped out. Still, I wasn't too disturbed. It was doubtless the influx and influence of the American military, I told myself, that accounted for the presence in northern France of this Yankee roadside pastime. In a few days, when we drove down to Ciboure, a fishing village, we would surely be out of range. There, among the proud and notoriously independent Basques, the children would be exposed to a novel way of life. I knew, or thought I knew, that the principal sports of the region were bullfighting and pelota, and I looked forward to the carefree role of a spectator sportsman.

En route to the Pays Basque, we naturally relied for guidance on the comprehensive guidebooks put out by the Michelin tire company. It was Terry, I believe, who first observed that among the many helpful symbols used in the Michelin books to mark the towns in which there are three-star restaurants, cathedrals, châteaux, tire-and-tube sales agencies, and other points of special interest was a symbol for miniature-golf courses. (Although Terry cannot read French, he was not hard pressed in making this discovery; the French for "miniature golf" is *"golf miniature."*) I myself was unaware that he had come upon this intelligence until we drove, one evening, into the outskirts of Les Sables-d'Olonne—a beach resort that Terry had earlier selected as a promising spot in which to spend the night. "Ah, there it is," he muttered.

"Where is what?" I asked.

"The golf course!" he shouted. "They had it in the Michelin!"

My sons were all for stopping at once and playing a round, but they deferred sulkily to my insistence that we first find overnight accommodations. Once we had arranged these, I stalled the boys off until after dinner, by which time Tony had gone to bed and the course Terry had seen on the way into town was closed for the day. Terry and Joey were disconsolate. To cheer them up, I took them for a walk. As we went, I said magnanimously that if the course hadn't been closed, I'd have played it with them. It was by then past ten o'clock, and the only public gathering place that still seemed to be open was the casino. I felt safe. With a son's hand in each of mine, I was strolling lightheartedly past the casino when Joey, guided by some intuition, broke loose from my grip, dashed behind the building, and returned with a smug, triumphant grin. He had found a *golf-miniature* course back there, and it was open for business.

There were no other people around when the three of us teed off, but before we had holed out on the fifth, a crowd of onlookers had assembled—paupers, I surmised at first, straight from the roulette and baccarat tables, and with nothing better or cheaper to do than gape at foolish alien night owls. It was soon clear, though, from our gallery's cries—now of *"Bravo!,"* now of *"Dommage!"*—that, whatever their economic status was, they were avid miniature-golf fans. I have never heard of anybody in the United States getting a kick out of watching strangers play miniature golf, but the way that gang in Les Sables carried on, you'd have thought they were following the likes of Sam Snead and Ben Hogan in the Masters. As a matter of fact, they threw me off my game. On the twelfth hole (a corker, by the way—a dog-leg to the left, with the cup cunningly guarded by two iron pipes), I blew up. Terry had a three and Joey a four; I took a seven. Later, my wife found it hard to believe me when I told her I'd have had the kids back at the hotel earlier but for the pleas of our aficionados that we play a second round.

I was too tired the next day to grasp the full implications of Terry's gleeful announcement, as we started out on the road once more, that the Michelin reported *un golf miniature* in Saint-Jean-de-Luz. When we got there, I dis-covered that *"un"* did not quite cover the situation. I had never seen such a hotbed of miniature golf as the Basque country—or, at any rate, the Basque country of France. (Spain is not hospitable to such frivolity.) It was indicative of the seriousness with which the French regard the sport that the score card at one of the two courses in Saint-Jean it-self carried the printed injunction *"La direction se réserve le droit de rembourser le prix des tickets à toute personne dont l' attitude deviendrait gênante pour les autres joueurs et de les prier de quitter le jeu."* (The main Saint-Jean course, again located within a chip's throw of the municipal casino, was a real toughie. Par forty-eight, and devilish hazards. I have bitter but respectful memories of the hole where you had to drive across some water into a heap of wire netting, whence your ball, if you were lucky, dribbled onto a winding ramp that led toward the cup, a good ten yards away.)

In addition to the two courses in Saint-Jean, the boys

quickly found one in Ciboure, within walking distance of our house—and a mighty familiar walk it became, too. All three of these installations were jammed day and night— for the most part with non-English-speaking players—and at one or another of them a tournament was usually under way, the winners' scores being solemnly proclaimed in the local papers the next day.

Soon after we arrived, I read a news story about an impending tournament. It said no pros would be admitted. I had never thought of there being miniature-golf pros, but thereafter, not wishing to compromise our amateur status by getting mixed up with even a semi-pro, my sons and I steered clear of the tournaments. We generally had little trouble getting onto one or another of the many courses that, along with the towering Pyrenees and the sweeping ocean, make the Basque landscape distinctive. (Some of the neighborhood boosters have an unusual scale of scenic values. According to a miniature-golf item put in the papers by a town father of Guéthary, a resort just north of Saint-Jean, *"Notre golf constitue vraiment une attraction de premier plan et contribue au renom de notre station."*)

At nearby Biarritz, the fashionable summer playground of King Edward VII and his set, the boys and I found two courses, and in its northern suburb, Anglet, two more. (Anglet is a small community, but it harbored two firms that specialize in the construction of miniature-golf courses.) The Anglet courses lay side by side in its beach area, which is called La Chambre d'Amour—in memory not of Edward VII but of two ardent, ill-fated lovers who chose to dally at the water's edge and neglected to pay attention to the incoming tide.

Both of the courses at La Chambre d'Amour were spacious, well-tended, challenging layouts, comparable, in their way, I should say, to the Pebble Beach and Cypress Point links in California, which, between them, occupy a good deal of the acreage of the Monterey Peninsula. These are uni-versally recognized as elegant courses, and the pair at Chambre d'Amour were equally high-class. For instance, the fine for losing a club there was two thousand francs, com-pared to a mere thousand at Ciboure—not that I am certain how one would go about losing a club in miniature golf.

Yielding to the boys' entreaties, I took them to lunch one day at a Chambre d'Amour restaurant situated next to one of the courses. The food was excellent, but the main reason for my sons' interest in the spot turned out to be their having heard that its patrons were allowed to play the course free after a meal, going around as many times as they liked. I took a nap in the car after lunch, and so cannot supply pre-cise statistics, but it is my impression that before I dragged the boys out of there, toward sunset, they must have come close to emulating the feat of a Stateside fellow who was said by *Sports Illustrated* to have played eight rounds of full-scale golf that same summer without a rest.

When we got back home, people keep asking my sons if they found the Basque country appealing. They usually re-plied that it was wonderful, and that they would never for-get it. And they probably never will. Some of the details of our adventures may fade from their memories, but I don't imagine anybody *could* forget a shot the likes of the ace Terry scored one afternoon on that maddening sixth at Ciboure!

Travelling in France is so widely considered a great gas-tronomic adventure that the reminiscences of many home-coming Americans tend to resemble a stomach pump. This attitude isn't indefensible, though. Indeed, it is often defen-sive, inasmuch as the first question asked of the returnee from France by at least one out of every four stay-at-homes he encounters is, "Tell me, how were the snails?" Even be-

fore we left, I felt smugly confident about how the boys
would answer *that* one. In a little farewell speech I planned
to deliver at our shipboard *bon voyage* party, in fact, I had it
in mind to say that while I was looking forward to our sons
enjoying a good many novel experiences abroad, these could
hardly be expected to include the sampling of *escargots,* since
the boys had long before come to garlicky grips with them.

I never did get to make my speech, owing in large part to
the lack of an audience. The fact that only a handful of people turned up to see us off was disappointing in another respect, too. Our travel agent had gravely warned me that if
we proposed to have an—ah—reception in our stateroom before embarking, I should know that it was not the *Flandre's*
practice to sell—ah—beverages to passengers before casting
off. I prudently sent myself a gift-wrapped case of champagne. Alas, we left on a blisteringly hot Saturday forenoon,
when nearly all our friends were, sensibly enough, swimming in the Atlantic, or at any rate not hanging around A
Deck of the *Flandre.* One of the few exceptions was a convi-
vial joker who brought us a can of snails. "In case they run
out over there," he said, cackling hilariously. I accepted them
as graciously as I could and stuffed them deep into one of our
suitcases.

Another well-wisher was a lady who had stayed in town
because she had to go on to a wedding reception. Realizing
that our pitifully small crew of celebrants would never make
much of a dent in my case of champagne, I urged her to take
a couple of bottles along with her. "I'd probably get in Dutch
with customs," she said, "and anyway, that would be like
carrying coals to Newcastle, wouldn't it?" We still had nine
bottles when we sailed. My wife and I gamely polished off
most of them, although, as we watched our fellow passengers
lapping up good French champagne that they had bought
on board, both before and after embarkation, for a fraction

of what our domestic stuff had set us back, we felt as if we were carrying offshore oil to Louisiana. We finally unloaded the last few bottles on a pair of college boys who were on a tight budget.

My sons first met up with snails at Cape Cod. All three boys have an affinity for shellfish. Terry has been wolfing raw oysters since he was three, and at four nearly had a tantrum when his mother and I said two dozen were enough at one clip. Tony has the same reaction to fresh clams as a pre-breakfast snack that many children have to cookies. Joey is the snail boy. (He was also our family's *mahi-mahi* boy until, while gorging himself on broiled *mahi-mahi* not long after marvelling at the lovable and almost human trained dolphins at Marineland, he discovered chokingly that *mahi-mahi* is dolphin. He pushed his plate aside then and said he felt like a cannibal.) Joey's initiation into snails occurred when he was six, and he and I went out onto a Truro beach to gather mussels, so the kids could have *moules marinière* for supper. On the rocks where the mussels were clinging, we also found some sea snails. We carted them home, too, and threw them into the mussel pot. Joey and his brothers pronounced the snails delicious, to the consternation of a visiting inland aunt, who watched the boys eat them with the same restrained revulsion that some relatives have toward nephews with bad table manners. Joey became so fond of snails that I was able to argue him out of a preference for going to camp, rather than Europe, merely by informing him that in France, as all adults knew and he would soon perceive, *escargots* were practically the staff of life. I promised him that before he got back home he would have snails galore, and *au beurre noir,* too.

I do not wish to pretend that my children can, or will, eat anything. Tony, for instance, had a mild stomach upset in the Loire Valley, from eating steak—although it was, to be sure, a *tournedos flambé* that his older brothers had ordered for him and that had apparently been not only doused with but suckled on cognac. Joey, for his part, does not much like omelets. His mother and I were saddened when, at Mère Poulard's celebrated *auberge* on Mont-Saint-Michel, he spurned one of the omelets that have made the island almost as memorable to tourists as the abbey itself. Instead, he had *fruits de mer assortis,* a seafood pot-pourri that was served on a platter the size of a tray. It comprised nearly every kind of shellfish I had ever heard of, and a few unidentifiable new acquaintances. Joey gobbled them all down with gusto, including one *fruit de mer* that was so fresh it was still crawling. He complained only that his molluscoid compote was not sufficiently comprehensive, since it included no snails. I tried to explain that the French eat mostly land snails, and that we were at that moment out at sea, but he was not appeased. "You promised me snails," he said, pouting. "You never keep your promise."

At that, he had a right to be sore. During our stay in Paris, every time we took the children to a restaurant and asked for *escargots,* we'd been told either that they weren't on the menu or that the supply had run out. I was beginning to wonder if the French had allocated most of their snails to the export trade, the way the Scottish do with their native whisky. I suppose that if I had made some all-out effort in Paris— like, say, taking the kids to the restaurant called L'Escargot —we'd surely have found snails, but I kept reminding myself that we had plenty of time ahead of us and that there was no need to get panicky. En route between Mont-Saint-Michel and the Basque country, though, and in the Pays Basque itself, we just never did seem to be able to catch up with a snail, although the children had no trouble ferreting out such obscure delicacies as banana splits and bubble gum.

Until a few days before we had to leave France, it was the

same frustrating story: *pas d'escargots*. Then, one night at
Saint-Jean-de-Luz, a long and neatly aimed putt of Terry's
was deflected, as it headed toward the cup, by some bumps
on the remote, dim-lit playing surface. When we got close, we
saw what the bumps were. Snails! I knew we were getting
warm. I was tempted to pluck the snails right off their perch—
especially since I still had to putt out myself—but I held myself in check. The next day, I escorted the children to a café
abutting the golf course, and ordered *escargots* for *tout le
monde*. To my delight, the waiter nodded. After a while—
it was almost as if he'd had to go outside to get some snails
—he served us. We all fell to eagerly—except Joey,
who toyed with his food for a while and then pushed it aside.
For a moment, I was horrified. Could it be that, after all, he
disliked the rubbery creatures? Was some subconscious
father hostility involved? Then it occurred to me that he
must be sick. When I suggested this, Joey denied it, saying,
as children will, that he was simply not hungry. An hour
later, in gratifying substantiation of my diagnosis, he had a
temperature of a hundred and three.

That was the nearest Joey came to eating *escargots* in
France, as he reminded me grumpily not long afterward,
while we were standing on a pier in New York waiting for
our baggage to be inspected. "You're always breaking prom-
ises," he said. A customs officer began poking through our
suitcases, and as he peered into the bottom of one bulging
bag, my eye was arrested by the glint of metal. It was the can
of snails we'd been given on the *Flandre,* and had quickly
forgotten. When the customs man had moved on to the next
bag, I fished the can from its hiding place, and opened it
with Terry's scout knife. Then and there, Joey finally had
his fill of snails. He was stowing away the last one when a
friend rushed up to welcome us back. "Tell me," he yelled
as he approached us, "how were the snails?"

"Just as good as Daddy promised," replied Joey, licking his lips.

I felt that the trip had been a success after all.

Linguistically, my wife and I were only slightly better prepared for our excursion than a friend of Jinny's who'd spent a good deal of time with us on our 1949 trip to Europe, and who, like my wife, had been much taken with the pub jargon they'd overheard in England. They had decided that, all things considered, "God bless, lovey!" was their favorite British toast. When they crossed the Channel, they resolved to acquire at once a suitable indigenous replacement. My wife's crony, alas, had a pitifully small grasp of French—so small that on first being exposed to *"A votre santé!"* she was obliged to ask for a translation. When she was furnished with one, she rejected the phrase; in her experience, she declared, alcohol and health had always been mutually exclusive.

Soon after our arrival in Paris, the two ladies were invited to have a drink by an American gentleman long resident there. He called for them in his car and, en route to the café he had selected, noticed that his tires needed air. As he pulled in to a gas station, my wife's companion happened to be asking him to tell her some colorful native toast. Preoccupied with his tires, he didn't hear her, and the next words he spoke —addressed to a filling-station attendant who had sauntered up—were *"Gonflez nos pneus."* The lady didn't repeat her question, and when they reached their destination and were served their first apéritifs, it became evident why she hadn't. Lifting her glass, she smiled all around and cried, *"Gonflez nos pneus!"*

Travelling with our sons, Jinny and I made equally free with the French language from time to time, even when we knew what it meant. We had left home too soon to receive

with our passports a letter that President Eisenhower was
sending to outbound Americans that year, urging them to
think of themselves as ambassadors and to behave accordingly. But we heard about this venture in mass diplomacy
and resolved that, even without credentials, we would do
everything we could to foster an atmosphere of international camaraderie. We quickly perceived that there was
plenty of scope for such action. Not long before we landed in
France, General Hans Speidel, of West Germany, had been
appointed commander of the NATO ground forces for Central Europe, and as our boat train passed through Rouen on
the way to Paris, we saw at a grade crossing a freshly painted
sign that said, "DANS CETTE VILLE SPEIDEL A FAIT ASSASSINER
DEUX HOMMES." Terry saw it, too, and asked me to translate
it. I was reluctant to inject a note of strained community relations into the start of the boys' first foreign junket, so I
replied lamely, "It says something like 'Stop, look, and listen.' "

We were not the only American clan to tour Europe that
summer in a German-made car. Both Max Lerner and Arthur M. Schlesinger, Jr., we learned after we returned
home, were carting their families around in Volkswagen
Microbuses, and, in the best diplomatic tradition, were sending back dispatches. Mr. Lerner said, in his column in the
New York *Post,* that he was put in mind of the Reign of Ter-
ror while driving his Microbus through Paris traffic, and in
the New York *Times* Mr. Schlesinger—who somehow associated *his* automotive experiences with the rapacious travels of Attila's Huns—stated that American families roaming
around in Microbuses had become a commonplace sight in
Europe. I didn't think he intended to convey the impression,
though, that Europeans commonly take Americans for Huns.
     I hated to find myself at odds with either of these amiable

and eminent social historians, but I didn't find driving our Volkswagen around Paris any scarier than reading an ordinary headline in the *Post,* and as for an American family like ours being a run-of-the-mill spectacle in Europe, I have often seen more Americans in Microbuses in Cambridge, Massachusetts, than I did along some three thousand miles of French and Spanish roads.

A not atypical European reaction to *our* Microbus occurred as we were driving through the Spanish Pyrenees one day, between Irün and San Sebastián. High in the hills, we came upon a Spanish Army detachment on maneuvers. Most of the soldiers were crawling on the ground, but at our rumbling approach the officer in charge looked at us, popeyed, and shouted a command, and all his men rose up, staring and blinking and gesticulating with undisciplined abandon, as if they had never seen so outlandish an apparition. Around the next curve, a Spanish Army band, composed mainly of drummers, was practicing at the roadside, and as we bore down on the musicians, they broke ranks, shouted *"Ole!,"* and beat their drums like wild things. It didn't look like a commonplace, conditioned reflex to me.

In any event, incidents like this, while agreeably spirited, could have done little to cement friendly relations between the United States and Spain, inasmuch as the soldiers in the Pyrenees, like most of the Europeans we encountered, undoubtedly took us for Germans. This was especially true of people we had passed. Not only was our car of German make; it had been registered in Hamburg, and, accordingly, bore on its back a prominent identifying "D," for "Deutschland." In rural France, when I looked into the rear-view mirror I would occasionally see a farmer stare wrathfully after us as he became aware of the origin of the vehicle that had roiled his flock of chickens. And once, when we halted in a small town, a bystander, possibly but not necessarily a Communist or Poujadist, shouted *"A bas Speidel!"* To avoid getting into a discussion of the complexities of mutual security, I took the liberty of translating this for the children as "You can't park there!"

After a while, we discovered for ourselves that we were not exactly an ordinary, recognizably American sight—or, at any rate, not what we were subsequently to learn constituted such a sight according to the Schlesinger thesis. On the move, we would wave at American tourists in American cars, but they never waved back, as they normally would at compatriots. German tourists, on the other hand, to whom Microbuses clearly were a familiar, nostalgic sight, would always wave eagerly at us, or give us a *gemütlich* raised-arm salute. If they overtook us from behind, they would honk furiously when they saw the "D." One time, when we had stopped at a fork of the road to study a map, a hiker in *Lederhosen* came marching up to us and asked affably, in German, if he could help us get our bearings. On learning that we were not what we appeared to be, he was successively astounded, hurt, and indignant, as if we had played some cheap, disloyal trick on him.

A few such unsettling experiences led my wife and me to conclude that if we were to avoid confusion and promote international harmony, the only sensible course was for us to pretend to *be* German, except when we seemed likely to have to speak it. To make our imposture as credible as possible, I at once began to coach the family in gestures and salutations that I believed would be helpful. But our impersonation, though occasionally successful, could hardly have been the sort of thing the President had in mind.

No sooner had we decided on our masquerade than we were emboldened to test it. Driving through Saint-Jean-de-Luz, we saw one of the very few Microbuses we were to come across during our journey. It was parked, and its driver was at the wheel. As we drew abreast, I tooted the horn, all the children leaned out the window holding their left hands high, in what they had perceived to be *echt-Deutsch* style, and my wife cried merrily, *"Heil!"* Unfortunately, the occupant of the other car turned out to be Max Lerner.

Shortly after that, we had a chance to improve our sorry record. One day when Jinny was driving, we crossed a bridge near Orleans and passed a French Army truck headed in the opposite direction. It had stopped, and a soldier was scrambling off the tail gate. We deduced what he was up to an instant later, when we saw a military hat lying at the edge of the road just ahead of us. My wife slammed on the brakes, jumped out of the car, and, while I watched in bewilderment, picked up the hat just in time to hand it to the soldier, who was running up to retrieve it. He poured out his thanks in rapid French, ending with *"Merci mille fois, Madame!"* Then, before Jinny could reply, he looked at the car. *"Danke —Danke—"* he began gropingly. Then he tried what was probably the only other German word he knew. *"Danke— schön?"*

My wife beamed at him in commendation. *"De rien,"* she replied, with a gracious *macht-nichts* inflection, and climbed back in the car and drove us away. "It seemed like a diplomatic thing to do," she said after a moment. "I may not have resolved any large issues, but that's one Frenchman, at least, whom General Speidel shouldn't have any more trouble with."

Our next-door neighbors, who are ardent camera fans, were going to do Canada that same summer, and we realized that our only hope of averting a whole-winter-long view-by-view circumnavigation of the Gaspé Peninsula lay in taking strong countermeasures. The defensive weapons we accordingly outfitted ourselves with included one movie camera and three still cameras. How we smirked as we marched up the gangplank! We'd show them.

As it turned out, we'd have done better to leave the cameras home and take along a photographer. I am now convinced that this must be the practice, whatever they say to the contrary, of those tourists who return home with pictures of the whole family smilingly assembled in front of this or that wonder of the world. Who takes those pictures, anyway? In the only group photograph we managed to bring back, we are all fast asleep. A waggish acquaintance snapped it one afternoon while we were sprawled across a sofa in the lounge of an English Channel boat. It is not only an excessively candid photograph but one that suggests its subjects may have been strangled by the camera-case straps in which they are all nightmarishly entangled. I never dared show this to our neighbors, naturally. They would have laughed themselves giddy at the notion of anybody's dozing off when there might have been a scrapbook item just across the horizon.

We tried, though. Leaving New York, for instance, we took pictures of the Statue of Liberty with such unremitting intensity that Terry complained an hour later he'd hardly had a decent naked-eyed squint at the monument. I told him he could look at it on the way back, and that anyway the important thing was to have it in pictures, for the Hot-Stove League. I had barely got him soothed when Tony discovered he'd been duped. While we were stockpiling our impedimenta, he overheard so much camera talk that he begged for one of his own. His mother and I gave him a fifth, broken old camera we found in a closet and told him it was for his very own exclusive use. Unfortunately, he met up with a fellow passenger on the ship who turned out to be one of those types who is forever sticking his nose into other people's light metres. This meddler babbled to Tony that the camera he was focussing on a stack of deck chairs was a worthless shell, and the jig was up.

Tony was outraged. He announced that he not only insisted on being a front-line fighter in our photographic crusade, but that he wanted live ammunition, too. He kept his precise tactical plans to himself until we made our first assault on Paris. We had gone to the Zoo—there is absolutely nothing like animal shots for torturing your friends—and Tony suddenly made a grab for my movie camera. I had already taken a lot of splendid footage that day, and so, after some spirited discussion, I said indulgently that he could finish off the reel. He finished it off, all right. When I opened up the camera that evening to change film, I discovered that our zoölogical memorabilia had somehow slipped off their spool—conceivably while Tony and I were wrestling for possession of the camera. The entire film was ruined.

I went into a terrible sulk after that, and refused to have anything more to do with cameras in Paris. Unfortunately, the rest of my shoulder-weary tribe followed my shirking example. As a result, the only pictures we had of the city were postcards. Postcards, of course, are perfectly proper to send to people, but, as any child can tell you, it is dreadfully *infra dig* to show them to anybody.

Our mission was further handicapped by the fact that Joey had told his schoolteacher about our trip. She urged him to bring back his own pictorial log of his adventures. If there is anything an eight-year-old hates in midsummer it is homework, or what he can construe to be homework. Most of the shots we finally did get him to take, accordingly, were influenced by bribery. If his classmates ever got to see his version of Big Ben, they must have been puzzled, since the clock hands were effaced by an outstretched human hand with a sweetmeat in it. In a way, I was sorry that that had to be one of Joey's few pictures that came out sharp and clear; when his brothers saw it, a month or so after it was taken, they claimed I owed them each a piece of candy.

Terry had a Polaroid Land camera, which can produce a finished print in sixty seconds. He set sail with around forty packets of film, and returned home with the majority still unexposed. His camera was quite heavy, he said, and it slowed him down to carry it. Most of the time, I had to tote it. One of the best of his slim collection of souvenir photos showed a parking lot outside the palace at Versailles. I made him take that one to see if the camera still worked after I had accidentally dropped it. Terry also had a rather unusual, albeit murky, shot of the Pyrenees, framed in the windshield of our Microbus. We all knew at the time he took it that he'd have done better if I'd stopped the car, or cleaned the windshield. But we were hungry and wanted to push on toward lunch. This shiftless attitude may have kept us from winning a prize in the *Saturday Review's* travel-photography contest, but we sure had a good lunch.

Terry was partly discouraged in his picture-taking by the circumstance that, when he was on foot, he found it difficult to take more than a single picture at any one spot. As soon as he pulled a finished print out of his magical machine, a crowd would gather around to gawk at the contraption, and would block his view of the scenery. The only person who didn't treat him like a freak was a soldier from Needham, Massachusetts, whom Terry met while climbing around the ruined battlements of the château of Chinon. The soldier had a Polaroid Land camera himself, and they greeted one another as effusively as if they'd been a couple of dish-lipped Africans converging by chance in the lobby of Claridge's. Terry thought the château at Chinon was one of the coolest sights of France, but his only souvenir of it was a picture of his comrade-in-arms from Needham.

Toward the end of our stay abroad, my wife and I decided to go to a bullfight, and, although by then we were
tired of lugging cameras around, we borrowed the movie
camera from Tony and loaded it with color film. What better riposte could there be to the glories of Banff and Lake
Louise, we calculated, than the sight of a brave bull's gallant
stand against the inevitable! (When we tried to make up to
our children, who'd been told they couldn't join us on that
particular excursion, by promising them a full pictorial report, they were terribly offended. After all our conversation
about how we were going to bedevil our neighbors, the boys
interpreted our pledge to mean we didn't like *them*.) On
reaching the arena, we didn't quite catch the entrance parade on film, owing to some difficulty I was having in loading
the camera, but by the time the picadors had come on I was
ready for them. I was just starting to acquire some mighty
colorful—in fact, blood-red—footage when Jinny seized the
camera. She said she thought she might find the whole business more bearable if, instead of having to gaze directly at it,
she watched through the view-finder. I grumpily assented,
but implored her, for our future peace of mind, to keep on
shooting. She did, but the entrepreneurs of bullfighting, who
generally do not like to have movies circulated that show all
the gory details, need not have worried. In our developed
footage, there were a few furtive, tantalizing glimpses of
blood-soaked bulls, but these were followed by inordinately
long close-ups of the back of a spectator's head; and when
the matadors went in for the kill, the scene invariably
switched to a painstaking study of cloud formations.

Not long after that outing, we all decided to leave our cameras in our luggage, even if it meant taking our lumps afterward. From then on, we had a wonderfully carefree, if irresponsible, journey. The pictorial proof of this was that
what we brought home was so skimpy that I knew we could

only justify our enjoyment of our travels by telling our neighbors they'd have to take our word for it—not that we had
much hope of their ever turning off their slide projector long
enough for us to get a word in. On our return, though, we
learned that the folks next door lost nearly all their film
when some blackguard looted their car in Québec. It was a
tough break for them, but the winter that followed was
quiet and companionable out our way.

At Home
with
the Ethnocentrics

In the winter of 1959, fortified by a wind-proof, water-proof, hooded, belted, fleece-lined coat that had buttons, zippers, and draw strings and that a clothing salesman promised me would keep a duck-hunter snug under the most imaginably adverse operating conditions, I went to Alaska, to have a look at what was then the newest state of the Union. I hadn't been there long when I heard a radio broadcast of a high-school basketball game. At the outset, the announcer said there were sixteen hundred spectators present. Later, one of the players made a fancy shot, and the announcer burbled, "I saw him! And so did everybody in Alaska!"

Alaska is not quite that sparsely populated an outpost, but to a New Yorker—even to many Alaskans—it seems remarkably undermanned. Tibet, a country with high marks for remoteness and inaccessibility, has a population of about three million and an area almost twice that of Texas. This makes Tibet almost the same size, geographically, as Alaska, but more than ten times as densely populated. According to the most accurate counts available at the time of my visit, (and these weren't very accurate), the forty-ninth state's five hundred and eighty-six thousand square miles harbored over twice as many big-game animals as people—something like five hundred and seventy-five thousand of the four-footed creatures, as against a mere two hundred and twenty thousand or so bipeds.

It is, of course, impossible to determine precisely how many moose, caribou, and bear there are in Alaska at any given time, and it is only a little less difficult to count its people. Because much of Alaska's employment is seasonal and much of its labor force migratory, the population may fluctuate by thirty thousand in a single twelve-month period, ebbing in the quiet of winter to less than two hundred thousand, or below the level of Worcester, Massachusetts. And at any time it is hard to make an exact head count in an area that, like Alaska, has less than half a person per square mile. Fifty people per square mile is the average in the rest of the continental United States—a far-off, southerly region to which Alaskans refer as "Outside." (In thus sweepingly assigning all outlanders to a single categorization, Alaskans resemble Cape Codders. But a non-Alaskan moving to Alaska may at once become an Alaskan, or Insider. A non-Cape Codder does not become a Cape Codder simply by moving to Cape Cod.)

Despite their comparative loneliness, some Alaskan wide-open-space lovers are already shuddering at the prospect that their state, one-fifth the size of all its forty-eight older sisters put together, may someday become as heavily colonized as, say, Jersey City (1950 pop.: 299,017), and, like the basketball announcer, many of them try to minimize even the present scarcity of residents.

The example of Congress notwithstanding, the Department of Defense has been taking its time about recognizing

Alaska as a full-fledged state; long after statehood became a fact, enlisted men stationed there still got foreign-duty pay. Many Alaskans themselves, military and non-military, seemed to me confused about their status, and this was understandable, their geographical status not having changed a whit. By airplane, Alaska's most widely used means of transportation, Anchorage and Fairbanks are still nearer Tokyo than Washington, D.C. When Alaskans spoke of "the States," it was safe to assume that they were not including their own state. When they spoke of their own, many of them still referred to it as a territory. A resident psychiatrist called Alaska "the territory become state"—perhaps as good a way as any of expressing Alaskans' schizoid attitude toward their vast locality.

Alaska encompasses four time zones: Pacific (the easternmost), Yukon, Alaska, and Bering (the zone in which lie most of the Aleutian Islands, a twelve-hundred-mile-long part of Alaska so much closer to Japan than to the rest of the United States that, from the Japanese viewpoint, at least, nothing could have been more logical than the wartime assault on Attu and its environs). Nome, the state's most westerly city of consequence, is west of Honolulu.

Alaska's coastline is longer than that of the whole rest of the United States, if one excepts Hawaii—which some Alaskans, I found, were quick to do, regarding it as a Johnny-come-lately state. A statistician in Washington has computed (and it would probably take another statistician to understand why he bothered) that in Alaska, despite its tiny population, nearly as many hunting licenses are issued annually per lineal mile of rural road as in New York State. New York, with its 105,566 miles of roads, at the last count, need not feel too bad about this, for Alaska, though it had seven hundred landing facilities for airplanes while I was there, had only 5,153 miles of road, of which but 959 were paved. Most Alaskans who had cars used them almost entirely for intra-urban travel. "Drive out and let us show you some excellent buys in used aircraft," said an ad in an Anchorage paper. Within the state boundaries, practically all first-class mail has long moved by air, at non-airmail rates. To transport mail, or anything else, on the ground would be a formidable task. Looking at a road map of Alaska, one had the impression that the cartographer had become bored after a few minutes' work, pushed aside his bottles of red and blue ink, and gone hunting.

Most of the Alaskans I met were fairly well resigned to their surface immobility, but some of them dreamed of a bright, four-lane future. One of the most touching symbols of this aspiration was visible in Nome, a city that can be approached only by air between October and June. (In the summer months, there is water traffic.) Nailed to the office door of the mayor of Nome was a metal road marker reading "Route 97." The citizens of Nome hoped passionately that someday the highway so designated would connect them with Fairbanks, nearly five hundred miles to the east. The road extended seventy miles from Nome in that direction, and another portion of it extended about the same distance west from Fairbanks. Between these outstretched arms extended a trackless expanse of three hundred and fifty miles, and, as far as most Alaskans were concerned, no roads led to Nome.

Soon after statehood was achieved, Wien Alaska Airlines, one of ten scheduled carriers operating in Alaska (aviation is the state's largest non-governmental industry), announced the inauguration of passenger service linking Galena, Ruby, Kokrines, Koyukuk, Kalakaket, and Nulato. Of these six communities, Nulato, with a population last calculated at two hundred and fifty-two, was the largest. By Alaskan standards, such settlements are not small; according to state law, a community that wants to incorporate as a first-class city need have only four hundred residents; the minimum for a second-class city is fifty. In the whole state there are a mere eleven cities with as many as twenty-five hundred people. Few, diminutive, and far apart as they are, I found Alaska's cities nevertheless considerably more cosmopolitan than my Outside notions of them. Some new arrivals are pleasantly surprised by the amenities they find, while others are a bit let down to discover so many trappings of civilization. I met one young couple who had pulled up stakes in Massachusetts and driven northwest. "Coming up the Alaska Highway," the wife said, "we camped out, and fished for salmon, and spotted two moose and a bear, and we were just beginning to feel like real pioneers when we rolled into Anchorage and had to get change for a parking meter."

Anchorage, with more than thirty-five thousand residents in the city proper and another twenty-five thousand or so, mostly military, on its outskirts, is Alaska's biggest city, and its commercial hub. It is so confident of its future role as Alaska's chief metropolis that in 1960 it tried to push through, but got turned down on, a referendum that would have shifted the site of the state's capital to its expanding city limits and away from the southeasterly seaport of Juneau. In Anchorage, there were not only parking meters but radar-controlled traffic lights and radio-equipped taxis, to say nothing of forty-four churches, and a high school that cost five and a quarter million dollars—just about two million less, as I was frequently reminded, than the United States paid Russia, in 1865, for Alaska *in toto*.

The school's facilities included a Link trainer for fledgling pilots and a two-thousand-seat auditorium with a hydraulic stage elevator. "When Mary Martin was here, she said our stage had everything Radio City's has," an Anchorage city official told me. Anchorage also had close to three thousand licensed pilots, eight airfields, and four seaplane bases. Of the two thousand-odd seaplanes in the United States, nearly a fifth called Anchorage anchorage. A banker there was likely to have a plane, or maybe two planes (one for his wife), and so was his dry cleaner. Doctors and dentists would pilot their own craft on calls to outlying patients, inquiring beforehand, with equal urgency, about landing conditions and respiratory conditions.

Most of the buildings along Anchorage's two main avenues were modest one-or two-story affairs (with a rather large scattering of bars and pawnshops among them), but there were two fourteen-story apartment houses, and a hotel the same height was under construction. By and large, the people who live in Anchorage seemed delighted with their town. "Places this size Outside couldn't touch the cultural activities we have here," a wholesale merchant told me. "We've got our little theatre and our community chorus, and we had Jan Peerce last year, and we brought in some first-rate professional wrestlers. Oh, there's something going on here all the time! We have three Lions Clubs, and we have the Soroptimists, and Rotary and Kiwanis, and the Elks and the Moose, and the Legion and the Knights of Pythias and the Sons of the Revolution, and I forget offhand who-all else. We have just about everything. I could take you to two hundred and fifty homes here where the standard of living is just as good as that of any upper-middle-class home in the States. Our Coke bottler has wall-to-wall carpets and a grand piano. And as for our high school! When Bob Hope was here, he said its stage was just as good as Radio City's!"

Fairbanks, two hundred and fifty miles inland from Anchorage, and connected with it by the only government-owned-and-operated railroad in the United States, is Alaska's second metropolis, with a population of fifteen thousand, and with several thousand more people at outlying military posts. It was once a booming gold town, and some of its street names—Minnie Avenue, Harriett Avenue, Nita Avenue, Bonnie Avenue, and the like—hark back to the frivolities of the Robert W. Service era. The gold-mining industry has lately been in the doldrums, and Fairbanks has become an intellectual center. Four miles outside of town is a suburb named College, the seat of the University of Alaska.

The university, a land-grant institution, was founded in 1922 as the Alaska Agricultural College & School of Mines. Its president, at the time of my visit, was a former gold miner, and beneath its campus runs a tunnel in which students are still taught to blast holes and extract ore. In 1959, it had more than eight hundred students, three-fourths of them Alaskans, and its curriculum was fairly broad. "Everything from Anthropology to Zoology!" a dean once trumpeted. This gamut encompassed courses in prospecting and wild-life management, but there were none in philosophy or psychology, and the faculty included only one history teacher. Despite such gaps, the university was a lively, up-and-coming establishment, and one of its few serious problems was that, being the only seat of higher learning in the mammoth state, its athletic teams had nobody within reasonable travelling distance to compete against.

In quite a few respects, the whole sprawling mass of Alaska seemed to me to resemble a small town, with all the passion and pride that characterize so many cozy New England villages. Everyone there appeared to be acquainted with everyone else. A businessman in Juneau, which is a city of eighty-five hundred and the only American state capital within a few minutes' drive of both a gold mine and a glacier, told me one evening, "One of the nicest parts about living in this town is that you know everybody. It's sort of like watching a movie when you're a pal of everyone in the cast. If you drop in at a murder trial in our courtroom, you'll know the judge and the D.A. and the defense counsel and most of the jury, and the chances are that you'll also know the defendant and that you knew the corpse." A lady in Juneau who invited me to dinner startled me by asking offhandedly, "Would you rather eat at our place or the Governor's? I thought you might like to see the Mansion."

The intimacy and affection that Alaskans share extend far beyond city limits. Although it is eleven hundred and twenty miles from Juneau to Nome, one Juneau man told me, with obvious pride, "I'll bet I know more people in Nome than my Los Angeles relatives know in the whole state of California." Alaskans, except for the dwindling few prospectors and other misanthropes who still pursue solitary lives in the wilderness, cannot abide being separated for long from other Alaskans. "The only time I've ever felt homesick in my life was on Election Night in 1948," a Fairbanks man told me. "I had had to go Outside on business, and I found myself in Times Square. There must have been half a million people milling around, but I suddenly realized I didn't know a goddam one of them, and even though I was a Democrat and should have been kicking my heels with joy because Truman had won, I felt so miserably alone that I went back to my hotel room and killed a bottle of whiskey." Some introspective Alaskans attributed their penchant for sticking together to their winter climate. "After you've been here awhile," a Fairbanks woman said, "you come to realize that if you don't cuddle up with other people—I mean figuratively, of course—you're going to freeze separately." It may be significant that Alaska's most enthusiastically supported private charity is the Salvation Army.

The most enthusiastically supported non-charitable fund drive in Alaska is a guessing game started in 1917 and conducted ever since by the citizens of Nenana, a settlement of three hundred or so inhabitants, seventy miles from Fairbanks. The contest is simple enough. The object is to predict the exact minute at which the spring breakup of the ice on the Tanana River, which runs through Nenana, will get under way. Each winter, a tripod is set on the frozen river and connected by a cable to a clock in a small tower ashore. When the ice moves, the tripod is jostled and the cable stops the clock. Alaskans love to gamble, and in 1959 more than a hundred and sixty-five thousand entries were filed, at a dollar apiece. Long-shot players pick dates as early as March and as late as August. The form players, after consulting meteorological charts, records of magnetic storms, astrologers, icemen, and their own dreams, usually choose a time late in April or early in May. For a promising day like May 1st, there will be fifty entries riding on every minute of every hour.

In theory, Outsiders are not permitted to bet, but I was urged, as I suspected many a transient had been before me, to take a little flier, using the name of a Fairbanks intermediary. My agent, after sniffing the air, cocking an eye at the sky, and spitting groundward (contrary to his and my expectations, the expectoration did not freeze in flight, but did instantly on hitting the earth), recommended May 3rd, at 5:42 A.M. He was not too far off, it developed. The ice on the Tanana buckled at 2:26 P.M., on May 8th. Eleven individuals or groups of individuals, my man subsequently informed me, had picked the right moment. The winners split ninety-three thousand dollars among them—the amount that remained in the kitty after the citizens of Nenana, which has practically no other source of municipal income, had deducted what they considered reasonable expenses.

Although the weather in Alaska is a subject of never-ending fascination to Alaskans, they deplore the widely held belief that they live on an ice-gripped tundra, huddling in igloos. In Eskimo language, "igloo" means "house," or "home." Most Eskimos, therefore, live in igloos. But most Alaskan Eskimos have never glimpsed, let alone dwelt in, an igloo fashioned of snow blocks. The only igloos of this sort ever seen in the state are put together every so often by boosters of tourism, to beguile transients. (Alaskans often seem to go out of their way to propagate myths that they professedly seek to exorcise. In March of 1959, the wives of the state's senators turned up at a Washington, D.C., costume party bundled in fur parkas—garments that are rarely seen or needed at any time of the year in the state capital, where the temperature range doesn't differ much from that of the national capital.)

On the chilliest of long winter evenings, Alaskans can get themselves all heated up explaining to visitors that while, in certain parts of the state at certain times of the year, the days may be a mite short and the temperatures a trifle low, at other times the very same places have gloriously long hours of hot and dazzling sunshine. The total value of Alaska's agricultural crop amounted to a scant four and a half million dollars in 1958, but it is undeniable that in the state's warm season things grow prodigiously, often crazily—eleven-foot sunflowers, eight-pound turnips, sixty-five-pound cabbages—while the hillsides abound with wild flowers and with indigenous bushes that sprout edible berries called bearberries, timberberries, crowberries, soapberries, and salmonberries. "My mother-in-law came to see us one August," an Anchorage man told me, "and she sent her garden club a postcard saying that in a twenty-foot radius she had spotted ten varieties of wild flowers she'd never even heard of before. What do you think about *that?*"

The most violent contrasts in weather occur above the Alaska Range, which separates north and south Alaska, and whose noblest ornament is Mount McKinley, twenty thousand feet high and the tallest peak on the continent. In Fairbanks, north of the range, the temperature has got up to ninety-nine degrees and down to minus sixty-six. It is a rare winter in Fairbanks when the thermometer does not dip to fifty below—and, for that matter, on the first day of spring in 1959 (a rare spring, to be sure), the mercury hit minus thirty-one. The Fairbanks *News-Miner,* the world's northernmost daily paper, chose a Coleridge quotation— "And the spring comes slowly up this way"—to head a full page of wry seasonal photographs it ran that day. One shot showed a housebound girl holding a bathing suit, with snow visible through a window behind her; another showed a woman forlornly inspecting a seed catalogue; and a third showed a man pouring into his car radiator a first-of-spring portion of anti-freeze.

In winter, an automobile owner in Fairbanks has special problems. He must equip himself with a heating device he can plug into his car's engine overnight, and with plastic squares, containing air bubbles, which he can fasten to its windshield by day, so he can see. The *average* winter temperature is six below. But the cold is far from unbearable, as I found, although my duck-hunter's gear may have had something to do with it. There is so little wind most days that snow piles up on top of fence posts. Even so, when the thermometer reading is minus thirty, dogs have to be prodded to go out for an airing. At forty below, a mother whose child has inadvertently gone off to school without his mittens has conniptions. At fifty below, a pipe-smoker may find that the moisture in his breath has turned to ice inside his pipe stem. Rivers are used as roads, and fire hydrants are fitted out with warming hoods.

Fairbanksians seem to thrive on their climatological abnormality. They sometimes say, more or less in jest, that after a prolonged cold spell, when the mercury rises to minus ten or thereabouts, they all shuck their coats; and on one minus-eight morning I did see a teenager there stride cheerfully along in his shirtsleeves—with the sleeves, what was more, rolled up to the elbows. One winter night, when Fairbanks policemen questioned two men they found curled up in sleeping bags on the frozen Chena River, which winds through the city, the pair explained drowsily that they stood to win a hundred-dollar bet if they could survive a whole

night out there. They survived very nicely, but didn't collect; a condition of the wager was that the temperature
reach forty-five below, and it unsportingly refused to drop a
single degree beyond minus thirty-five.

As befits a state that in some ways so far exceeds
the American norm and in others falls so far short of
it, Alaska is full of incongruities. One may hear over the
radio that a meeting of the Dog Sled Mushers' Association has
been postponed because of snow, or one may hear a woman
living north of the Arctic Circle say, on a day when the temperature stands at minus twenty-two and a cutting wind is
blowing in off the Bering Strait, that she is simply dying to
go Outside soon, because her husband has given her a mink
coat for Christmas and she wants a chance to wear it. I was
having lunch in a restaurant one day with a big, burly
hunting guide, who interrupted a hair-raising account of
being charged by a grizzly to tell a waitress he didn't think
he'd have a drink, because it might make him drowsy. Then
he changed his mind and commanded, gruffly, "Oh, bring me
a snort." On being asked what sort of snort he craved, he
ordered a Daiquiri.

Alaska is a youthful state in more ways than one. Those
of its settlers whom census-takers have caught up with average a firm-skinned twenty-seven. And they are an uncommonly self-perpetuating lot. A popular two-line joke that I
heard several times there began, "You only have one child?,"
and ended, "Yes, but we've only been here a year." (A substantial number of Alaska babies are, in the vulgar idiom,
Army brats. Of fifteen births reported one day in the Vital
Statistics column of the Anchorage *Times,* two had occurred
in a civilian hospital and thirteen in a military one.) Relatively few present-day Alaskans were born in the state,
aside from the thirty thousand-odd aborigines—Eskimos,
Indians, and Aleuts (who have both Eskimo and Indian

blood) . Members of these three ethnic groups are all known as natives, a term that is never applied to whites born in Alaska. This has nothing to do with racial intolerance, which is negligible in Alaska, although few natives have ever entered a state-run old folks' institution called the Pioneers Home, perhaps on the reasoning that you can't be a pioneer on your native ground.

Many authentic pioneers have retained their Outside characteristics. Alaskans from Texas still wear broad-brimmed hats and cowboy boots. I heard a Bureau of Indian Affairs agent who was charged with protecting reindeer discuss wolf control and warble-fly extermination with Eskimo herdsmen in tones that savored of the Bronx, where his hegira began. One of Alaska's pioneer doctors was a Virginian; a number of other Virginia physicians followed him north, and though many of their latter-day fellow-practitioners have come from other states, Alaskans like to say that all their doctors have Virginia accents, and that some of the accents are stronger than they were when the doctors arrived.

Alaska's incumbent and first elected governor, William A. Egan, is a fairly exceptional Alaskan in that he was born there—in the city of Valdez, where he still runs a grocery store. (Egan is known to many of his electorate as Eagle Bill, a nickname he acquired when, as a member of the territorial legislature, he spoke up in favor of continuing a long-standing local bounty for killing eagles, which Alaskan salmon fishermen regard as dangerous predators. The bounty was discontinued after Outside patriotic societies, screaming louder than any eagle, rose in their star-spangled wrath to denounce this insult to the national bird.) Egan's second-in-command, Secretary of State Hugh J. Wade, comes from Iowa. Before Wade moved to Alaska, he held a variety of jobs, and when, at the onset of statehood, Egan was seriously ill and Wade assumed his duties, Alaska found itself being

governed by a man who was once influential in selling Eskimo Pies.

Diverse though Alaskans' origins may be, there are some
traits that can perhaps be ascribed to many, though certainly
not all, of the state's contemporary residents. Alaskans have
firm opinions on practically every subject under the sun, and
no inhibitions about airing them. One of the new state's two
senators in Washington, E. L. Bartlett, told me, "Alaska
today is a state in a state of ferment." He paused, and added
cheerfully, "But then it always will be." When Bartlett,
whom everyone in Alaska seems to call Bob, was the Territory of Alaska's non-voting delegate to the House of Representatives, a post he held for fourteen years, he used to get
so much mail from his constituents that enfranchised Congressional colleagues from much more populous areas were
awed and envious. (Alaskans make more phone calls per
capita than any other Americans.)

The esteem in which Alaskans hold individualism was
exemplified by the obituary of an eighty-four-year-old resident of Nome, who was found dead in her home one day
after she'd stubbornly refused to be moved to a hospital,
and whom the Nome *Nugget* eulogized as "a proud and independent woman to the very last."

Alaskans are tough. "Most of us here have gone through
migration," a newspaper publisher told me, "and migration
is a wonderful screening process. It eliminates the weak sisters. Of course, it also makes the people here quite a handful
to put out a paper for. Most Alaskans, to hear them tell it,
can edit a paper better than any editor, and sell goods better
than any storekeeper, and now that Hawaii's come into the
family, it wouldn't surprise me if some Alaskans claimed
they could do a better hula than Hilo Hattie herself."

Alaskans are informal, and unpredictable. In Anchorage
I saw a wedding convoy of three confetti-decked vehicles—
two gleaming limousines and a pick-up truck. In Fairbanks,

a waitress I'd never laid eyes on before said to me in one breath, "Everything O.K., sweetie?," and, three or four breaths later, "Thank you very much, sir." In a Fairbanks building owned by a bank (inside its front door, where an Outside bank might have an armed guard, this one had an enormous stuffed grizzly, with bared fangs), space was occupied by two establishments called Ed's Bakery and Ray's Supermarket; Ed was the bank's executive vice-president and the chairman of the board, and Ray was one of his fellow-directors.

It was a very few years ago that an Alaskan judge astounded some of his more freewheeling colleagues by announcing that thenceforth he would wear robes while sitting on the bench, and that the attorneys appearing before him had to put on coats and ties. "People up here like to dress the way they feel like dressing," a nattily dressed Fairbanks businessman told me. "There was a reception one summer for the Secretary of the Interior, who in the territorial days was sort of Mr. Big in Alaska, and I turned up in a sports shirt. A couple of days later, I ran into a guy who said, 'You know, for a Cabinet officer and everything, you really should have worn a white shirt and a tie.' I said, 'Man, he was here in my country. When I go to his country, I'll dress his way.'" A member of President Eisenhower's Cabinet once nettled Alaskans by telling them that their chances of attaining statehood would be enhanced if they were less brash and learned to behave more like ladies and gentlemen. Soon afterward, Adlai Stevenson arrived in Alaska and, on being advised of the Republican's tactless injunction, made much political capital by beginning a speech with an emphatically inflected "Ladies and gentlemen . . ."

Alaska has a rough-and-tumble heritage, and by no means all of its inhabitants are distinguished by ladylike or gentlemanly attributes. The consumption of liquor in the state runs high, and on occasion the papers casually refer to this or that individual, by name, as "a habitual drunkard." Eskimos have been frequent offenders; it is not known whether this is because they have a low tolerance for alcohol or because they live from day to day and, accordingly, when they get hold of a bottle, finish it off. On the fringes of Anchorage, there are saloons that stay open all night and put on burlesque shows at three or four in the morning. Until recently, the girls in these places upheld a venerable Alaska tradition by coaxing bleary customers to buy costly drinks, such as champagne at fifty dollars a bottle; the proprietors were glad to take payment in the form of a check, if the customer was steady enough to execute a recognizable signature. (Alaskans love to write checks; they write more of them, proportionate to total bank deposits, than any other people on earth.) Just after statehood, the tyro Alaska state legislature, mindful of the area's new dignity, outlawed the B-girls. The bill deposing them was introduced by a lady member of the House of Representatives. The day it came up for a final vote happened to be the day the Hawaiian statehood bill was expected to be passed by Congress, and, in sisterly acclamation of that event, the legislator had come to work wearing a sarong and a *lei,* and toting a ukulele. When she learned that her anti-B-girl bill was on the calendar, she hastily excused herself, changed into a severe suit, and returned to steer her legislation through.

Many American judges hardly ever get to try a first-degree-murder case; most Alaskan judges have lost track of the number they've handled. Certainly there have been enough to justify the old Alaskan wheeze that if you are going to shoot something and don't want to get into excessive trouble, make sure it's a man and not a moose out of season. I arrived in Alaska just too late to take in the trial of a prostitute who, after a client had enjoyed but declined to pay for her services, had pummeled him savagely with a whiskey bottle. She was accused of assault but acquitted on the ground that her victim had reneged on a business contract. I did get there in time to hear at first hand about a former athletic coach in Fairbanks who was arrested for bank robbery, and—as further evidence that statehood had not altogether dimmed Alaska's reputation as a haven for unsavory characters—about a former criminologist on that city's police force, who for a time also ran a credit bureau there, and who'd been arrested for passing bad checks.

By and large, Alaskans are tolerant of such rogues. "We have more than our share of fast-buck boys," a banker told me, "and we have skin-game operators all over the place, and we have far too many lawyers—around a hundred and fifty, the last I heard—but all in all we're a pretty good bunch of people. Up here, we feel kind of the way a family does about its members. In Juneau, I was sitting in the state senate one day and a speaker referred to some drunken old slobs at our Pioneers Home as ne'er-do-wells. It did my heart good when, on another legislator's recommendation, the senate agreed to amend the record by substituting the word 'unfortunates.' You see, we Alaskans love all Alaskans, even the no-good ones. I suppose it's because, when you come right down to it, we have a chosen-people complex. If I ever had to pick one adjective that would most nearly sum up the lot of us, I guess it would be 'ethnocentric.' "

"Chauvinistic" might be another good word. Advertising copywriters for Alaskan firms, when they run out of routine appeals, fall back on such testimonials as "We're in love with our wonderful state—Alaska." The University of Alaska in 1958 gave an honorary degree to a woman whose major achievement was having written the lyrics to the "Alaska Flag Song"—an anthem that, on June 30th of that year, the day Congress passed the statehood bill, had the same lachrymogenic effect on many Alaskans that the "Marseillaise" had on Parisians on August 25, 1944. Being so close to the North Pole, Alaskans loyally denigrate the South Pole, and they resented all the hoopla lavished on that spot during the International Geophysical Year. I saw on display in the university's museum a campus pennant that an undergraduate who took part in an antarctic expedition had planted theatrically, if temporarily, at the South Pole. The polar influence is strong: a published notice I saw about a bartenders' union's election said, "Poles Open, 12:01 P.M. 'til 8 P.M."

Alaskans are so fond of their homeland that they are almost as partial to Eskimo-carved ivory trinkets as tourists are; what's more, they call large hot dogs "huskies," and smaller ones "pups." Bourbon is their favorite drink, and when, soon after statehood became a *fait accompli*, the purveyor of one brand, Beam's, brought out a special pottery container in the shape of a green star, with a "49" emblazoned on it, Alaskans with a sense of taste that would ordinarily have made them recoil from moose-embroidered pillows or other such hideous souvenirs gobbled up the stuff. An Anchorage organization eager to be known by an indigenous-sounding nickname calls itself the Parents Association for Retarded Children of Alaska—for short, PARCA.

Alaskans are avid readers, and they particularly enjoy reading about themselves. Edna Ferber's *Ice Palace* has had brisk sales there, and Senator Ernest Gruening, who was Alaska's territorial governor for fourteen years, conveyed to me his belief that the book, which he and others have called "Alaska's *Uncle Tom's Cabin*," had a lot to do with the state's being admitted to the Union. Some Alaskans I talked to thought, on the other hand, that statehood did more for the book than the book did for statehood. Their reservations about Miss Ferber's novel were not based on its portrayal of Alaska (which the author liked much better than she did Texas) but were expressed in such judgments as "poor job of plotting" and "inadequate character development."

The House of Adler, Alaska's best-known bookstore, which was opened in Fairbanks thirty years ago by a refugee perfume salesman from Greenwich Village, sold a tidy six hundred copies of *Ice Palace,* but it also sold well over a thousand copies of *Alaska Now,* by Herb Hilscher, an Alaskan of modest celebrity Outside. Alaska's four bookshops often fill entire displays windows with local-interest titles like *Alaska Past and Present, Alaska Sourdough, The Real Book of Alaska, Ootook—Young Eskimo Girl, Panuck—Eskimo Sled Dog,* and *Where Else But Alaska?* There is no telling how a John Gunther book on Alaska would sell Outside, but Alaskans would undoubtedly dote on it, and some of them hope that Mr. Gunther will tackle the assignment sooner or later, if for no other reason than to take advantage of a title that he would be hard put to it to justify elsewhere—"Inside Inside."

Traditionally, the floral symbol of Alaska has been the forget-me-not, and rarely has a symbol been more apposite. Until the forty-ninth state became equally sovereign with Maine (white pine cone and tassel) and California (golden poppy), Alaskans chafed under the yoke of a distant but omnipotent federal government that, to many of them, seemed dismayingly oblivious of their existence, and at times almost insultingly obtuse about their problems. When Congress amended the immigration laws in 1951, for instance, under prodding from Senator Patrick A. McCarran, of Nevada (sagebrush), in order to keep America undefiled by undesirables, it was decreed that all travellers arriving in the United States from Alaska, regardless of their citizenship, had to be screened by the immigration authorities. Alaskans, not surprisingly, regarded this as a galling affront, especially since the McCarran Act said nothing about deterring Outside undesirables from going *to* Alaska. One Anchorage man became so incensed by all this that he testily handed out municipal-garbage-dump permits to his touring

friends, urging them to exhibit these when asked for identification papers. At one of an interminable series of Senate-
committee hearings that preceded statehood, a Republican
National Committeewoman from Alaska won bipartisan
admiration at home by testifying, tearfully, how thrilled
she'd been late in 1952 to be invited to President Eisenhower's first inauguration; with what uplifted feelings she'd
boarded a southbound plane; and how much of a shock it
had been when, at Seattle, she was treated little better than
an alien suspected of opium-smuggling and perhaps a trace
of moral turpitude to boot.

Now that Alaska is a state, its citizens' distress over such
federal indignities is being swiftly replaced by anxiety lest
Washington leave them too much to their own sketchy devices. In 1957, the *News-Miner,* which, in the heart of a colorful state, goes in heavily for color-printing and splashes
its pages with red, green, blue, yellow, brown, pink, orange,
and lavender ink, declared, "Alaska today is like a giant bud
—ready to burst into bloom under the magic sunshine of
statehood." The author of that pronouncement may not
have been thinking of the forget-me-not, but that small and
gentle blossom has proved to be as apt a state posy as it ever
was a territorial one. One Alaskan remarked to me, "Some
of us look at ourselves as though we were a boy who has suddenly grown up and whose father takes him aside and says,
'Listen, Son, you've been nagging at me all these years about
how you wanted to go off on your own and be a man. O.K.,
you win. Now run along and be one.' We can't help wondering if we've had the proper training and if we may not
have to come crawling abjectly back to the old man for help
—in our case, of course, not Father, but Uncle."

There seems little likelihood that this well-heeled old
relative will leave Alaska high and dry for quite some time,
if ever. For one thing, the Alaska Statehood Act passed by
Congress stipulated that Uncle Sam was to retain title to

more than two-thirds of Alaska's three hundred and seventy-five million acres. Of Alaska's annual gross product, which amounts to around five hundred million dollars, federal spending accounts for three hundred and fifty million. The most openhanded of the federal agencies has been the Department of Defense, whose outlays are so vital to the Alaskan economy that, as one Alaskan told me, "Peace could slaughter us." Alaskans were the first to concede that there were grimly ironic overtones to the last sentence of Section 20 of Article I of their state constitution, which says that "The military shall be in strict subordination to the civil power." The fact was that the civil power, once Alaska became a state, couldn't have begun to make ends meet if it hadn't been for the seventy thousand contemporary Alaskans—one-third of the total—who were members, dependents, or civilian employees of the armed forces. This reliance was even more pronounced in 1943, when the population consisted of a hundred and fifty-two thousand service men and seventy-four thousand civilians. In 1939, by stark contrast, there were five hundred and twenty-four men in uniform in Alaska. Every year since the Second World War, nearly three hundred million dollars from the military's mighty reservoir of funds has drained beneficently into Alaska's parched economy.

Alaska, which one resident described to me, with mixed feelings, as "the last happy hunting ground of the federal agencies," has harbored other Washington agencies in large and lucrative force, and there have been, in fact, so many bureaucrats active in the state that they regularly step on each other's toes. The Department of the Interior has had jurisdiction over natural gas in Alaska, but the Post Office Department could not use a cheaply available local supply of this fuel to heat its branch in the Far North village of Barrow, because the branch was in a private building and Interior had decreed that the gas might be piped into none but federally owned structures. Only an Act of Congress could resolve this prickly situation. Among similar anomalies called to my attention were a couple of isolated public schools run by the national Fish and Wildlife Service, and a couple of others where white children were educated under the aegis of the Bureau of Indian Affairs.

Moreover, the Statehood Act was not a model of clarity. It conveyed to Alaska the large white Colonial mansion in Juneau that has traditionally been occupied by the governor, but it neglected to yield up the furnishings (uneasy lies the gubernatorial head that sleeps in a federal bed), and Congress had to pass a number of amendments to correct this and other discrepancies. Alaskans were a trifle disappointed, though, when Congress turned over to them, with no strings attached, the large stone building in Juneau that houses the governor's office and both chambers of the legislature. The building needed extensive repairs, and Alaskans had hoped that the federal government would hang on to it long enough to foot the bill.

Alaskans first formally besought Washington to grant them statehood in 1916. Upon being turned down, they grew discouraged for a while, but between 1945 and 1957, Bob Bartlett, their delegate to Congress, who, voteless though he was, could introduce bills, faithfully and unavailingly came up with a statehood bill every year. In 1955, the territorial legislature decided to take a unilateral step toward statehood by calling a constitutional convention. Alaska has never been a wealthy region, except in terms of natural resources. Its first state budget was fixed at twenty-six and a half million dollars, or slightly more than one per cent of New York City's. As a territorial ward of the federal government, it could have got its guardian Uncle to foot the bill for the convention. But the legislators in Juneau wanted their constitution to be their own affair, and accordingly they appropriated three hundred and fifty thousand dollars for the convention, out of their own modest tax receipts. (Alaska has a blessedly simple way of computing state income taxes; the levy comes to a flat fourteen per cent of an individual's federal tax.) This legislative decision was traceable to the same stubborn pride that prompts some contemporary Alaskans even to seem to disparage their own children. "My kids couldn't possibly feel the way I do about Alaska," one normally doting father there told me. "They're Alaskans by chance. I'm an Alaskan by choice."

Because the 1787 Constitutional Convention at Philadelphia had fifty-five delegates, Alaska patriotically decided on the same number. (A replica of the Liberty Bell, crack and all, stands outside the capital building in Juneau.) Because the state constitution of New Jersey, which since its adoption in 1946 has been widely acclaimed the very model of such a document, evolved from a convention at Rutgers, Alaska decided to draft its constitution in an academic setting, at its University. The constitution that emerged from the convention, in February, 1956, provided for, among other things, a minimum voting age of nineteen and an uncommonly strong executive branch of the state government, in which the secretary of state is the only elected official besides the governor, who appoints all other officers, and thus wields unusual political power. Two months after the convention ended, a special election was held, and Alaskans ratified their brand-new constitution.

Not all Alaskans were in favor of statehood; it was endorsed by a vote of only three to two in a 1946 referendum, and even after attaining statehood, quite a few residents would have been just as happy if territorialism had persisted. This group included some who feared that statehood would attract too many new settlers, increasing the budget, raising the taxes, and generally spoiling Alaska's clubby atmosphere. Four of the territory's six daily newspapers

were militant opponents of statehood, but the publishers of
the two largest ones were among its most ardent advocates. Robert B. Atwood, of the Anchorage *Times,* made
some thirty trips to Washington to plead the cause before
congressmen and the President, while C. W. Snedden, of the
News-Miner, travelled all over the forty-eight states urging
publishers to write editorials in favor of immediate statehood, and considerately offering to furnish suitable exhorta-
tory copy. "It wasn't too tough a mission," Snedden told me.
"Who would run an editorial *against* statehood? That
would be like blasting motherhood." In Washington, D.C.,
one day, Snedden stopped in to see Representative Joseph
W. Martin, Jr., who was then the majority leader of the
House, and who was a stubborn adversary of statehood.
Martin had taken the position that most Americans didn't
much care what happened to Alaska, but he confessed to
Snedden that he was beginning to waver; why, he said, his
own home-town paper had just printed an editorial strongly
endorsing Alaska's petition! This made Snedden feel especially good, since he had written the editorial in question.

It was June 30, 1958, at 8:04 P.M. Eastern Daylight Saving Time, that the Senate followed the lead of the House
and passed the bill admitting Alaska to the roster of states.
This was 2:04 P.M. Alaska Standard Time in Fairbanks, and
the *News-Miner,* an evening paper, was about to go to press.
Snedden held up the press run long enough to insert a complete account of Alaska's triumph. Then he called the Eiel-
son Air Force Base, just outside the city, and learned that a
jet bomber was about to take off for Washington. He rushed
a bundle of papers to the base, stowed them aboard, and had
his statehood story on every Congressional desk the following
morning. Throughout Alaska, there were wild celebrations.
In Anchorage, the citizens put a torch to what those who
had assembled the fuel insisted was a forty-nine-ton bon-

fire. (Actually, Anchorage had two forty-nine-ton bonfires; a couple of days before statehood came through, some pranksters ignited the first pile of logs that had been collected.) In Fairbanks, the Air Force gave the civic authorities a batch of the bright-gold dye that castaways from plane crashes at sea spread on the water to attract the attention of searching aircraft. The Fairbanksians joyously dumped the dye into the Chena River, but unfortunately the substance will work only in salt water, and the Chena turned a bilious green instead of gold.

Alaskans were not so resentful as might have been expected that the forty-nine-star flag was doomed to enjoy such a brief moment of official glory before Hawaii joined the Union. There was some mild grumbling, inevitably, because Arizona had been able to remain the youngest state for forty-six years, while Alaska enjoyed less than a year as baby of the family. "Now that we're no longer the newest state, but merely the biggest," one Alaskan remarked to me, "why, we're nothing but another Texas."

By far the majority of Alaskans, however, were delighted to have Hawaii piped aboard the ship of statehood. (The two areas have at least one natural attribute in common: in neither are there any snakes.) In February, 1959, eighty-eight Alaskans who had banded together as the Alaska Friends of Hawaiian Statehood chartered a plane and flew from Anchorage to Honolulu, to give aid and comfort to the Hawaiians, who were then nervously awaiting the verdict of Congress. One of the leaders of this evangelistic delegation was a wartime Army lieutenant colonel, subsequently an Anchorage real-estate operator, named Marvin R. Marston. (Marston is known throughout Alaska as "Muktuk," which is the Eskimo word for whale blubber. He got the nickname by once outeating a champion Eskimo *muktuk*-eater. *"Muktuk"* is not to be confused with *"mukluk,"* which is Eskimo for "leather boot," although an Alaskan joke has it that the only difference between the two items is a single consonant in their names, inasmuch as they taste just alike.)

Colonel Marston, who, I learned, had grandly forgiven one Hawaiian paper for referring to him as "Old Whale-meat," was organizer of a unique martial body during the Second World War. This was an outfit that is usually re-ferred to as the Eskimo Scouts—its original, formal desig-nation was the Alaska Territorial Guard—a volunteer group of some thirty-seven hundred Eskimos who operated out of sixty-five villages, collecting and passing along intelli-gence and standing ready to repel invaders. The volunteers were sometimes known as Gruening's Guerrillas. Marston spent three and a half years recruiting and training the Scouts, and they made up a spectacularly varied unit, their ages ranging from thirteen to eighty-two. The thirteen-year-old was signed up on the recommendation of some senior Eskimos, who said that anybody who had already shot seven caribou, as the youngster had, could presumbly bring down a Japanese. The octogenarian got in after brushing aside Marston's doubts as to whether his legs would hold up in a fight. "I'm not planning to run anywhere," the old man said mildly. "I'll shoot them when they get to me." He then hauled himself creakily to his feet, plucked a rifle out of the hands of a friend standing nearby, knocked a beer can off a fence post a hundred yards away, and sagged contentedly back down.

There are still around a thousand Eskimo Scouts avail-able for duty, some of them organized into groups of no more than nine and some residing in villages—Tuntutu-liag, Kwigillingok, Akiak, Tuluksak, Kasiglook, and Eek, to name a few—so tiny that they do not appear on maps and most Alaskans have never heard of them. For quite a number of Eskimos, wartime allegiance to the Scouts repre-sented the first experience of belonging to any social unit larger than the family. Under statehood, however, it has been estimated that only about ten per cent of Alaska's Indians, Aleuts, and Eskimos still lead a traditional, primitive existence. (It wasn't so long ago that the Alaska Coca-Cola bottler, who also distributes stronger stuff, had a special Rainier Beer bottle cap designed for the illiterate-Eskimo trade. There was a picture of a reindeer on the cap, and this, it was rightly surmised, would impel some thirsty zoöphiles to ask bartenders for the Reindeer beer and be served its homonym.) The remaining ninety per cent of the natives have taken an increasingly active part in community affairs, and many Alaskans have been dismayed by this new sophistication. Travel by air, for instance, is now as old hat to the Eskimos as travel by dog sled, and when a group of them took their first train ride, in the course of a visit to Anchorage, they were puzzled by the absence of safety belts.

When Alaska's first state legislature convened, in January, 1959, there were six Eskimos and one Indian in the forty-man House, and two Eskimos and one Indian in the twenty-man Senate. One of the Eskimos in the House had never cast a vote until, the previous October, he cast one for himself. When the Senate elected its president, the two nominees were an Eskimo and the Indian. The Eskimo won, conceivably because, although a carpenter by trade, his favorite avocational reading for some years had been Robert's Rules of Order. The Eskimo legislators usually go down the line together on sectional issues, and they have become known, informally, as the Ice Bloc.

Most of the natives in that first legislature were Democrats. In 1953, the territorial legislature had been predominantly Republican. But though Alaska achieved statehood under a Republican national administration, the change was actually voted by a Democratic Congress, and much of the leadership in the statehood campaign had been provided by such Democrats as Gruening, Bartlett, and Egan.

As a state, accordingly, Alaska was at the start almost as overwhelmingly Democratic as though, instead of being partly above the Arctic Circle, it had been wholly below the Mason-Dixon Line. Alaska's electoral votes were all but conceded to Kennedy during the 1960 campaign. The fact that they were won by Nixon may be attributable to Alaskans' engaging perverseness, or to the rancor of the voters in Anchorage, where a large segment of the electorate dwells, against their Democratic statesmen who torpedoed the proposal to have the capital moved out of Juneau. Or it may simply be attributable to Nixon's election-eve flight to Anchorage. Above all, Alaskans love to have other Americans remember that they're part of the family.

The loneliest men in that first state legislature seemed to be not the ten natives but the seven Republicans. In one strongly Democratic precinct, a Republican showed up to register for a primary election and, after revealing his party affiliation, said jokingly to the official in charge, "I guess I'm in the wrong precinct." "Hell, you're in the wrong world," was the reply. Despite such Democratic popular strength, though, Alaska hadn't, and still hasn't, a single consequential Democratic newspaper. (In that respect, it is pretty much like most other American states.) The last such, a weekly in Juneau, folded a few months after my visit. It was published in a former church and edited by a former sheet-metal worker. (Alaskan journalism is full of such oddities. Sitka has a daily whose entire working staff consists of a man and his wife; Nome has a thrice-weekly paper run by a peppery little grandmother.) Labor unions, especially those in the building trades, have been a powerful political factor, and Alaska Republicans have commented tartly on the circumstance that, owing to a delay in appropriating the lawmakers' salaries after the 1959 legislature convened, some Democrats made ends meet by borrowing from the state's chief union lobbyist. When I asked one Democratic solon point blank if he was beholden to organized labor, he said, "Certainly not. I'm controlled by the principles of labor." Or so I took his answer to be until I mentioned it to an Alaskan Republican, who suggested that what his adversary had told me was, "I'm controlled by the principals of labor."

When the legislature meets, Juneau hums. The town's, and Alaska's, biggest hotel is the Baranof—it was named after the Czar's first governor—and a dimly lit chamber there, called the Bubble Room, is the legislators' favorite retreat. The hotel used to cool Bubble Room drinks with million-year-old ice chipped from the nearby Mendenhall Glacier; a chunk of this would stay in a glass without melting for hours at a stretch. To the distress of traditionalists and slow drinkers, the Bubble Room switched to ordinary, highly soluble ice, but it was a compensating solace to some Alaskan statesmen that, not long after statehood, the oasis, theretofore closed until the cocktail hour, began opening its doors at noon. During legislative sessions, the Bubble Room is jammed with legislators and lobbyists, and the latter, in the semi-darkness, sometimes find themselves sending free drinks over to people who aren't lawmakers at all, but simply travelling salesmen with thoughtful and thirsty expressions.

Alaskans on all levels are wonderfully hospitable, and twice during the maiden session of the legislature its members, who perhaps did not want to incur an undue sense of obligation, gave parties at the Baranof for the lobbyists. For one of these shindigs, the hosts had their constituents ship in regional delicacies from all over the state—caribou, elk, reindeer, moose, porcupine, bear, ptarmigan, king crab, shellfish, salmon, sea cucumber, and so on. Five hundred people, many of them transients who just happened to be strolling through the hotel, milled about, contentedly sipping drinks and nibbling at the feral *smörgåsbord*. The only untoward incident occurred when an Army colonel, conceivably believing—not without justification—that the military is so all-powerful in Alaska it can do and have whatever it wants, complained loudly about his cocktail to a shirt-sleeved bartender. When the bartender brusquely told him to mind his manners, the colonel stormed off to the Baranof's manager and demanded that the sassy servitor be fired. With some glee, the hotel man advised the complainant that the bartender was the chairman of the Alaska Senate Committee on Commerce and Labor.

What has concerned everyone in Alaska lately—legislators, lobbyists, and laymen alike—is the condition of the fledgling state's economy, which even a local booster group has described in print as "shaky." Alaskans are so cash conscious that in 1959, when their biggest winter sporting event, the North American Championship Sled Dog Race, was won for the first time by an Outsider, a veterinarian from Massachusetts, who took a purse of twenty-five hundred dollars, one woman standing at the finish line grumbled, as the new champ came pedalling past her behind his team of ten frost-breathing Huskies, "He ran a fine race, but I just hate to see him take the money out of Alaska."

Most of the new state's business activity has been in the retail-merchant and service fields. "All we do here is take in each other's wash and fix each other's watches," one Alaskan remarked disgustedly to me. It has been the hope of many Alaskans that tourism will bring in a welcome flow of Outside dollars, or Outside laundry, or Outside broken mainsprings. In 1959, nearly sixty thousand tourists visited the area, most of them in the summertime. One reason the visitors don't leave behind as many dollars as Alaskans might wish is the scarcity of roads; since the majority of visitors travel in and out by air, the number of souvenirs they can buy is apt to depend on airline baggage allowances. Moreover, there were at last reckoning only thirty-eight establishments that could fairly be described as hotels or motels in the entire state. A travel agent from Texas, who went to Alaska to arrange for a group tour he was going to shepherd north, found when he got to Anchorage that the sole accommodations he could book thereabouts were at a motel nine miles out of town. When I was in Alaska, just two hotels had bellhops. "If a person is very fussy about service, he shouldn't come to Alaska," a man told me in Fairbanks, where neither of the two main hotels had any bellhops, and the more centrally located had no dining room. "Sure, we want tourists, and we need tourists, but the trouble is that there are damn few people here who know how to take care of tourists. We just don't have any servant types around."

Exceedingly few large American businesses have had branches in Alaska, and people there regarded it as a happy portent when Woolworth's announced that it was about to move into Anchorage. The total deposits of all seventeen banks in the state came in 1959 to a mere seventy million dollars, and, according to the most up-to-date figures issued by the Bureau of Internal Revenue, in 1955 only twenty-six Alaskans had adjusted gross incomes of more than fifty thousand dollars. There has not been a single brokerage office or stock ticker in the state; Alaskans who have wanted to play the market have had to be shrewder than most in order to come out ahead, for the cheapest way they could keep abreast of quotations was to phone Seattle, fourteen hundred miles from Anchorage.

But while people of substantial wealth have been scarce, the desperately impoverished have been equally few. The closeness between the top and bottom strata was illustrated by the sandwich menu of a Fairbanks coffee shop. It offered three triple-deckers. There was a Career Girl's Special

(egg salad, bacon, lettuce, tomato, mayonnaise, and potato salad), at $1.25; an Executive's Special (roast beef,
lettuce, tomato, mayonnaise, and potato salad), at $1.45;
and a Banker's Special (turkey, bacon, tomato, crisp lettuce,
mayonnaise, and potato salad), at $1.55. While the price
range was narrow, the menu did at least provide evidence
that bankers in Alaska, like bankers everywhere, prefer
their lettuce crisp.

Alaska is known to have all but one of the thirty-three
raw materials that the United States considers strategic and
critical. (It has not been credited with diamonds, which
achieve the strategic status because of their industrial uses.)
Formerly, salmon fishing and gold were the principal sources
of income. Because of overfishing, however, the salmon catch
has fallen off by nearly two-thirds in the last two decades.
Although gold mining has been in a similar slump, Alaskans
continue to think and talk a lot about it too, and the U.S.O.
conducts leisure-time gold-panning expeditions for servicemen. In Fairbanks, real-estate agents still tout gold
mines in newspaper ads illustrated with photographs of
heaped-up nuggets, and every few years a rumor of a get-
rich-quick strike sweeps one section or another, but it has
been a long time since anyone really profited from such an
outcry—except the bush pilots who cart their avid brethren
around.

A while ago, a homesteader, upon being asked how he
proposed to support his family of nine on a tract he had applied for, cheerfully replied that he expected to find gold.
His optimism may not have been much more unjustified
than that of many other homesteaders. Alaskans disagree
among themselves as to how many homesteading families,
each of which moves onto a hundred-and-sixty-acre plot
and is expected to cultivate a part of this within three years,
actually make a go of it. According to a 1955 report on homesteading on the Kenai Peninsula, south of Anchorage, fifty-

nine per cent of the land on which homesteaders had previously encamped was unoccupied or abandoned when the
report came out, and thirty-one per cent more was being
used for residential purposes but wasn't being farmed.
"All too many find that Alaska is a hard bargainer, taking
their savings and their hopes and giving them in return a
bit of land which they are powerless to use," the report
said. When a caravan of migrants from Detroit reached Anchorage in 1959, after a miserable trip, it was accorded a
rousing public reception, but privately many Alaskans expressed concern about the newcomers. "If these people
were friends of mine," one highly placed state executive
told me, "I'd feel guilty if I didn't say to them, 'For God's
sake, go back to Michigan.'" Some Alaskans thought it was
ironic that when the hard-pressed caravan's principal truck
broke down along the Canadian stretch of the Alaska
Highway, its contents were transferred to and delivered to
their destination by, of all vehicles, a new garbage truck that
happened also to be en route from Michigan to Anchorage.

Like gold, most of the minerals with which Alaska is
richly endowed seem to have feeble commercial potentiali-
ties right now. (A valuable by-product of mining, though,
has been the excavation of a rich store of prehistoric relics.
The chief paleontologist at the University, after sending
many such treasures to Outside museums, had enough left
over to edge his driveway with fragments of mastodon
bones.) "Until we get some dependable surface transportation in this state, aside from dog sleds, all the ore we have
is nothing but dirt and rocks," one mining man told me de-
jectedly. "Dogs just don't grow big enough to pull it. We
have some hills on the southeast coast so loaded with mag-
netite ore that ships passing near them get pulled off course.
We have enough tin and bismuth near Nome to keep the
United States supplied for years, but until somebody
builds a road or a railroad out that way, they're just so much

tundra. The sad and simple truth is that we still don't have anything you can't get somewhere else at a much lower cost. Maybe our best hope is for the rest of the free world's resources to be rapidly exhausted."

For the last few years, many Alaskans have looked to oil for economic succor. Geologists have estimated that there may be oil under as much as a hundred and thirty million acres of Alaska, or slightly more than a third of the state. In this case, Outside capital has come along in a big way, mainly because oilmen never operate in a small way, and around ten million dollars a year is now being spent in Alaska by oil companies. In the summer of 1959, fifty helicopters under hire to roving geologists buzzed busily in and out of Anchorage. That city has not only a Petroleum Club but also a Petroleum Wives' Club, and the University of Alaska has added to its curriculum a course in petroleum engineering. There was one successful oil strike, on the Kenai Peninsula, but there have been rather spectacular setbacks, too, among them a dry hole that cost its bruised entrepreneurs six million dollars. Quite a few people—both Alaskans and Outsiders—have profited handsomely from oil, but almost entirely by speculating in oil leases rather than by selling oil, practically none of which has yet been sent to market.

Nearly everything is expensive in Alaska, in large part because of shipping charges. Ninety-two per cent of all food consumed in Alaska, except for fish, is imported. In the other forty-eight continental states, freight rates are equalized so that consumers far removed from a producer pay the same retail price for his goods as those close by. Except in the case of a very few items, such as cigarettes, chewing gum, canned soup, and certain candy bars, equalization has been slow in coming to Alaska (and to Hawaii). The shipping charge on Grand Rapids furniture ordered by Alaskans amounts to more than the price of the furniture. It has been costing a salesman based in Seattle slightly over a dollar a pound to pay for lugging north the samples he shows the widely scattered customers along his route. And some salesmen, because Alaskan storekeepers, even in isolated villages, have been as choosy about the merchandise they stock as the proprietors of Madison Avenue specialty shops, have had to cart around nearly a ton of samples. Alaskans do considerable complaining about the freight charges that figure so importantly in their lives. Being genial folks, they also do considerable joking about them. A favorite character in Alaskan mythology is a barber who, on being asked by a customer why he demanded two and a half dollars for a haircut, replied, "It's the freight."

The farther north in Alaska one goes, the stiffer prices get. If, for purposes of comparison, the cost of living in Seattle—a rather expensive community compared to most of the United States—is set at an index figure of 100, the index for Juneau is 123.5; for Anchorage, 140.8; for Fairbanks, 153.5; and for Nome a whopping 166. During the winter, when Nome is isolated save by air, fresh milk may cost eighty-eight cents a quart there, and it is not uncommon in that city, as in other Alaskan outposts, to hear a child ask its mother a question that in most parts of America would sound either strange or plaintive: "Mommy, would you make me a glass of milk?" Nome is so far off even the beaten Alaska track that it had only one practicing lawyer when I was there. When legal trouble was brewing, he would try to pacify the disputants, knowing that if he failed and they went to court only one of them could engage him, which meant that the other would have to fly in counsel, at considerable expense, from several hundred miles away.

Nome was a boom town at the turn of the century, with prospectors for gold swarming all over the place. It boomed again during the war, when it was a refuelling station for planes being ferried from Fairbanks to the Soviet Union.

Nome is a place where the manager of the Northern Commercial Company, Alaska's leading chain store, can say—
in fact, can only with difficulty be restrained from saying—
that he sells refrigerators to Eskimos. But with local prices
staggeringly high and sixty per cent of the labor force unemployed, nobody has been buying much of anything, and
there has been a hollow ring to the cheer that Nome's
high-school students lustily, almost defiantly, intone: "Clap
your hands! Stamp your feet! Nome! Nome! Can't be beat!"

One bright spot in Alaska's inflated situation is that if
prices are lofty, so—when jobs are available—are wages.
During the relatively short summer construction season,
migrant workers from Outside hustle to Alaska, drawn less
by the exhilarating scenery than by the exhilarating pay
scale. The University of Alaska has been concluding its
academic year in mid-May, so that its students who want
summer jobs can grab them before the influx from Outside
reaches engulfing proportions. Plumbers and carpenters can
earn twelve thousand a year without overworking, and such
specialists are so much in demand that they can afford to be
pretty lordly about responding to calls for help. A common
phrase in Alaska is "Do it yourself or get mad." When one
of Nome's two hotels burned down several years ago, the
proprietor, though he had had no previous experience in the
building trades, gamely set about reconstructing it with his
own hands. With both labor and materials so expensive, a
contractor-built house that in 1959 would have cost eleven
thousand dollars in Los Angeles cost twenty-six thousand in
Anchorage. Alaskans can, and without much goading will,
tell you the precise dimensions of their houses and those of
their neighbors; a man's wealth is often judged by the floor
space he can call his own. One man in Anchorage, who had
moved his family into new quarters not long before, told
me smugly that he now presided over exactly two thousand

and fifty-six square feet. I gathered that he would have considered any description of his home as a two-thousand-square-footer outrageously inaccurate.

Most Alaskans seemed to agree that much of what ailed them could be cured by the establishment of some year-round manufacturing industries—ideally, industries that could produce goods both for local consumption and for export. If the ships that ferry materials to Alaska could return south with a back haul, Alaskans reasoned, the northbound freight rates would decrease. This was the dream of many Alaskan businessmen, and I guess still is, and maybe will be for a long time to come. There were others I talked to, however, who believed that their state's greatest potential source of economic strength lay not in the direction of their sister states but in the Far East. One of the few large investments that have been made in Alaska in recent years was a forty-one-million-dollar capital outlay by a Japanese syndicate, representing two-thirds of the backing of a lumber mill at Sitka—the first major Japanese-sponsored industrial establishment on United States soil. Other Japanese capitalists have shown interest in developing Alaskan coal and Alaskan iron, and there has been much vague but stimulating talk about a Hong Kong financier who was reputedly flashing a fifty-million-dollar letter of credit around Anchorage and indicating that he was itching to use it.

Money is going to have to come from somewhere. An economic report that came out early in 1960 gloomily declared, "Alaska is entering a very difficult stage. Truly, a financial crisis looms ahead." Beyond 1961, the report predicted, Alaska—unless a golden-egg-laying goose materialized soon —wouldn't even be able to pay for its operating expenses, let alone make any capital improvements. And those the state hoped to make, according to the report, were modest enough. In fact, the only one planned through 1966 by the

Office of the Governor was the installation, at a cost of twenty-five thousand dollars, of a new elevator at the Pioneers Home. The elevator in use wasn't big enough to accommodate a stretcher.

The southeastern, or panhandle, section of Alaska, a five-hundred-mile-long tract that includes Juneau, Sitka, Ketchikan, Haines, and a host of smaller seacoast towns, has often been called a satellite of Seattle. As far as many Alaskans are concerned, the whole state is a satellite of Seattle—or, as some people put it, a Seattleite. In the summer of 1946 a delegation of Alaska businessmen chartered a plane and, carrying along the then Governor Gruening and a plentiful supply of straw hats (to show they came from a temperate zone) and moose steaks, flew to Chicago by way of Edmonton, Great Falls, Fargo, and Minneapolis. Their objective was, like that of Columbus, to establish a trade route to the east. To the anguish of various Seattle groups firmly opposed to any such deviationism, the Alaskans accomplished their mission, and soon Northwest Airlines was flying passengers and freight between the Midwest and Anchorage three times a week, giving Seattle a wide berth and saving three hundred and twenty-five miles on each flight.

But the rebellion was short-lived. By 1953, Northwest had cut back to a schedule of a round trip a week along the straw-hat-and-moose-steak trail. Ever since, Alaskans have been muttering about sinister pressures, and, to back up such allegations, they have pointed out that the Post Office Department, possibly at the behest of the legislators of a state much more powerful politically than Alaska, has never authorized the shipment of mail to Alaska through any relay station but Seattle. That city, which has a population of seven hundred and fifty thousand, or more than three times that of all Alaska, has for years been the seat of, among other Northwest trading empires, the Alaskan salmon industry.

The blame for the overfishing that has caused the slump in this business is placed by many Alaskans squarely on the absentee owners.

An official of the Seattle Chamber of Commerce once solemnly asserted, "Alaska is Seattle's best customer, and Seattle is Alaska's best supplier." At first hearing, this sounded like a fine, fraternal, you-help-me-and-I'll-help-you relationship; when Alaskans considered it some more, they realized that it was merely a gallingly redundant reminder that Seattle sells and Alaska buys (often, Alaskans lament, at prices unilaterally fixed by the supplier). Alaskans have had enough troubles of their own not to laugh at other people's misfortunes, but they could not completely stifle their chuckles when the news arrived (through a Seattle paper— thirty cents for the daily edition, sixty for the Sunday) that a United States senator from the State of Washington had broken three bones by dropping a case of canned salmon on his foot.

Pleased though they may be with their fellow-citizens and their physical surroundings, Alaskans reveal mixed feelings when asked about their state's role in the Union. "A fair half of us are living in the past, and the other half are living in the future," one old-timer remarked to me, "so the present doesn't worry us a bit." The cheery theme of a teachers' conference in Fairbanks in the spring of 1959 was "Tomorrow Is Here!," but one of the principal speakers was a Juneau economist named George W. Rogers, who had written shortly before, "Alaska is not something that is or has been; it is a promising potential of something that can be."

Many Alaskans, optimistic about the destiny of their much-loved land, have been furious at the sour-mouthed busybodies who have proposed that, since most states have abbreviations, a logical one for Alaska would be Alas. But there has been so little unanimity among Alaskans that even the state's taxi-drivers have neglected their traditional

pose of omniscience and freely admitted to uncertainty. One
of them told me, "Sometimes I fear we'll end up a disgrace to
the nation, and then I stop and look around and say to myself, 'Oh, what a marvellous, glorious state this can be!' "

Most Alaskans, while awaiting transfusions of capital from
Wall Street, Tokyo, or Hong Kong, and the development
of a new benevolence among the entrepreneurs and shippers
of Seattle, seemed to me to be reasonably content with what
they had. What they had, mainly, was animals and scenery,
which afforded them ample recreation and solace, and
would, they hoped, do the same for future swarms of tourists. Game is so abundant in Alaska that some guides, on taking hunters into the bush, inquire in advance, as though they
were shoe salesmen, just what size their customers want. The
bush pilots who fly sportsmen in for the kill make a handsome living; one of them has bought a new airplane annually for the last seven years. When it's springtime in Kotzebue, on the Arctic Ocean, there may be as many as thirty
small planes parked on the ice at a time.

I flew to Kotzebue, from Nome, on a scheduled airline
flight; but, printed timetable notwithstanding, my plane
turned out to be a single-engine job, with a capacity of
three passengers, and skis for landing gear. We detoured,
approaching our destination, because the pilot had heard
that a similar craft, under charter to some Outside polar-
bear hunter, was lost out over the ice, and maybe we could
spot it. (We couldn't, but we later heard it was all right.)
The first polar-bear hunter I encountered at Kotzebue was a
leather-faced Texas farmer on his first journey to Alaska,
and the first day he was there he flew out over the ice and,
with his first shot after the plane had landed, brought down
the first polar bear he'd ever seen outside of a zoo. After the
ice begins to break up, some hunters track polar bear by
boat, cruising up alongside their prey and shooting without

getting their feet wet. The airplane polar-bear hunters, who at least dismount, have nothing but contempt for these deck-chair sportsmen—a scorn that is perhaps exceeded only by the derision heaped on *them* by Alaskans who believe that the one sporting way to bag a polar bear is to go after it, Eskimo-fashion, with dog sled and spear.

Nowadays, fewer and fewer Eskimos go after anything Eskimo-fashion. I met a man from Anchorage who made a jaunt to Kotzebue and was disgusted at having an Eskimo boy try to cadge a dime off him. Many of the Eskimos there were ardent motion-picture fans, with a special addiction to Westerns. Kotzebue had a population of only twelve hundred, nine-tenths of it native, but it had two movie theatres. Not very long before, one of them had stationed guards at its exits when a particularly ancient picture was showing, so that its audience wouldn't be able to escape and patronize the rival theatre. There was no television in Kotzebue (as there was in Fairbanks, Anchorage, and Juneau), and Radio Moscow, which had been sending out programs in Eskimo, came through better than most American stations. The only year-round hotel in town occupied the second story of a general store that, presumably because a local market existed for the stuff, stocked Rudolph the Red-Nosed Reindeer Toilet Water. There were just two other places in Kotzebue that sold merchandise of any kind. (One of them flaunted the slogan "Remember—Before You Buy—Try Us.") Up to 1956, the only electricity in Kotzebue was that furnished by privately owned generators. Then the federal government installed a power plant, and the local citizenry had quite a time buying strings of blinking Christmas-tree lights, although there is not a tree of any species within a hundred miles of the place. In the wintertime, the residents dump their garbage on the ice; when the ice breaks up, the stuff floats out to sea. Kotzebue has no water supply. Its water has always been hauled in from a nearby river—often by dog sleds laden with chunks of ice. The children there bathe in melted snow. The village had one taxi, one dishwashing machine, and five churches—Quaker, Pentecostal, Baptist, Catholic, and Episcopal. The local Catholic priest was president of the Chamber of Commerce—the world's northernmost Chamber.

To the dismay of those Alaskans who hate to see the encroaching refinements of civilization, Kotzebue had built an up-to-date jail. "We're very proud of our jail," a Kotzebue civic booster told me. "The day it opened, our Mothers' Club held open house there and served coffee and doughnuts."

Kotzebue was scheduled to get a new hospital soon, for the treatment of natives from all the villages within reasonable distance of it—a few hundred miles, by Alaskan standards—and in that respect would be better off than a good many Alaskan communities. (Its environs were also scheduled to get a new harbor, blasted out by nuclear fission, and in *that* respect, since nobody could say precisely how the fowl, fish, and animals would react, let alone the humans, Kotzebue may have been less privileged.) Medical service in Alaska has, by the very nature of the place, been limited. Until fairly recently, it was customary for relatively well-to-do Alaskans to send their wives to Seattle to have their babies. When Governor Egan was on the point of death, after two operations in his own state, he was flown to Seattle for a third, life-saving round of surgery. More than one Alaskan doctor ruefully confessed to me that it was all but impossible to lure a first-rate specialist to so thinly populated an area as theirs unless he was infused with the missionary spirit or loved to camp out. In all of Alaska, there were only two pediatricians in private practice and only one psychiatrist—a woman who could not handle too many patients because she had nine children of her own. Some Alaskans appraised their professional men by unique criteria: I ran into one businessman who spoke glowingly of his family physician, whom he regarded as absolutely topnotch because of the agility with which he could track down and dispatch a caribou.

All Alaskans—doctors, lawyers, Indians, thieves—had their pet animal stories. In Anchorage, I was told three times of a half-tame moose—assigned to a different sector of town in each telling—that regularly came around to a housewife's kitchen door for potato handouts. One day, the story went, the housewife was out of town, and the moose, hungry and impatient, pushed its nose against the door, a plate-glass one, and demolished it. (In the bedroom of one Anchorage home I did visit, I noticed a rifle perched on a ledge behind the bed. The paterfamilias explained that his neighborhood was full of prowling moose, that his bedroom had a picture window, and that he kept the weapon there just in case.) A member of the state legislature from the northwest was convinced that near Unalakleet, there lived a creature built along the reputed lines of the Abominable Snowman of the Himalayas—a manlike creature at least six feet tall, covered with thick fur. The legislator told me that while he had never actually laid eyes on the critter himself, it had been sighted several times by witnesses whose veracity he trusted as much as he did that of any of his fellow-solons. The people who claimed to have seen this monster, I gathered, did not find it especially abominable. It was, after all, a fellow-Alaskan.

Not long after I had made a visit to Kotzebue, I met a lawyer in Fairbanks who was the only Alaskan I ever heard admit that he didn't care for big-game hunting. "Some of my friends consider me a real nut because I don't hunt and I don't fish and I don't fly a plane," he said. "Personally, I think it's my own business whether I shoot a polar bear or not. When you stop to think about it, a polar-bear rug can be very impractical. First you have to have a large enough room, which can be expensive up here, and then you have to be careful whenever you walk through your own house that you don't trip over the damn thing's head."

I heard no such heretical views about Alaskan scenery. While taking their routine rides through the skies, Alaskans of many years' residence hop from one side of a plane to the other, pressing their noses against the windows in order not to miss any new views of the magnificent terrain that they so contentedly call their own. Alaskan geography can make even doctors, whose prose is ordinarily on the stuffy side, become rhapsodic; one of them has written, "We are given the opportunity now to insure that no longer need the un-recorded medical voice be sent plaintively wailing across the waters of the Inland Passage to quiver in the Susitna Flats, or be sent rumbling toward the peaks of Mount Mc-Kinley only to wither and be dissipated in the Wilderness." What he meant was simply that a new Alaskan medical jour-nal was coming out. (It subsequently recorded, among other unusual clinical experiences, a physician's vain struggle to save the lives of some Eskimos who had contracted botulism from eating beluga-whale flippers that had been preserved in seal oil.) Allusions to Mount McKinley, such as the doc-tor's, are not lightly made in Alaska. The degree to which it and its adjacent heights have affected Alaskan prose styles can be measured by a decree handed down by one bygone judge, who after hearing the garbled pros and cons of a spat between two drunken gamblers indited, "Above the mists of inebriety which befogged the mental landscape of the principals in this case at that time rise a few jagged peaks of fact which must guide the court notwithstanding their temporary intellectual eclipse."

Mount McKinley is the state's No. 1 symbol, even though, wearing a year-round crown of snow and ice, it contributes little to Alaskan efforts to convince tourists of the mildness of local weather. The motto of the University of Alaska is "*Ad Summum,*" and the undergraduate yearbook is called *Denali,* an Indian word meaning "Great One," and a common pet name for the big mountain. Alaska's favorite painter, the late Sydney Laurence, specialized in portraits of the Great One. A Brooklyn man, he came to Alaska in 1904, with Paris and the Boer War behind him, and before his death, in 1940, he is believed to have painted the mountain some ten thousand times. Alaskans, who bought most of the paintings, never tire of Mount McKinley, or of mountains in general.

"You remember that old child's game king-of-the-mountain?" a Fairbanks man asked me. "Well, here in Alaska we're all equal—not in the sense of having the same material possessions, but in the sense of feeling that when it comes to the land we live in, we're all sitting on top of the heap. Land fascinates me. There are parts of this country that I guess some people might call bleak, but I call them pretty. I like to divide my time between prospecting and hunting for mountain sheep, and I sometimes catch myself wondering why. You can't make any money prospecting nowadays, and it's certainly not that I like killing animals, especially sheep. Sheep hunting is the hardest damn work in the world. Still, it gets you up high. The best thing, I guess, is that though I'm prospecting part of the time and hunting sheep part of the time, I'm looking at scenery all of the time. When you get on top of one of these mountains on a clear day and look out for miles and miles, and there's nothing, absolutely nothing, that's taller than you are, it's the most beautiful experience a man can have."

Recollections
of
an Intourist
Tourist

My wife is what people who study consumer habits would call an impulse shopper. She is inspired to some of her giddiest whims by window displays or roadside billboards; and it was characteristic of her to tell me unexpectedly, early in July of 1958, that she'd just read a magazine advertisement for a tour of the Soviet Union, and why didn't we go? I could think offhand of no logical argument against going, especially when she pointed out that nearly five thousand other Americans would probably be making a similar trip that summer. Some of these, it developed, were to go in posses— of athletes, for instance, and of astronomers—bent on engaging in their own mysterious rites. Others were individuals on special missions—a washing-machine salesman hoping to sell washing machines, Mrs. Roosevelt hoping to sell the brotherhood of man. The vast majority, however—if the word "vast" can be applied, even relatively, to a trickle —consisted of run-of-the-mill tourists like Jinny and me.

In a sense, the most challenging aspect of a trip to the Soviet Union is its aftermath. I know people who have been to Saudi Arabia and Sierra Leone, but on their homecoming they could hardly have been grilled to anywhere near the extent we were. Not only is the person who returns from Russia expected to discourse at length on his personal experiences (even color slides are tolerated) but he is expected to be an inexhaustible source of intimate, throbbing, hair-raising, up-to-the-minute behind-the-scenes intelligence about what is really going on There—and, indeed, what is going on in parts of There several thousand miles from any part he laid eyes on. My wife and I thoroughly alienated one stay-at-home neighbor of ours by insisting that we knew nothing more about the whereabouts and state of health of Marshal Zhukov than we gleaned from the New York *Times;* the neighbor was sure we were holding out on him.

As if in preparation for the encounters with the Hot-Stove League that lie ahead, the hit-and-run tourist is likely, while in the Soviet Union, to try to secure and stow away some exclusive nuggets of information. I recall the chagrin I felt in Leningrad, when, at the end of a culturally uplifting afternoon, Jinny and I ran into an Englishman who announced that he had just gone on an automobile outing to two palaces. Two palaces! A car! We were consumed with envy.

"*We've* just seen the icons at the Russian Museum," I said, putting up a brave front.

"Been there," said the Englishman witheringly.

In Moscow, several days later, we again ran into the Englishman, and the smug fellow got his comeuppance. A few hours before he got it, my wife and I, along with a crowd of other tourists, had visited the All-Union Agricultural Exposition—a sprawling, permanent, World's-Fair type of exhibition on the outskirts of the capital—and there an American girl I'll call Geraldine (I am not using her, or any other tourist's, real name) had asked our guide if it was true that there was a shortage of wool in the U.S.S.R. The guide, a steadfast Communist, reacted warily to any question he thought might be loaded. And since Geraldine took great delight in twitting guides, any question of hers, he had learned, was almost sure to be. "Shortage? Shortage?" he parried, though his English was normally quite good. "I do not recognize this word."

After Geraldine had prodded him awhile, he finally gave a little ground. "We have shortage of nylon, but of wool, satin—no," he said. Later, back at our hotel, I heard the two-palace Englishman remark to Geraldine that he had seen some colored stockings in a show window of GUM, Moscow's main department store. He wondered if they were nylons. "Probably not," said Geraldine crisply. "I thought everybody knew there's a shortage of nylon in Russia." The Englishman was crushed.

In the lobby of Moscow's Hotel Metropole, Jinny and I overheard a colloquy between two American men.

"I've just been fifty miles outside of Moscow," said the first. "That's where you see what's *really* going on."

"How did you manage to swing it?" asked the other.

"By yelling at Intourist," his companion replied. "It's the only way to deal with these people. Tomorrow I have something even hotter on the fire, but I can't tell you what." And he strutted off, exuding smugness and mystification.

The second man turned to us. "There's a typical example of a closed mind," he said, nodding toward the first fellow's back. "Personally, I've found Intourist very obliging. That guy is one of those Americans who come here merely to confirm their antagonistic preconceptions about this country." He paused. "Say, you wouldn't happen to have any notion of where he's going tomorrow, would you?"

My wife and I spent just ten days in three Soviet cities—Moscow, Leningrad, and Kiev—and had no more warrant to speak authoritatively about the U.S.S.R. than a foreigner would have to expound on the U.S.A. after ten days in Washington, New York, and Kansas City. But since the shortness of our stay did not disqualify us as experts—at least among people who had been there nine days or less— we spent much longer than that answering questions about the place. After a few weeks of this, we could pretty well predict what questions would be asked, though not necessarily in what order.

DID YOU HAVE MUCH TROUBLE GETTING A VISA?

It was a little disconcerting to have to confess that there was really nothing to it. We simply applied for one through the New York travel agent who arranged the Russian phase of our trip, which had to be paid for in advance. The jaunt we signed up for was Tour No. 102, encompassing Leningrad, Kiev, and Moscow, in that order—one of a series of excursions conducted by the Company for Foreign Travel to the Soviet Union, which is more commonly known as Intourist. The visa application was a one-page printed form, and the only questions that might have been interpreted as having sinister implications dealt with whether the prospective tourist was born in the Soviet Union or had relatives currently living there.

Not that an affirmative reply to either seemed to matter much. Among the thirty-five members of Tour No. 102 was a Russian-born American citizen, a Mrs. Armstrong. She was a registered nurse from New York, and her principal reason for returning to her native land was to see a brother—an engineer living in Moscow—from whom she had been separated for thirty years. The Soviet government not only gave its nod to this reunion but allowed the brother to proceed to Leningrad and mingle freely with all us outlanders, thus exposing himself to whatever ideological poisons we might exude.

The day Mrs. Armstrong reached Leningrad, she came down with a sore throat. Intourist referred her to a Russian doctor, who, for no fee at all, wrote out a prescription for some cough medicine, and this, she informed the rest of us, was first-rate. As the only member of No. 102 who had occasion to consult a local physician, she would always have the edge on us in any future symposia on Soviet therapy. "The Russian doctors are very partial to mustard plasters," she told me one day in Kiev, and she was probably saying the same thing to some invalid on Park Avenue the next month.

It may well have been that it was easier for a tourist to gain admittance to the U.S.S.R. that summer than to the U.S.A. Take the case of François, a young French law student on No. 102. As the winner of some scholarly competition, he was enjoying his prize—a trip around the world. When our tour ended, he was to take the Trans-Siberian Railway to Peiping, and from there he would make his way, by stages, to South America. He wanted to visit the United States, too, for he had never been here, but our State Department had turned him down after learning that it would have to share him with both Russia and Communist China.

François was not the only French citizen in the Soviet Union who seemed bemused by the official American attitude—which some Europeans took to be the unofficial one, too—toward tourists who set foot on Communist soil. With us on No. 102 was an American girl named Gloria, who lived in New York and had a job with the United Nations Secretariat. In Leningrad, a transient Frenchwoman Gloria got to talking with asked her earnestly, "What will happen to you when you get home? Will you lose your job for having gone to Russia? Will your friends refuse to have anything to do with you?" Since these questions were addressed to Gloria and not to me, I will skip them.

WAS IT DIFFICULT TO GET THERE?

Moscow is connected with half a dozen other European capitals by regularly scheduled non-stop flights. Jinny and I planned originally to fly in from Helsinki, but the Soviet airline Aeroflot, on which we were tentatively booked, was casual about confirming reservations, so we turned to Sabena, the Belgian airline, which flew us from Brussels to Moscow in five and a half hours. We had better luck with Aeroflot on our way out, and took one of its TU-104 jets from Moscow to Copenhagen. The crew included three stewardesses, who, at eight in the morning, served us a meal of bread, butter, caviar, cold beef, pears, plums, cookies, cheese, and hot tea. We were given heavy linen table napkins, but, taking the edge off these bourgeois amenities, the plane was unaccountably full of flies. Maybe the napkins were supposed to be used for dispersing the flies.

Although we went to Russia at the height of the tourist season, our plane out of Brussels, a DC-7, was two-thirds empty, and of its two dozen passengers all but four were Russians. The airline had apparently taken this unbalanced national representation into account, for while the Martinis served en route were brown and unappealing, the vodka was delicious—so much so that Jinny, who had previously barely tolerated vodka even when liberally diluted with tomato juice, at once fell under its spell. Before the trip was over, she was toting a bottle around in her purse, as a tonic against exhaustion.

On the plane, some Russians sitting near us chose vodka, naturally enough, and drank it in dainty sips—a disappointing contrast to the robust, bottoms-up technique we had expected. They also surprised us when, after Jinny had consulted a Russian phrase book we'd brought along and toasted them with a halting *"Ya pyoo 'za va' she zdaro 'vye!,"* they responded with a genial "Cheers!"

Aside from their manner of imbibing, there was nothing dainty about the Russian passengers. They were all men, possibly returning home after a fling at the Brussels Fair, and they were so uniformly burly that they might have been shaped in the same bulging mold. All were wearing the broad-shouldered, bell-bottom-trousered suits to which Soviet tailors seem addicted. Around the chest, they measured five centimetres more, on the average, than they would have in 1926—an esoteric comparison that I cite with confidence, having read it, after the plane landed, in the letters column of the English-language edition of a Russian propaganda weekly called *New Times.* The writer of the letter in question, with obvious awe, attributed this gain of two inches in chest circumference over a period of thirty-two years partly to "the free creative labor of the Soviet citizens."

The non-Russians on the plane, a fairly puny lot, were, in addition to my wife and me, an uncommunicative American girl, travelling on a diplomatic passport, and Lester, an exceedingly communicative twenty-year-old college student from California, who wouldn't have been with us if we hadn't taken off late. Ten minutes after our scheduled departure time, he raced up to the ticket gate, looking very American in chino slacks, a blue blazer with brass buttons, and soiled white shoes. His face was purple. While he was getting his wind back, an airline official, pointing to him and addressing the Russian passengers collectively, said *"Amerikanets."* The Russians swung around, in a formidable body, to gaze at him.

"Gosh!" gasped Lester. "Are all those guys Russkis?" Keeping a wary eye on them, he told the airline man he was majoring in psychology and was on his way to the U.S.S.R. to join an Intourist group—No. 102, it later turned out. The airline man asked him if he planned to write a psychological treatise on his journey. "If they ever let me out," said Lester.

"Well," said the Sabena man airily, "just remember that if you get arrested, you're guilty until proved innocent."

"*Really?*" cried Lester.

Jinny walked over to him and said, "Don't worry, we're Americans. We'll look after you." Much as I admired her compassionateness, I was tempted to say "Really?" myself.

Few, if any, of the Russians could have understood much of this byplay, but on the plane, as if to reassure the young man, a couple of them took seats near him, smiling, and one transferred a Lenin's-head pin from his own lapel to Lester's. By the time we were aloft, Lester was chattering away at his new acquaintances—if not exactly to them, since they couldn't understand him. "Is it possible—*est-ce possible* —how do you say it? Get a car?" he asked one of them. "Drive yourself around?" The Russian looked blank. "Automobile?" persisted Lester. "*Voiture?* Machine?"

"Ah, *machina, machina!*" said the Russian. He and Lester were both so elated at having hit upon a word more or less common to their respective tongues that they passed it back and forth several times, like a peace pipe.

Lester was to have some diverting adventures in the Soviet Union. After a twenty-minute layover in Moscow, he and my wife and I flew on together to Leningrad, to join up with Tour No. 102. Our second day there, she and I were having lunch when Lester flopped down at our table. His face was magenta, and he was carrying a sheaf of American magazines. "I've found a Russian girl!" he told us enthusiastically. "She's the best-looking girl I've seen in a long time! I wouldn't be ashamed to take her home." When we inquired how he had met this dazzler, he took a deep breath and said, "Well, I saw her walking on the other side of the street, and I walked across at about eighty miles an hour, and I was too winded to talk—not that she could have understood me anyway—so I just flashed my vote-winning smile. And—listen to this!—half an hour later I was walking right in her own neighborhood with her, holding her hand. How can you beat a country like this!" Lester paused to take a swig of a sweetish, bottled fruit drink called Mandarin. "Her name is Tania," he went on, "and I have a date to meet her this afternoon. She's an engineer, and she's also a painter, and she can play the piano. She made me feel almost ignorant. Boy, when I get back to school, I'm really going to have to hit those books! I'm going to give her these," he concluded, exhibiting a *Saturday Evening Post*, a *Ladies' Home Journal*, a *Science and Mechanics,* and a Mickey Mouse comic book. "I knew it would be a good idea to bring them with me."

Within forty-eight hours, though, Lester had seen the last of Tania. Maybe she made him feel too ignorant. In any event, while she apparently accepted most of his proffered gifts, he still had the Mickey Mouse, and he was presently bestowing it upon another attractive indigene, a chubby-faced, dark-haired young woman named Olga, who was a schoolteacher but, in Lester's estimation, less overpoweringly intellectual than her precursor. (It was the consensus of the other Americans on No. 102, who naturally took a chauvinistic interest in Lester's involvements, that neither of these ladies was a tramp.) Lester got on so famously with Olga that he tarried overlong with her the night we were all supposed to fly from Leningrad to Kiev, and missed the plane. He turned up in Kiev twenty-four hours later, and I asked him if he'd had much trouble catching up with us. "Naw," he said. "Oh, the dame that's the big cheese at Intourist tried to give me a hard time. She wanted to know what had held me up, and I told her it was none of her damned business. It wasn't as though she was my mother."

I asked him if Olga had been sorry to see him go. "She wanted me to come again next year and take her back with me," he said. "I'm not so sure, though. You know, Olga's home was depressing. It was terrible. Why, I was over there after lunch one day and they hadn't even done the breakfast dishes. I'll be glad to get out of this country. I don't like being depressed."

DID THEY LET YOU TAKE ALL THE PICTURES YOU WANTED TO?

Before we left the States, we had heard, from people who had been to Russia, that we might be subjected to all sorts of inconveniences in the name of security. Being stripped and searched at the border was one of them. Living in bugged hotel rooms was another. Having any English-language books or periodicals we might try to bring into the country confiscated by customs was a third, and a fourth was running into the same difficulty with whatever undeveloped film we might try to take out. Maybe our experience was atypical, but at least three of these prophecies failed to pan out. (We had no way of checking on bugs.) On the plane to Moscow, we were asked to fill out a customs declaration, but the only inconvenience it caused us was linguistic. It was printed in Russian, Polish, and German, and of these three languages the only one we were acquainted with—and but noddingly, at that—was the last. Concluding that we were supposed to own up to any munitions, opium, or hashish we might have on us, we responded with a forthright *"Nein."* As it turned out, we could have brought in enough opiates to keep the Russian masses happy for some time, since nobody so much as peeked inside our luggage. It wasn't inspected when we left, either.

We carried very little reading matter with us, partly because we had been warned of its probable fate but primarily because there wasn't any room left in our bags once we had packed all the instant coffee and aspirin and other provisions that we'd heard highly recommended for such a trip. (We never used any of them.) Our library, in fact, consisted only of two Erle Stanley Gardner paperbacks and a Paris *Herald*

Tribune we'd bought in Brussels. All three items, to be sure, were swiftly appropriated by a genial, red-haired Intourist man who met us at the Leningrad airport and took us to our hotel, but his mood was plainly covetous rather than confiscatory. He badgered us for them so unrelentingly that by the time we reached the lobby, we decided we had better let him have them if we hoped to do anything in that city besides listen to his wheedling. When, at last, we capitulated, the Intourist man insisted that this cultural transfer take place privately, in our suite (he may have known that our rooms were *not* bugged), and the instant it was completed, he thrust his trove inside his suit coat. If he ever got around to doing the crossword in the *Herald,* he probably found one five-letter entry a cinch: "Executed Russian leader." The answer was "B-e-r-i-a."

The acquisitive Intourist man was also fond of cigarettes. He was quite knowledgeable about extraterritorial brands. He preferred Marlboros to Winstons, and thought the French were a narrow-minded race because the Frenchmen he had met were undeviatingly partial to Gauloises. I learned one footnote to Russian folklore from him. As he was leaving our suite, his clothing lumpy with books and butts, I went to the door with him and held out my hand, and he spurned it and jumped back inside. A truly furtive fellow, I thought, but I turned out to be wrong, for he told me that it was considered bad luck in his country to shake hands while standing on a threshold. We shook hands on unobjectionable ground, and then he was gone.

To get back to photographs, we were allowed to take all we wanted, wherever we wanted, and to bring our film out of the country undeveloped. Nearly every member of No. 102 had a camera, and while a number of Soviet citizens expressed intense interest in our equipment, it was in the hope of buying it from us. A few glowered when we snapped them without a by-your-leave, and two Russian sailors turned their backs on me one time, but they may have been shy, or A.W.O.L.

The most dedicated photographer among us was a teacher named Alec, a Virginian living in Stockholm, where he gave private English lessons to children. Alec was the exposure man of our group. Almost before the wheels of our sightseeing bus had stopped rolling, he would disembark, consult a light meter, and make some such pertinent proclamation as "*f/8* at a fiftieth." He had been to the Soviet Union before, and he told the rest of us, not without satisfaction, that the police had once detained him for four hours on a charge of taking pictures illegally. He never did say what it was he had been shooting on that occasion, but it may have been his captors, because he liked nothing better than to bag Russian cops. On the bus, he would always occupy the back seat; squirming around, he would click his shutter at any policeman framed momentarily in the dust-streaked rear window.

Alec seemed determined to take at least one picture in the course of No. 102 that would get him in hot water. On a train carrying us from Kiev to Moscow, he huddled in a compartment with his camera at the ready and peered ahead, alert for any taboo installation that might loom up along the tracks. After he had snapped one hulking factory, he swiftly hid his camera and, catching the eye of our porter—a woman —he pointed questioningly toward his subject as it disappeared behind us. The porter said something in Russian that sounded like "*Atom-stantsia.*" Alec was ecstatic until Mrs. Armstrong told him that what the woman had said was "Let me have your empty tea glass, please."

WHAT SORT OF TOURISTS DID YOU BUMP INTO OVER THERE?

The Soviet Union puts out a surprising number of foreign-language publications, but the nearest thing to a society column I saw in any of the English-language ones was a department in the twice-weekly Moscow *News,* published by the

Alliance of Soviet Societies of Friendship and Cultural
Relations with Foreign Countries, headed "Our Guests."
Except for a few visiting dignitaries and their accompanying kin, if any (the president of the Burmese-Soviet Cultural Society, for instance, and the Icelandic Minister of Fish-
eries and Trade, both with wife and daughter), the guests
who rated mention were identified by group rather than as
individuals—a delegation of Czechoslovakian agricultural
and industrial workers, a delegation of Yugoslavian textile
workers, a farm delegation from Finland, a youth delegation from Peiping, a delegation of scholars from the Democratic Republic of Vietnam, a theatrical troupe from the
Korean People's Republic, and a delegation of British
mothers.

In the dining room of our hotel in Kiev one day, we sat
near another delegation of Britishers, about two dozen of
them, including some grandmotherly-looking specimens.
One of the males in the party, a mustachioed elder of military bearing, spotted an acquaintance in our party, an Englishman named Michael. The old boy came over, exchanged
a few words with Michael, and then toddled off. When he
was out of earshot, Michael said, "Rum bunch, those," and
told us that the group was made up of Leftists who were so
ideologically compatible with the Communists that they
had been given a civic reception in Leningrad. They were
on a forty-day swing around the Soviet Union, he continued,
and the trip was almost wholly subsidized by the Russians.
"It's costing each of them only twenty-five shillings a day,"
he said. (Tour No. 102 was available on a first-, second-, or
third-class basis, and it was costing even our third-class tourists the equivalent of a hundred shillings a day.) "I shouldn't
be surprised if, at those rates, some of these chaps stayed on
here permanently. No great loss to the United Kingdom if
they do, I should say. Still, I rather hope they don't. I

shouldn't want too many Russians to get the notion that they're typical British subjects."

Tour No. 102 was ignored by "Our Guests," possibly because we weren't a homogeneous delegation, possibly because we were paying full freight. On our roster were twenty-three Americans, six Canadians, two Englishmen, two Swedes, one Frenchman, and one Japanese. The only married couple besides my wife and me were Mr. and Mrs. Bronsky, who hailed from British Columbia and had brought along their three daughters, the youngest of whom was seven. The father, who was of Russian descent, always wore a metal maple leaf in his buttonhole, to make clear where his allegiance lay. The Bronskys were travelling on a single passport, and the Soviet official in Canada who had put the family visa on it had omitted to take note of the seven-year-old. None of the Bronskys could read Russian, though, so they did not become aware of this oversight until they reached Leningrad, where Intourist began matching visaed names against visible noses. Mr. Bronsky eventually got things straightened out, but only after he had spent several anxious days ascertaining whether he would be allowed to take a seven-year-old girl out of Russia when there was no proper evidence that he had ever brought one in.

Most of the Americans on No. 102 were students or teachers. Three of them wore beards—two black, one red—and some Russians may have deduced from this that beards are a prominent part of the contemporary American scene. (Maybe they are, at that.) One of the black beards belonged to a teacher from Washington, who had been escorting eight American boarding-school students—four boys and four girls —around Europe. By the time he reached Leningrad, he had only six in tow, because in Stockholm, as he was about to set out with his whole brood, he had received frantic wireless messages from the fathers of two of the girls, enjoining him not to shepherd *their* daughters beyond the Iron Curtain.

The least homogeneous member of our tour was the Japanese. An exceedingly affable businessman named Tsutuki, he was in a paradoxical position; English was the language our guides used, and he knew some Russian but not a word of English. Nonetheless, he nodded affirmatively whenever anybody asked him anything, in any language. The general belief among the rest of us was that Tsutuki had signed up for some other tour, had been assigned to ours by mistake, and was too polite to call the error to Intourist's attention. Several of us hoped that the impetuous Lester would double-check before acting on the response Tsutuki made to a question of his. The question was "Can an American readily travel from Vladivostok to Tokyo, with a side trip, perhaps to North Korea?" As usual, Tsutuki nodded vigorously.

HOW COULD YOU GET ALONG IF YOU DIDN'T KNOW RUSSIAN?

We encountered our share of the misunderstandings and frustrations that crop up in any country where one doesn't know the language. In Moscow one night, my wife and I were all set to go to the theatre—to see a play we had mulishly bought tickets for because an Intourist woman had counselled us not to. We thought at first that she was trying to talk us out of it for political reasons, but I later believed it was just that she knew the play, a comedy, would be harder than some others for foreigners to appreciate, since much of its effect depended on double-edged dialogue. If so, she was right, but while we didn't get the jokes, we got the point; the characters were mostly Czarist noblemen portrayed at their dissolute worst—drinking heavily, abusing social inferiors, and indulging in all kinds of frivolous pursuits, some of them downright scandalous.

We had heard that the theatre was only a few blocks from our hotel, but we were late in getting under way, so we

took a cab. Another No. 102 man, a free-lance writer named
Herbert, who specialized in articles on child care and was
looking into the Russian angle, was going to the same show,
and he hopped into the front seat. When a non-Russian-
speaking tourist in Russia hires a taxi, he generally either
asks a native to write out his destination for him or, if he is
going to a theatre, shows the driver his ticket. Herbert did
the latter. The taxi man nodded, said something that we
took to mean "Must hurry!" (too bad, we thought; the curtain's up) , and lurched off. We had travelled a mile or so, at
a spanking clip, when it occurred to my wife to ask Herbert,
whose grasp of Russian orthography we knew to be minimal,
just what he had shown the man. It turned out to have been a
Kiev-Moscow railroad ticket. As soon as the driver got the
idea that we didn't want to catch the night express, he
laughed so hard he had to stop the car.

Such misadventures, however, were rare. We could usually
find somebody who fathomed English or French or German.
German saved us when we flew into Moscow from Brussels,
and had only a few minutes to make a connecting flight to
Leningrad. The only Intourist agent we could find spoke not
a word of English, and although neither Jinny nor I knew
much German, with enough pleading *Bitte's* and *Danke
Schön's* and *Schnell's,* we got him to get us aboard a plane. It
wasn't until we were airborne that we reflected that, for all
we positively knew, we might be on a flight to Tashkent. Our
stewardess could furnish no reassuring enlightenment. When
I said to her, pointing in the direction we were heading, "Leningrad?," she merely pointed forward herself, to a sign in
the cabin that, I later learned, said "No smoking."

The Russian alphabet can be assimilated without much
effort, however, and while transliteration is many versts removed from translation, it helped. The Russian words for
"apothecary" and "restaurant" are practically the same
as ours, and it was nice to know that the characters

"Хрщев" stand for "Khrushchev." It would be equally nice
to know precisely what he stands for. (The editors of the
phrase book in whose pages I came to grips with the alphabet were apparently hedging their bets on the durability of
Soviet leadership. Introducing that spectacular "щ," which
stands for the consonantal cluster "shch," they instructed us
to pronounce it as in, of all evasive proper names, "Ash-
church.") In the matter of language, Tour No. 102 was
lucky. Besides Mr. Tsutuki, four of its members knew some
Russian—a circumstance that the rest of us took avid advantage of. Perhaps the most sought-after fellow in the group
was an upstate New Yorker named Elbert, who had studied
Russian at Princeton and had an idiomatic command of it.
On learning from Elbert that "compote," "omelet," and
"coffee" are just about the same in Russian as in English or
French, several of us took to ordering this manageable trio
every morning. It made breakfast monotonous, but it made
us feel articulate.

Our main communication links with our often unintelli-
gible environment were the various guides Intourist assigned
to us. The principal one was a thin-faced blonde—in her
early thirties, I should guess—named Nina. A teacher in
Leningrad during the school year, Nina took us in tow there
and led us on to Kiev and then to Moscow—an accomplish-
ment that, considering how greatly we outnumbered her
and how unaccustomed most of us were to disciplined travel,
may have been comparable to Hannibal's getting his ele-
phants over the Alps. Nina seemed unusually worldly for a
Russian woman. She was trimly, if not flamboyantly, dressed,
and she went in for makeup; she painted her fingernails, and
used mascara rather liberally. Her delight was boundless
when two American women on No. 102 dug into their hand-
bags and edifyingly plucked forth a rub-on perfume dis-
penser and an eye-blacking machine called, I believe, a Mas-

cara-matic. If these were hardly earth-shaking artifacts, Nina seemed to think they were.

While Nina tended to get rattled in unexpected situations, she could handle the expected to perfection; her mind was a tidy storehouse of data. She reeled off the names of five blue-blooded malcontents who were exiled or executed (and which happened to which) after the uprising against Nicholas I in 1825; she knew the names not only of all the nobility who had once occupied the palaces now occupied by the workers' bureaucracies but of the architects of these stately hives; and she knew the precise number of columns that hold up, or adorn, St. Isaac's Cathedral, now the State Antireligious Museum, in Leningrad. "A hundred and twelve of them, all monoliths," Nina told us, as proudly as though she came from a long line of pre-revolutionary engineers, or columnists. "St. Isaac's was built by serfs. You know that we had serfs."

"Yes, but we'd like to know how many people have been executed in Russia *since* 1825," called out Geraldine, our heckler.

Nina didn't flinch, but by the time she was finished with us, she had no great need for mascara. Her eyes were dark and hollow in a face that had become drawn and pallid. Before taking on the thirty-five of us, she confessed, she had never had to cope with more than two alien tourists at a time. She spoke wistfully of a seventy-eight-year-old American whom she'd recently escorted on a leisurely jaunt to Yalta, Odessa, and a few of the other cities that the Soviet Union now lets foreigners enter. "I almost came to look on him as a father," Nina said.

There seemed little likelihood that a similar affection would blossom between Nina and any of our gang; if she had familial feelings about us, they were those of a long-suffering parent toward a batch of incorrigibly truant children. Her seventy-eight-year-old charge had been hard of hearing, she said; there was nobody thus handicapped in No. 102, but before Nina said goodbye to us, she had had to yell so much that she nearly lost her voice. Among other things, she was obliged, by one Soviet regulation or another, to keep our passports in her possession during a good part of the trip. As she was juggling a couple of dozen of these one day, a fellow-tourist—a Canadian woman who taught in a school for children of Dominion soldiers stationed in Germany—whispered to me that a guide was liable to an eight-year prison term for mislaying a passport. Just then, Lester came crashing along, jostled Nina's elbow, and sent two passports slithering across the floor. Nina grimly retrieved them, thereby perhaps saving herself sixteen years in Siberia.

From time to time—particularly when she was not worrying about passports—Nina displayed flashes of vivacity. Until her vocal cords got frayed, she sang with us. She also danced with us, and joked with us. (She would not drink with us; whatever her other standing orders may have been, she was evidently not allowed to tipple with the tourists.) She was especially fond of watery jokes—possibly because she had been born in Leningrad, a city that, as she informed us without faltering, is composed of a hundred and one islands connected by three hundred and sixty bridges. (Many of the bridges had life preservers hung on their railings—an accommodation that the Western world, as far as I know, nowhere furnishes its accident-prone citizens.) In the Russian Museum in Leningrad one morning, while we were examining a boiling expanse of ocean painted by a seascape man named Aivazovsky, Nina took seven-year-old Dottie Bronsky by the arm and drew her away from the canvas. "So do not stand too close," Nina told her mirthfully. "You might get splashed."

Another morning, Nina led us to Petrodvorets, a Versailles-like summer playground of the Czars outside Leningrad, on the Gulf of Finland. The Nazis knocked the place to pieces during the war, but the Communists have been faithfully restoring it, and a great many ornate fountains are now in shimmering operation. Pausing alongside a muscular bronze Triton who was prying a stream of water from the jaws of a writhing bronze sea monster, Nina remarked gaily, "Somebody told me this sculpture is supposed to represent dental aid. I like that joke." A few minutes later, it became clear that she also liked practical jokes of a watery cast. Catherine the Great had had a few hidden fountains installed at Petrodvorets (or Petershof, as it was called when Leningrad was called St. Petersburg), for the impish purpose of dousing her guests. When a victim ambled along a pebbly path, an attendant screened by foliage would press a button and release a drenching spray. Nina, in cahoots with an invisible colleague, gave several of us the treatment as, like lambs behind a Judas goat, we followed her through the pleasant, handsome palace grounds. *Après Nina le déluge.*

One thing Nina did not jest about was politics. Her English was splendid—that was what she taught in school—but whenever one of us asked her a question touching on current events, she would reply, politely but firmly, "I don't understand." For example, Leningrad was full of soldiers—astonishingly full, in view of the Russian's recent protestations about the demobilization of their armed forces—and one day I asked Nina whether there was a very large military garrison in or near the city. Oh, no, she replied. Then why were there so many uniformed men on the streets? "I don't understand," said Nina. Later that day, we were looking at the Maryinsky Palace, which had been transformed into the headquarters of the Leningrad City Soviet. "Our city has three times been awarded the Order of Lenin," said Nina, with obvious pride; and indeed three giant medals were pinned to the building's broad façade. While we were gaping at the decorations, a sixteen-year-old prep-school student named David asked Nina if the local electorate, in choosing members of that august body, had a chance to vote for more than one candidate.

"I don't understand," said Nina.

"I must have a long talk with you one of these days about politics," David told her solemnly.

"Oh, I know nothing of politics," Nina said.

She seemed grateful when a fourteen-year-old girl named Diana began telling her something of two-party politics in America. "My parents are Democrats absolutely *surrounded* by Republicans in Litchfield, Connecticut," Diana told her in a hushed tone. "Mother registers Republican, of course, but actually she's a Democratic spy." Nina blinked.

IS IT TRUE THEY ONLY LET YOU SEE WHAT THEY WANTED YOU TO?

Few people would think of going to London or Paris for the first time without visiting Westminster Abbey or the Eiffel Tower. The formal itinerary of a guided tour in Russia is largely limited to landmarks like the Kremlin and the Moscow subway, but these, after all, are what the tyro tourist has been hearing about for ages and wants to see anyway. And Intourist did not insist that we inspect solely what it put before us. True, our visas confined us to the three cities covered by Tour No. 102, but once we arrived in any of them, we were free to ignore the prescribed agenda and go off on our own. In fact, at practically no moment during our trip were all thirty-five of us together. Lester, for one, hardly ever materialized for an organized jaunt.

A surprising number of the organized jaunts involved palaces. In *The Russian Revolution,* Alan Moorehead quotes Maxim Gorki's advice to the proletariat in 1917: "Citizens . . . take care of the palaces—they will become palaces of your national art; take care of the pictures, the statues . . . preserve the monuments, the buildings, the old things, the documents—all this is your history, your pride." Gorki's counsel had been conscientiously heeded. Fresh gilt adorned the spire of the Admiralty in Leningrad and the domes of the Kremlin cathedrals; to spruce up the glittering summit of St. Sophia's Cathedral, in Kiev, the Communist regime—so a guide told us—had contributed seven kilos of pure gold. The historic museums we saw were invariably crowded, and most of the visitors were not foreigners but patently proud Russians—countrywomen, in boots and babushkas, shoulder to shoulder (and what shoulders!) with urban art students flourishing their sketchbooks. We saw as many soldiers and sailors in the art galleries on Palace Square, in Leningrad, as one might see in the shooting galleries on Times Square.

Leningrad—a dignified, gray city full of historic and cultural shrines—has often been compared to Paris. The famous art collection in the Hermitage Museum is in many ways a counterpart of that in the Louvre. The Russian treasures are stored in a onetime royal dwelling, the Winter Palace, that hugs a bank of the city's principal waterway, the Neva River. The Winter Palace is just about as heroically proportioned as the Louvre, but to us it seemed far more cluttered. Though practically every square inch of wall was in use (the lighting was atrocious), thousands of the Museum's two million-odd works of art were not on display, for lack of space. The collection also appeared to be more haphazardly catalogued than the Louvre's; while we were in Russia, the curators of the Hermitage were expressing their delight at having unearthed, in some unexplored recess, an original da Vinci sketch that they hadn't known was on the premises.

We had only a little over two hours in which to inspect the Hermitage. Nina had warned us we would have to gallop, and she set a stiff pace. Very nearly at a trot, we went past a bunch of paintings that, she said, her government was about to send back to Germany. There was some confusion among us as to whether she said the works got to Russia in the first place because they were saved by Soviet soldiers during the war or seized by them; in the tumult, we had no chance to pin her down. The Moscow *News,* a few days later, said "saved" was the word; it ran a testimonial article by the Ambassador Extraordinary and Plenipotentiary of the German Democratic Republic to the U.S.S.R., in which the East German legate said, among other things, "Now these treasures are being returned to the German Democratic Republic. By this action they are being returned to the German people as a whole; for the German Democratic Republic is by right the sovereign German state."

The speed at which we were moving did not let us do justice to the marvels of the Hermitage. I do recall striding briskly past assorted Titians, Rembrandts, Raphaels, and El Grecos, as well as two glorious da Vinci oils, on the main floor, and a group of orange-red dancers by Matisse, on the top floor, where the servants' quarters must have been when the Winter Palace was a going concern. All the French Impressionist works—a magnificent sampling, in the view of this particular sprinter—were displayed up there, presumably because they were less esteemed by contemporary Soviet critics than the Older Masters in the downstairs parlors.

HOW WERE THE HOTELS?

Each Soviet city to which foreign tourists are admitted has at least one Intourist hotel. In these, the visitor never has any truck with the main desk. Instead, he gets his mail, buys his theatre tickets, and complains about the plumbing at the Intourist Service Bureau in the lobby, and leaves his room key with an attendant, customarily a female one, on his floor. The custodian of keys on the third floor of the Hotel Europa, where we stayed in Leningrad, was a puzzling trusty. One afternoon, Herbert, the child-care man, wanted to enter his room. Suspecting that the custodian knew no English, he showed her a slip of paper (the right one this time) with his room number written on it. "That's not your room," the woman told him, in English. He insisted that it was, and had been for three days. "You're mistaken," she said. Here, one would have said, was a case of black or white, with no gray compromise possible. Nevertheless, the Russian woman hit upon one; she handed him the key he wanted and, as he went down the hall, called after him, "All the same, that's not your room."

The Astoria is widely reputed to be the best hotel in Leningrad, but the red-headed Intourist man who escorted my wife and me to town from the airport, feverishly smoking our cigarettes, said he personally preferred the Europa. He knew, of course, that we had been assigned there. The Europa struck us as somewhat less elegant than the Astoria, but it was unquestionably of first-class dimensions. It covers a whole block. Our quarters were spacious, too—big bathroom, bigger bedroom, great big sitting room. On one wall of the sitting room was an oil painting of a bejewelled lady who, like the furniture, was overstuffed. Beneath the glass top of a broad mahogany desk was a list of house rules, printed in English, French, German, and Chinese. No visitors were permitted between midnight and eight in the morning, and the playing of musical instruments was forbidden between midnight and ten.

One confusing element of Soviet hotel life was the capricious elevator service. At the Europa, the operators, seemingly according to their mood, might or might not take aboard downward-bound passengers. In Kiev, at the Hotel Ukraine—where we had no sitting room, a bedroom as small and crowded as a ship's cabin, and a tiny bathroom with a shower but no shower curtain—the elevators were self-service. The doors above the main floor could not be opened from the outside, so there was no chance of wangling a ride down unless somebody happened to stop at your floor. We

were on the sixth floor, and walking down to the lobby, after
several hours of ambulatory sightseeing, was something of a
chore. Getting to the café in the Hotel Ukraine also took
some doing. The easiest way, we discovered by trial and error, was to go out into the street, walk half a block, and cut
back into the hotel through the barbershop.

Moscow is the most cosmopolitan city in the U.S.S.R., I
suppose, and our hotel there, the Moskva, had manned
(womaned, to be precise) elevator service operating con-
sistently in both directions. The Moskva is only a couple of
blocks from Red Square, and its lobby is suitably scaled to
the neighborhood; it could accommodate a good-sized parade. At the Moskva, we had another majestic suite. The sitting room had a button you could push for room service, another for a valet, and still another for a chambermaid. (We
tried room service for breakfast one morning. The waitress
who answered our summons knew not a word of any language familiar to us, but it all worked out very nicely. We
had compote, omelet, and coffee.) The sitting room also contained an upright piano, which looked brand-new. Unfortunately, it was locked, although if we had asked, maybe we
could have had it opened—at least from ten in the morning to midnight.

In our bathroom the pièce de résistance was a tub that
must have been eight feet long. It was the kind of appliance
that deserved sculptured lion's paws for feet, but its dignity
had been cruelly ruffled; it was propped up on two rough-
hewn wooden blocks. Through the bedroom and sitting-
room windows we could see, on the north side of Red Square,
a corner of the Historical Museum—a red stone pile out of
which half a dozen Newport homes could be carved without
making much of a dent. Beyond the Museum loomed a section
of the Kremlin wall, and beyond that we could see two of the
seven lofty Kremlin towers, surmounted by huge red stars.
After dark, the stars, which revolved slowly in the breeze,

were brilliantly illuminated. It was an odd sensation to go to sleep with those meaningful sentinels so close at hand.

WAS THE FOOD TERRIBLE?

While it is true that our first exposure to a Leningrad restaurant quickly dispelled any illusion of being in Paris, the food we had there, and in the other cities, was not bad at all. For the most part, we took our meals in the dining rooms of our Intourist hotels—large, chandeliered chambers served by dinner-jacketed staffs and equipped with bandstands that, come evening, were occupied by hard-working dance orchestras. The music was predominantly American, but every so often a band would assert its independence of the West by emitting a jazzed-up version of "The Song of the Volga Boatmen." The bands played imitatively, and a bit raggedly. It was as if the instrumentalists had got hep to American music by attending movies in which the sound and action were imperfectly synchronized.

A tourist in Russia is supposed to pay for his meals with coupons that Intourist doles out. Though each has a stipulated value in rubles, the sum does not appear on the ticket itself. My wife and I were travelling first class, and while our accommodations were a bit grander than those of the second- and third-class folks on Tour No. 102, we quickly became aware of one important edge we had on them: We could order à la carte, while they were on a table d'hôte basis. Nearly every morning, they got hot dogs and sauerkraut for breakfast. (The Americans among them must have been amused if, after returning home, they spotted, as Jinny did, an Associated Press photograph of four United States Marine guards at our embassy in Moscow, gobbling franks. Jinny laughingly read me the caption, which said that the hot dogs had been flown into Moscow "after one of the Marines had remarked to an American tourist how they all missed frankfurters in Russia. Coöperation of a Moscow customs official and Daniel and Soviet airlines was needed to get the 25 frankfurters and 24 buns through the Iron Curtain." The A.P. never explained what happened to the missing bun.)

Our first-class coupons, we learned in due course, entitled us to fourteen rubles' worth of sustenance apiece at breakfast, twenty-four at dinner, four at tea, and sixteen at supper. (The official exchange rate for the ruble was four to a dollar, but tourists enjoyed a rate of ten to one.) We never had tea, but it didn't matter, for the coupons could be used at any meal. You could buy drinks with them, too, if you had any to spare, but you needed a lot of spares. One evening, in a Continental mood, I asked a waiter to bring us a bottle of dry red wine. What we got was sickeningly sweet, and we couldn't down much of it. When our bill came, we found that the bottle had set us back seventy rubles and twenty kopecks, or seven dollars and two cents. The twenty kopecks really hurt.

Given enough time—two hours, say—a Soviet waiter can, and probably will, deliver a satisfying meal, though the chances are he'll bring the entire order, from caviar through ice cream, in one trayload. This may save trips to the kitchen, but it crowds the table. Occasionally, though, the service we got was so indifferent that we darkly suspected our waiters of ideological discrimination. In Leningrad, for instance, four of us on No. 102 entered the dining room, and sat there, not even getting an opportunity to place our order, while two dozen Asians trooped in, had a big meal, and trooped out again, licking their lips and rubbing their stomachs. I thought they were probably Chinese, at first, but as they walked out past us Jinny nudged me and said, "Look at those shoes! Just like the ones you brought the boys from Korea!" Sure enough, several of the men were wearing the gondola-like, solid-rubber shoes I'd seen so much of during the war there. "But you brought them from South Korea,"

Jinny went on. "These must be North Koreans, maybe that theatrical bunch the Moscow *News* was welcoming." I had never been that close, knowingly, to so many live, uncaptured North Koreans, and I forgot all about being hungry.

Another time, the prep-schoolers in our group got so famished while waiting for their lunch that after a stranger at the next table—he had the air of a Bulgarian—had finished his meal and departed, they lunged for a few pieces of black bread and globules of caviar he had left behind. In their frenzy, one of them smashed a glass. When the teacher in charge of them went to the lobby a few minutes later to complain that his wards were on the edge of starvation, an Intourist woman cut short his lament to say sternly, "Don't tell me about *your* troubles. I hear one of them broke a glass."

We consumed a good deal of borscht in the Soviet Union, but it was green instead of red and made from cabbage instead of beets. This deviation from our notions about the soup puzzled quite a few of the tourists in our group; one of them later reported to the rest of us, after consulting a maitre d'hôtel, that the Russians call cabbage borscht Big Borscht, and beet borscht Little Borscht. We were on the Big Borscht Circuit.

The best food we had anywhere there was chicken à la Kiev, in Kiev—breast of chicken rolled in bread crumbs and deep-fried. As a rule, we did not tip our waiters; since they did not normally give us any change after accepting our coupons, they probably pocketed the difference between what these were worth and the cost of our food. In Kiev, I would gladly have tipped the waitress who served us that chicken, but when I handed her a couple of coupons, she did some rapid calculating and, reaching into the pocket of her uniform, pressed six rubles on me. I had never been tipped by a waitress before, and it was an exhilarating sensation.

WHAT DID YOU DO IN THE EVENING?

The best ballet and theatrical companies of the U.S.S.R. were on vacation, or at the Brussels Fair, during our visit, but my wife and I did squeeze in an opera, a ballet, an operetta, a straight play, a circus, and a puppet show—a far more strenuous postprandial program than we would tackle at home, or in most places we would contemplate visiting regularly. The puppet show, at the State Central Puppet Theatre, in Moscow, was the most engaging of the lot. The performance, entitled "An Unusual Concert," was a spoof of conventional concert-hall virtuosos. It was staged by Sergei Obraztsov, who was described in the program—a Russian-and-English one—as a "People's Artist of the U.S.S.R." His artistry was flawless, and funny. In Russian theatres, the electricians are customarily stationed, along with their batteries of lights, in upper boxes; the minuscule stage on which Obraztsov's puppets cavorted had its own adjoining boxes, and in one of them perched a puppet electrician, busily working tiny spotlights. The ballet and the opera were both put on, in Leningrad, by a visiting company from Lithuania. The opera was called *Vaiva,* and before we went to hear it, we asked an Intourist woman to synopsize the action for us. "It's a fairy tale," she replied. "I'm not sure of the plot, but I think it has something to do with good and evil forces, and a magic belt. '*Vaiva*' means 'belt' in Lithuanian, you know. The good forces win. It's their belt." Thus briefed, we carefully scrutinized each new waistline that came onstage, but it did us no good; practically every character was besashed.

Later that night, I picked up a copy of *Soviet Literature,* one of the English-language propaganda journals on sale at the hotel newsstand, and one that I had a particular interest in because, a decade earlier, it had expressed a particular interest in me. It had run a piece by R. Samarin dealing with the wartime literary accomplishments of several American writers, principal among whom were J. Hersey and B. Mauldin. One paragraph had gone:

"Among the most grossly false American books dealing with soldiering on the eve of the war are *The Army Life* (1942), by E. J. Kahn, *See Here, Private Hargrove* (1942), by M. Hargrove. Written, no doubt, with a view to distribution in the army, these books lay special stress on American soldier's devotion to the laws of bourgeois ideology in the U.S.A. The alleged 'democracy' of the American army is illustrated with particular cynicism in Kahn's book. The lieutenant who is training the recruits explains the peculiar beauty of the army hierarchy; it starts with the sergeant giving orders to the private, then, the lieutenant to the sergeant, and so on, until it rises to Roosevelt who gives orders to Marshall, Chief of the General Staff—thus coming full circle, the lieutenant adds enthusiastically, with the soldier-citizens giving orders to the President."

I hadn't quite got the connection between Samarin's second sentence and his third, but I passed that up, my attention having been diverted by a glance through the rest of his polemic. That brief look made me gratefully aware that Hargrove and I had, on the whole, got off far easier than Hersey, described as an "agent of American militarism," whose *Into the Valley* was called "a striking example of a literature that aims at corrupting the minds of the American soldiers," and Mauldin, who was credited with having believed that "the only constructive element amid the ruin and chaos" of war-torn Europe was "a drunken barbarian with his helmet set at a rakish angle and an idiotic leer on his unshaven face"—a reference to Mauldin's thoroughly lovable cartoon characters Willie and Joe, whom Samarin, in an impressive display of gross falseness, referred to throughout his article as "Billy and Joe." Poor Mauldin! Samarin also said that "Mauldin's

blether thus reveals as far back as 1944 the outline of that
plan of American-Nazi coöperation which has now in many
cases, and despite the protests of progressive circles in the
U.S.A., become an established fact." (I looked up "blether"
in the dictionary, and, by God, there was such a word. It
means "blather.") As for American war writing in general,
Samarin called it "bestial and false in substance," "amazingly
inartistic," and "a blend of imperialistic propaganda with
consistent hypocrisy, seasoned with mendacious ballyhoo
about the notorious American democracy."

When I first read the Samarin piece, his paraphrase of the
chain-of-command anecdote I had related sounded accurate
enough, but later, when I checked it against my text, I found
that my account did not start, as Samarin said, with a sergeant giving orders to a private; it started with a *corporal*
giving the orders, after having himself received them from a
sergeant. How, I wondered, could Samarin, a writer admit-
tedly concerned with excoriating falseness and presumably
concerned also with the sensitive feelings of the proletariat,
thus have purged from the ranks a grade of soldier traditionally considered the backbone of any respectable people's
army? Now, in my Leningrad hotel room after the opera, I
wondered anew who was purging whom. Enlightenment was
not long in forthcoming. As I opened *Soviet Literature,* a
printed supplement that had been tucked inside fell out. It
proved to be the text of a decision taken by the Central Committee of the Communist Party of the Soviet Union in regard
to "the Correction of Mistakes in Appraisal of the Operas
The Great Friendship, Bogdan Khmelnitsky and *With All
My Heart.* It had been determined on February 10, 1948, I
read, that the libretto of *Bogdan Khmelnitsky,* to cite just
one of the trio, was guilty of major ideological defects. On
May 28, 1958, though, the C.C. of the C.P.S.U. had decreed
that this ten-year-old denunciation was unjustified, being
"a reflection of the subjective approach to certain works of

art on the part of J. V. Stalin," who, I learned as I read on, "was in large measure influenced, negatively, by Molotov, Malenkov, and Beria." Had they put Stalin on my back, too?, I mused. In any event, I was sorry that *Vaiva* had escaped reappraisal; I might have learned what it was all about.

The circus we saw was—in delightful contrast to so many greatest shows on earth—a one-ring affair. What is more, it took place not in an arena that could be converted overnight into a hockey rink or a revival-meeting hall but in a cozy, circular, low-roofed building, in Kiev, that had apparently been designed with circus-going children in mind. The house was packed with kids, who loved every minute of it. So did we. There were some amazingly limber acrobats; a juggler who kept three flaming torches in play while atop a galloping white horse; some clowns who rose to extravagant heights of buffoonery (one of them had a donkey whose rear end had been costumed in imitation of a man feigning to be the rear end of a donkey); and a suave, tailcoated magician, who, among other feats, turned a lady into a lion. We were a mite taken aback not to find any trained bears among the acts, but in compensation there were some trained white doves and a pack of exceptionally well-tutored dogs.

There were more dogs in that one circus act than we saw anywhere else in the Soviet Union. In Leningrad, a city of three million people, we met up with just one dog, and it may have been a tourist itself, for it was a French poodle leashed to a French-looking woman. On the streets of Moscow, we saw no dogs at all (maybe all the dogs in town had been requisitioned for space travel), and on the streets of Kiev we saw just one—a small white animal, which my wife guessed was part of the circus act, out for an airing. It therefore came as a surprise to us to find the last page of one issue of the Moscow *News* devoted to stories about dogs, complete with pictures. There was even an All-Union Dog Show in the offing, we read. Many breeds were to be represented, in-

cluding some that I could tell from both pictures and text
were strikingly different from the breeds recognized in the
United States. There would be four kinds of Eskimos, for
example, and five kinds of borzois, and one entirely new
Soviet breed, the Estonian hound. It was only a question of
time, I supposed, before doggy delegations from North
Korea, Bulgaria, and maybe even the United States would
be making trips to Russia themselves. Not that this was likely
to produce any relaxation of international tensions. To judge
by the pictures in the Moscow *News*, the two big powers
might find it easier, in the long run, to reconcile their different standards than the All-Union Dog crowd and the
American Kennel Club.

DID YOU MEET KHRUSHCHEV?

No, but we never met him in the United States, either. To
our surprise, Jinny and I didn't even meet up with many
likenesses of Khrushchev. There were large photographs of
him, and of Marx, Engels, and Lenin, in the windows of
book and art stores, and at a museum in Kiev we saw a portrait of him as a young man done in woven silk—a painstaking honor the premises also accorded to Mao Tse-tung and
Paul Robeson. (Another work of art in this collection was an
oil painting glorifying the electric-light bulb.) But in a nation bursting with sculpture—though, to judge by quality,
pitifully short of sculptors—we saw not a single statue of
Khrushchev. Possibly there hadn't yet been time for him to
move from atelier to esplanade. In any event, Khrushchev was
still an iconographic nonentity compared to Lenin. Lenin's
image not only abounded in Leningrad—logically enough,
perhaps, though one would not expect to find a life-size
bronze Abraham Lincoln dominating the interior of a book-
shop in the capital of Nebraska—but is also all over Moscow
and Kiev, often larger than life. We must have seen Lenin
in every material that can be carved, chiselled, hammered,

or molded. We became so conditioned to him—in parks, pavilions, squares, and subway stations—that after a while we hardly noticed him at all.

We hadn't figured on seeing much of Stalin, but we saw more of him than of Khrushchev. Stalin had a head start, of course. He was still prominently featured in the intricate mosaics that adorn the ceilings of several of Moscow's celebrated subway stations. At the Byelorussian station, an Intourist guide named Boris, who was shepherding Tour No. 102 around that day, told us that the lofty mosaics there exemplified the life of the Byelorussian people—the White Russians. While he said this, he was pointing a finger upward without bothering to look, as if he had delivered the same spiel many times before. (Sightseeing guides in Russia, like those anywhere, are given to rote. Our second day in Moscow, a young woman took us out, and her first words as our bus began to roll were "You are now in the city of Moscow.") If Boris had glanced overhead, he would have realized that he was pointing not to some such timeless aspect of White Russian life as a girl milking a cow or an athlete clutching a trophy but, rather, to a picture of a woman painter standing at an easel with a flattering portrait of Stalin on it—an exemplification of Byelorussian life that is surely passé.

A couple of subway stops later, we came to the Komsomolskaya, or Young Communist, station, and, after saying that it was reputedly the most beautiful of all the fifty stations in the Moscow system, Boris remarked, with iconoclasm rare in an Intourist guide, "I don't like it myself—but maybe." The Komsomolskaya was unquestionably the most ornate of the stations we saw. Its ceiling had the biggest mosaics— eight of them altogether—and these alternated with formidable fancy chandeliers. "Each weighs a ton," Boris said, standing fearlessly right under one.

The Komsomolskaya mosaics memorialized significant

moments in Russian history. One panel, given over to the
victory parade in Red Square at the end of the war, indicated that Stalin's niche in history was more secure, no matter how strenuously his successors may have poked at it, than
that of many a contemporary of his. This mosaic showed a
platoon of Soviet chieftains reviewing their triumphant
troops as they marched past the Kremlin in 1945, and Boris
pointed out Stalin, Kalinin, and Kaganovich, among others.
Some of us, however, were more beguiled by half a dozen
blank spaces, where other leaders had once stood. The out-
lines of their heads and shoulders were still visible, but plain
red tiles had been substituted for their features. It must have
been a tricky alteration job. Geraldine, the member of No.
102 who loved to hector our guides, asked Boris to identify
the individuals who had been thus erased from Soviet subway art, if not from memory. At first, Boris professed not to
know who they were.

"Oh, come, now," said Geraldine.

"Well, I guess one of them was Beria," Boris finally said.
"And maybe Malenkov."

"And the others?" Geraldine nagged.

Boris dug in; he would yield no further. "And maybe some
other people about whom you know very well," he said. "I
am not going to tell you about those people."

The principal Soviet shrine of the cult of the individual,
of course, is the stone-cube mausoleum that Lenin and Stalin
share, on the west flank of Red Square. From noon to five
every day of the year, thousands of pilgrims file into
the tomb, in a column of twos. The stretch of the square
that they traverse is bordered with white stripes, and a corps
of policemen sees to it that the traffic moves in an orderly
fashion. Foreigners under Intourist's aegis are granted prec-
edence over the natives, and the day we went there, we were
squeezed in near the front of the queue, whose back end was
out of sight. Directly ahead of us were some Germans, who,

while we took pictures of the mausoleum and of two soldiers with fixed bayonets guarding its portals, took pictures of one another.

I had always assumed that Lenin and Stalin were just inside the entrance. Actually, the portion of their memorial that sticks up aboveground is a mere foyer. The burial chamber is a subterranean, icily refrigerated room approached by a dimly lit flight of broad, shallow steps. Of the two bodies, each stretched out supine in a massive bronze casket with a hermetically sealed glass top, Lenin's, in a plain civilian suit, is the first a visitor glimpses. To his left lies Stalin, wearing a beribboned military tunic. Both men looked small, serene, and somewhat unreal. At intervals of a few feet, stern-faced, rigid soldiers watched over such glory and grandeur as no Greek or Roman ever achieved. Now and then one of these sentinels would snap out of attention, step forward, and gently tap the elbow of an excessively curious or morbid visitor who was holding up the procession. Nobody said a word—not even the members of No. 102, who were ordinarily a high-spirited, wisecracking crew; even when they came up out of the mausoleum, they were uncharacteristically sombre. A few of them, to be sure, made feeble attempts at banter. One young man, a stress physicist from Alabama, who himself had a bushy red beard, mumbled, "Lenin needs a shave." But this was an exception to the prevailing mood, and a not terribly mirth-provoking one, at that.

DID YOU MEET MANY RUSSIANS?

It would be fairly safe, I think, to say that all English-speaking Russians are eager to chat with all English-speaking visitors. As one member of our group, an art teacher named Margie, put it one day, "You know, one of the best parts of being here is being a novelty. When you go to other countries, they've all *seen* Americans. Here, you're *some-*

thing." Many Soviet citizens—especially the younger ones—would gravitate toward the hotels where they knew foreigners stayed, and would buttonhole them on the street outside. For that matter, it was our impression that Russians would accost a foreigner on any street. Recognition required no particular deductive skill; with our Western clothes, our cameras, and our gaping mouths, we could be detected half a block away. In Kiev one night, a Russian man who picked several of us up insisted that we accompany him to a building where, he told us, we would find some real Americana. What he wanted to show us, it developed, was a poster heralding, in Russian, a forthcoming exhibit of the works of "РОКУЕ-ЛЛА КЕНТА, США"   which, after squinting a moment, we were able to decipher as "Rockwell Kent, USA." The Russian asked if we knew Kent, and when we all confessed we had never met him, demanded, "But is he not your leading people's artist?" We decided not to confuse the fellow by suggesting that to most of our people the hegemonic artist was probably Norman Rockwell.

Museums are a favorite hangout of Russians who want to practice their English. At the Russian Museum, in Leningrad, a young engineer latched eagerly on to my wife. Dismayed to learn that she was married, he latched dispiritedly, but volubly, on to me. Like many other Russians we encountered, he was exceedingly self-centered. He told me he was both a pilot and a research scientist, and had had something to do with one of the sputniks. "You know sputnik?" he asked. I said I knew. He went on to say that he played football, basketball, volleyball, and the piano, and was a prizefighter of no mean prowess. Then he switched to literature. He was familiar, he said, with Mark Twain, Theodore Dreiser, Walt Whitman, and three other writers, whom I was perplexed to hear identified—until I recalled that the Russians have no letter "h" and generally use "g" instead—as Victor Gugo, Goward Fast, and O. Genry. A moment later, he left abruptly. I thought at first that I had offended him because he had had to admit, in answer to my questioning, that he had never heard of Nathaniel Gawthorne, Sherlock Golmes, or G. Allen Smith, and I was relieved when I saw him swoop upon a seventeen-year-old girl in our party who had no rings on her fingers.

Most of the Russians we chatted with were extremely cordial, but every now and then we ran into one whose cup of grievance against the United States was so full that it spilled over onto individual Americans. At the Leningrad airport the evening we were to board a plane for Kiev, I fell into conversation—partly in English, partly in German, partly in gestures—with a Soviet Air Force colonel. We went through the usual ritual of such meetings—the tentative smile, the handshake, the exchange of cigarettes, the display of children's photographs, the establishment of origins. (He was from Minsk.) Presently, we got onto the subject of foreign relations, and his affability vanished as he rebuked me severely for my country's policies. "Russian people don't want war," he said.

"American people don't want war, either," I countered. With a snarl of disbelief, he turned on his heel and stalked into the waiting room.

I followed him in, and found most of the other members of Tour No. 102 standing around a piano, singing American songs. (There's no telling where one will run into a piano in Russia.) Several dozen Russians were listening. All of them seemed to be enjoying the recital, except one mother, whose baby had been roused by the din and was bawling, and the colonel, who stood by stony-faced. When our chorus soared —not too tactfully, perhaps—into the Wild Blue Yonder with the chantey that ends "Nothing can stop the Army Air Corps!" the colonel glowered. Then someone in the audience cried out, "Paul Robeson!" There were no Negroes on No. 102, so it was clear this was not a case of mistaken identity, but the shout was taken up by other Russians until we Americans felt obliged to make some appropriate acknowledgment. Most of the males among us, I imagine, had tackled "Ol' Man River" in the privacy of the morning shower, but the lounge of the Leningrad airport at midnight, with immense portraits of Lenin, Stalin, and Mao on the walls, was something else again. Nevertheless, for the sake of international amity, we proceeded to render the song as best we could, and the reaction—surely a tribute more to Robeson's popularity than to our performance—was stupefying. The cheers drowned out the infant's howls, and even the colonel permitted himself a fleeting smile, which turned into a broad grin when one of the women in our party—my own wife, I was astonished to perceive—then gave a further demonstration of native American culture by shedding her raincoat in the manner of a strip tease. *"Meine Frau,"* I said to the colonel, and he shrugged his epauletted shoulders in sympathetic, man-to-man rapport.

Our most comradely experience, all things considered, was an impromptu alliance we formed one noon with another faction of the Red Army. This took place at Petrodvorets. While we were looking around, two workmen engaged in sprucing up some of the dozens of statues that decorate the grounds, furtively approached Herbert and gave him a couple of postcard-size photographs—closeups of the bosoms of sculptured nudes. The men also gave him their names and addresses, and hinted that they'd like him to send them some reciprocal tokens of Western culture. He was slated to go from the U.S.S.R. to Paris, and figured he would have no trouble finding something suitable there. It was soon after Herbert amassed his rakish souvenirs that, at a gaudy set of fountains, we came upon the Soviet soldiers—half a dozen of them, armed with cameras. We took their picture. They took our picture. Several members of No. 102 posed in cozy embrace with the military. Cigarettes were swapped.

One soldier had a guitar, and he was easily induced to play it. Another, whose insignia indicated that he was an officer, went into a deep-knee bend and did the *Kazachka*. A dozen or so Russian passersby stopped to watch. A boy and a girl in our group gave a demonstration of rock 'n' roll, to the guitarist's inapt, but vigorous, accompaniment. Then, to exactly the same music, six of the tourists did a Virginia reel. A drunken Russian civilian vaulted into the clear space encircled by the spectators—some fifty of them by now—and danced a solo. The officer took a jew's-harp out of his pocket and joined in with the guitarist. Two members of our group did the fox trot, and two others, one of them a boy from Stockholm, the Swedish polka. (His partner, I was by now not quite so astonished to perceive, was my wife, a girl from East Rindge, New Hampshire.) A hundred spectators applauded. An accordion player materialized. One of the Russian soldiers did a high-stepping dance with the tipsy civilian. The officer danced with one of the American girls. Soon a dozen couples of mixed nationality were gaily skipping about. All at once, a stocky, leather-faced old woman in a quilted jacket, with a red armband girding one sleeve, pushed through the mob, which must have numbered close to two hundred. At a single, sharp command from her, the musicians stopped playing. The Russians, soldiers and civilians alike, drifted meekly away. There wasn't a murmur of protest. It was as sudden, and obliterating, as a summer thunderstorm.

DID ANY OF THEM DARE SAY WHAT THEY REALLY THINK?

The anti-Communist traveller in Russia is, of course, ever on the alert for signs of disenchantment with the system and the authorities. There is nothing very remarkable about an argument between a taxi-driver and a policeman, but it was somehow heartening to watch a cabby wrangle with a cop just a block from the Kremlin. (Bystanders got into the act, too, and the policeman did not seem especially put out when they joined the driver in yelling at him.) We were also pleased that one sidewalk acquaintance we talked with described the satellite nations as "the so-called people's democracies." A solitary epithet does not constitute much of a chink in the wall of conformity, but it was cheering all the same. Another time, while hanging around an Intourist office, I listened happily as one of the men on duty delivered himself of what sounded like a gripe against his government's policies. He was talking—in English, oddly—on the phone. "Do you know what's going on now?" he was saying, with some heat. "A special session of the U.N." There was a pause. "It *should* be broadcast—*now!*" he shouted. Another pause. "It *shouldn't* be jammed. But," he concluded, with bitter resignation, "who knows that?"

Every now and then, our Intourist guides seemed to think that we were awfully nervous about being in a police state. In Leningrad, a cannon is fired daily, at noon, from the Peter and Paul Fortress—the city's oldest structure, dating back to 1703. When we heard a muffled boom one day, none of us flinched or showed any other sign of alarm, but our guide quickly told us not to be frightened; it was merely a time signal. We had no idea what else she thought we thought it might be, but it was obvious that she had anticipated a jumpier reaction. Actually, the consensus in the ranks of No. 102 was that it was surprising that the guides did not tremble in *our* presence; had not Khrushchev and Mao, a day or two before we reached the U.S.S.R., appraised all Americans as sabre-rattling imperialist maniacs?

Boris, a lawyer by profession, always watched his words, as if they were being transcribed. Once, he got to talking about his nation's literary heritage. "Mayakovsky was a great Russian poet," he said. "Excuse me—I mean great Soviet poet," he corrected himself hastily. It was difficult for Boris to relax in our company. While we were aboard one subway train, which had metal bars, rather than straps, for standees to cling to, a schoolteacher on our tour told him an American subway joke. It was the old wheeze about the fellow who offers his strap to a lady and, when she thanks him but says she already has one, replies, "In that case, would you mind letting go of my tie?" Boris listened politely, but warily, as the story proceeded, apparently suspecting that it might have a nasty political twist. At its unexceptionable punch line, he laughed heartily—as much from relief, it seemed, as from amusement.

DID YOU FEEL CUT OFF FROM THE REST OF THE WORLD?

During our stay, the Moscow *News* ran a story about another tourist, Adlai Stevenson. "Mr. Stevenson . . . expressed the opinion that Soviet people were getting a one-sided conception of what was happening in the world," the paper said. One-sided or not, the Soviet people might have been getting *some* conception; the non-Russian-speaking visitor to the U.S.S.R. usually felt as far out of touch with current events as a miner trapped by a cave-in. The only English-language papers from the outside world sold on newsstands were the *Workers* of New York and London, and these, to an American or Englishman hungry for information, were no more nourishing in Russia than they are on their home grounds. The Moscow *News* belied its name. It contained mostly feature articles with titles like "Irkutsk Reservoir Filling Up Rapidly," "Chicks to Be Hatched All Year Round," and "The Arabs Will Come Into Their Own." About the only spot news we got out of it was the number of times Sputnik III had cruised around the earth at press time.

Almost every day, someone on our tour would ask our Intourist guides for a rundown on the latest news. We got precious little out of them. It was hard to tell whether their reticence stemmed from a reluctance to discuss controversial matters with us or from a simple lack of information. One day—a day on which, I later learned, the New York *Times* was hard put to it to squeeze onto its front page all the events that were shaking the globe—a guide remarked that she had read that morning's *Pravda,* and when we asked her for a summary of its leading stories, she replied that a hydro-electric station in Kuibyshev had commenced full-scale operations. Fine, we said, and what else? That was all, she told us. Boris was even less communicative. I spotted a folded copy of *Pravda* in his pocket one day, and asked him to translate the headlines for me, but although he was doing nothing more taxing than watching us watch some fountains spray, he said he was too busy.

In an English translation of a Stalin Prize novel (written by a man who was clearly no Pasternak) that my wife and I picked up in Leningrad, one of the characters, a philosophical old fisherman, says, "Reading the newspapers makes me sick; to think that while we here are working our hardest to make life better for people, those sons of sin across the ocean are stirring up trouble—testing out bombs, buying up the scum of the earth with dollars, and signing pacts against us on the sly." Apparently, not all Russians felt so testy about dollars—most of us on No. 102 were approached at least once by black-marketeers avid for greenbacks—but many Russians seemed, like that fictional fisherman, to be sick of their newspapers. For all its lighting fixtures and mosaics, the most eye-opening aspect of the Moscow subway system was that, in the hours we spent riding around on it, we never saw a passenger carrying, let alone reading, a newspaper.

WHAT WERE THE STORES LIKE?

We saw one sight in Kiev that no tourists before us had ever seen. This distinction, whatever it may be worth, was ours because we happened to be in the city the day its new municipal market opened for business. The market building, a gigantic, domed white stone structure with a glass roof, looks like a railroad station, and could hold a fair amount of rolling stock. Most of the food on sale was raised on collective farms, but our Intourist guide told us that in-dividuals with back-yard gardens might also bring in crops and sell them. We got to the market early in the afternoon. Outside the main entrance, half a dozen women in babushkas were peddling bunches of flowers, possibly from their back yards. By that time, the produce inside, displayed on row after row of waist-high counters, had been pretty well picked over. What was left—small, half-rotten apples, plums, and pears; a scrawny chicken or two; some loose eggs with cracked shells; and some bowls of sour cream, which house-wives sampled by spooning a bit onto their palms and lick-ing it up—was unappealing and expensive. No prices were posted, but the women behind the fruit counters wanted a ruble (ten cents) for a runty apple or pear and thirty ko-pecks (three cents) for a low-grade paper bag to carry it in.

The only appetizing fruit we saw during the whole trip was at the All-Union Agricultural Exposition, in Moscow. Most of the three hundred buildings in this enormous in-stallation, a permanent exhibition ground that not only fea-tures crops but has a big industrial section as well, are re-gional in scope, but some are not—the Sputnik Pavilion, for instance, given over in large part to photographs of the ill-fated Laika, and the main industrial pavilion, an edifice so huge that a heavy dump truck parked on a shelf along its façade had the relative appearance of a model truck on a toy counter. Fifteen ornate pavilions harbored the indigenous arts, crafts, fruits, and vegetables of the fifteen republics that make up the U.S.S.R. (Many Soviet products that we saw had regional brand names—the Kiev camera, the Estonia grand piano, the Moskva typewriter, the Volga automobile—and we saw eggs with "Bulgaria" stamped, in Roman letters, on their shells, to say nothing of cigarettes called Sputnik and

Laika.) In most of the pavilions we dropped into, there were mounds of fine fresh fruit—fat apples and pears, lemons the size of oranges, oranges the size of grapefruit—that looked not unlike those at the Farmers' Market in Hollywood; and attached to the Georgian Pavilion was a greenhouse with citrus trees growing in it. Boris told us that the piles of fruit in the pavilions were changed every four days, to ensure the acme of freshness, and we asked him what was done with the discards, since they seemed likely to be a good deal more interesting than anything we'd seen on sale anywhere. (In Hollywood, all the fruit's for sale.) They were available, he replied, at fruit stalls scattered about the exposition grounds. When we stopped at one such outlet, though, all it had to offer was some dried-up pears, at two rubles each, which looked dwarfish compared to the juicy giants we had ogled earlier.

Shopping in Russia was hard work. Except for the food stores, most establishments didn't open until eleven in the morning. Well before that hour, in mute testimony to a lack of depth in inventory, customers would line up outside. We saw a few attempts to emulate Western merchandising. In a show window of one Kiev department store were two slim, Anglo-Saxon-looking mannequins—a blonde in a house-coat serving breakfast coffee, from a gleaming samovar, to her husband, who was wearing a dapper dressing gown. Though the model was a good deal more attractive than most of the live women on the other side of the windowpane, her husband's fixed smile was focussed not on her but on a copy of *Pravda*, which the waxen wretch was holding right up to his face.

Most Soviet stores seemed old-fashioned by Western standards. In many of them, the cashiers did their totting up with a wooden abacus. The prices were high—two hundred and sixty rubles for a flimsy-looking pair of ski boots, fifteen hundred rubles for a ready-made suit. About the least expen-

sive consumer goods were books and phonograph records, for
their production is heavily subsidized. In Moscow, we bought
some long-playing records for seven rubles each, which was
the sum we later paid for a two-hundred-gram goblet of
sweetish champagne in the nearest thing we saw to an Ameri-
can-style bar—a table set up in one corner of a liquor store
and presided over by a woman in a white smock, who poured
out drinks of wine at so much per hundred grams. A two-
volume English-language edition of the correspondence of
Stalin, Roosevelt, Churchill, Truman, and Attlee during
what the Russians call the Great Patriotic War cost fifteen rubles in the U.S.S.R.—one-tenth what I had paid for
the same set in New York.

Shortly after eleven o'clock one morning, my wife and I
did some shopping at GUM, which stands just across Red
Square from the Kremlin. The big store is absurdly laid out.
Three stories high, it is about three blocks in length. Much
of that vast interior, though, is air space. A good deal of the
merchandise was displayed in tiny stalls huddled together
along the walls on mezzanines connected by a series of
bridges and catwalks. I felt inside the place as though I were
walking through a dirigible—and a perilously overloaded
one, at that. (My wife must have felt giddy, too: When I told
her expansively to buy herself a souvenir, she proceeded to
purchase a gold tea-strainer that cost a hundred and eighty
rubles, although we hardly ever serve tea at home.) The
summer day we were there, the store was more crowded than
I have ever seen Macy's the week before Christmas. One of
the stalls was hawking inflated balloons, but it was hard
to believe a customer could have carried one out of the place
intact. Like most tourists, we were eager to buy fur hats, and
in due course we found the fur-hat counter. It was be-
sieged by a throng ten deep, and trapped in the melee was a
white-bearded patriarch protectively clutching a straw hat.
He did not appear to want a fur hat. He was just trying to

keep the hat he already had from being shredded. After a harrowing ten minutes, during which, as foreigners, we were pushed up front, we bought our hats, and a few hours later we discovered that we could have bought exactly the same kind, identically priced, at an elegant, uncluttered furrier's on Gorki Street, the Moscow counterpart of Fifth Avenue. The only horde in this establishment consisted of a couple of dozen immobile women who were watching another woman—evidently a paying customer—try on a silver-fox neckpiece. It had a seven-hundred-and-thirty-six-ruble price tag. The customer swaggered and preened and examined her mirrored reflection from all angles, and the onlookers were agog with vicarious luxurious living. When she spread the pelt out on a table, they surged forward and stroked it tenderly.

KIEV IS IN SIBERIA, ISN'T IT?

No, it isn't. Kiev, the capital of the Ukrainian Republic, is about five hundred miles southwest of Moscow. It is a full-fledged metropolis, with a population of more than a million, a university in which twelve thousand students are enrolled, an amusement park, saloons where you can buy a beer by dropping coins into a vending machine, and the biggest Young Communist Headquarters building you ever saw. We found it—in warm weather, at least—a markedly gayer city than either Leningrad or Moscow. Many of the women were wearing flower-print dresses, and many of the men colorful, high-necked shirts with embroidered collars and cuffs. (We saw one Soviet car there with embroidered slipcovers. A talisman dangled at its rear window—a toy Mickey Mouse.) Even a statue of Lenin down the street from our hotel seemed to have a jauntier expression than its grim-jawed counterparts to the north. Spang in the middle of the city, which is bisected by the Dnieper River, were long stretches of white-sand bathing beach, dotted with cabañas, restaurants, and polychromatic umbrellas. We sailed along the river on a sightseeing boat one Tuesday afternoon, and there were as many swimmers in the water, or basking on the banks, as you would find at Jones Beach on a sunny August weekend.

Kiev was all but levelled by the Germans, and its reconstruction afforded the Soviet government a magnificent opportunity for large-scale city planning. There was much evidence in the new Kiev, such as the Young Communist palace, that the government can think big. Its main avenue, the Kreshchatik, is two hundred and sixty feet wide—the broadest thoroughfare in the entire U.S.S.R., our guide told us proudly. One side of the street is lined with apartment houses, and the other with stores and office buildings. Beneath the Kreshchatik, when we were there, a subway system was in the making, and it wouldn't have surprised me to hear that its chandeliers weighed two tons. A temporary wooden structure surrounding one of the excavations was so splendidly decorated with painted flowers that it could have passed muster as a pavilion at a fair. Kiev teemed with giant T-shaped cranes, which also towered over building sites in the other cities we visited. In Moscow, block-long, nine-story apartment houses were going up as abundantly as single-family dwellings on Long Island. The quantity of construction work everywhere was awesome, but we could not help wondering what the Soviet delegates found to talk about at an international congress of architects that was being held in Moscow at the time of our visit, for however advanced in theory the Soviet architects might have been, the best they seemed to have come up with in practice was Central Park West.

DID THE WOMEN REALLY DO MEN'S WORK?

Nowhere in the Soviet Union did we see a lawnmower —not even in the public gardens, where meticulously

tended flower beds were set off by lush and green, but raggedly trimmed, swards. Wherever grass was being cut, the
job was being done—at a snail-like rate—by squads of
scarfed-and-booted women equipped with scythes and hand
shears. We saw women masons laying bricks, and women
carpenters hammering away on new construction projects.
The biggest trailer truck we met up with in the U.S.S.R. had
a woman at the wheel. And then there was the woman porter on the sleeping car that took us from Kiev to Moscow—
a jolly woman worker, whose repeated smiles made her
mouthful of steel teeth memorable. The trip took about
fifteen hours, and every now and then the porter served us
tea, which she brewed in a charcoal-heated samovar at one
end of the car. In the morning, we started to take up a collection for her, but she got wind of this scheme and
announced that she would not accept a tip. She wondered
if we could give her a written testimonial instead. Nurse
Armstrong composed an appropriate tribute, and we all
signed it. When it was presented to the porter, she flashed a
magnificent metallic smile.

The sleeping car we rode in appeared to be brand-new,
and was quite comfortable, but even so it was not, as Nina
had made clear to Jinny and me before we left Kiev, what
we were entitled to. This was a *second*-class car, and our
pre-paid tour entitled us to ride in first-class rolling stock,
but it would be a great convenience to Nina if all the people on No. 102 could travel together, and would we mind
terribly much downgrading ourselves for one night? (Russians are very class-conscious.) Of course, she added, we'd
be entitled to a refund on the difference between what we'd
paid for a first-class Kiev-Moscow berth and what we got.
(Russians are very money-conscious.)

What we got, to begin with, was different compart-
ments. When my wife and I examined the tickets that Nina,
after fervent asseverations of her thanks for our having

made a sacrifice in the group's behalf, had handed us, we discovered that Jinny was to sleep with Mrs. Bronsky and the two older Bronsky girls. I was with Mr. Bronsky, Dottie Bronsky, and Mr. Tsutuki. Bronsky *père* vetoed that arrangement. Jinny thereupon swapped berths with Dottie, and found herself in a compartment with three men—a Canadian, a Japanese, and me. At that, the Swedish boy who'd danced the polka with her offered to swap berths with me, so that she could enjoy the novel experience of sharing a cubicle with three inhabitants of three continents. I vetoed that; travel can be too broadening.

Nina was conscientious. Jinny and I were scheduled to leave Moscow, a few days later, at six in the morning. We didn't finish dinner until eleven the night before, and while my wife went upstairs to pack, I arranged—or thought I arranged—with a woman in the lobby, sitting in a cage labelled "Hotel Administrator," to have us telephoned at four-thirty, and to have a cab on tap for us at five. When I got to our room, Jinny handed me a farewell note from Nina. "I have ordered the car for you for 5:45 to the hotel," it said. "You will find it yourself and say 'aeroport.' I haven't got the paper for you to refund your railway ticket, but I'll send it to you. I have asked the maid to wake you up at 5. Best wishes! Come to the U.S.S.R. once more. Caviar is 'ikra.' P.S.: Have you taken your passports?"

At midnight, Nina phoned, to make sure we'd got the message. I thanked her, and explained I'd already made alternate airport plans. "So don't worry," she said cheerfully. "I will cancel yours."

I begged her not to, but she said Intourist wouldn't hear of our throwing money away on a cab when it stood ready and eager to furnish us free transportation. She hung up, and called back a few minutes later to report that a car would indisputably be at the front door of the hotel at five.

Throwing money away was the least of our problems at

that point. Despite elegant tea-strainers, and a few jars of *ikra* we'd picked up in the hotel dining room in exchange for unused meal tickets, we still had a lot of rubles left over that we'd acquired in anticipation of a real Muscovite shopping binge. Jinny and I hadn't been told that we could exchange these for dollars at the Moscow airport, as we could have, and now, staring out at the Kremlin's chilly stars, we tried to figure out how we could possibly spend some money in Moscow between one and five in the morning.

"I have it!" Jinny finally exclaimed. "Room service! We'll buy two gallons of vodka!"

I pressed the room-service button, and in less than a minute, the telephone rang again. It was Nina again, evidently destined for another sleepless night. She said she understood we had summoned room service, and would we mind telling her what we wanted? Maybe our room wasn't bugged, but room service certainly was.

"Ten bottles of vodka, please," said Jinny.

Nina gulped and hung up, and ten minutes later a waitress arrived with the vodka. It was nearly two o'clock before we'd packed it all among our clothes and had gone to bed, but even so I woke at four-fifteen. This was just as well, for nobody roused us, nor, after we had carried our now substantially overweight luggage down to the lobby, did anyone know anything about any Intourist car. We finally hailed a cruising cab, and said "Aeroport." The driver had to stop for gas en route. He got it on a Moscow side street, where he halted next to a kiosk with a solitary pump. He pounded on the door of the kiosk, and presently a young woman emerged, rubbing her eyes. She gave him some gas, which, near as we could make out, he didn't pay for.

A few months later, we got a handwritten letter from Nina, identifying herself as "Guide-interpreter," on Intourist stationery. The document was headed "Statement," and it said, "This is to certify that on the portion of the trip from Kiev to Moscow 2nd class accommodations were provided for Mr. and Mrs. Kahn instead of 1st class." The idea of a refund, however small, in Moscow gold appealed to Jinny and me enormously, and we wrote a couple of letters to that end. After some months, we heard from the New York office of Intourist, which said, "Please be informed that we have forwarded [your letter] to our head office in Moscow for appropriate action and requested them to speed up a reply directly to you." More than a year after that, we received a copy of a letter that the Moscow office of Intourist had sent to a New York travel bureau, about me: "We should appreciate your efforts in looking for your client and informing him that the matter of refund can be considered by Intourist only on the ground of a statement, confirming that service was not used by him." If only I knew where Nina's Statement was!

In an issue of *Soviet Woman*—a monthly magazine that, according to its masthead, was "devoted to social and political problems, literature, and art," and was published in Russian, Chinese, German, Hindi, Japanese, Korean, Spanish, Urdu, and English—I read about a Soviet fashion show put on in Cairo. (A dress pattern was tucked inside the magazine—a design for a garment that its creator presumably considered equally suitable for Spanish, German, Indian, and Korean women.) *Soviet Woman* quoted several Egyptian reactions to the display of gowns. "Though made of inexpensive fabrics, they all were superb," one critic said. Another declared, "The Russian models are distinguished for their fresh, vivacious faces and unaffected manner. All of them are tall and slender." We ourselves saw very few tall or slender women—maybe they were all on overseas duty— and very few of any proportions whose gowns could be called superb. Most of the women were short and thickset, and, whether wielding a shovel or pushing a baby carriage, were garbed in drab, formless clothes. They looked about as fresh and vivacious as a warden in a girl's reformatory.

Still, we surmised that they had lively aspirations. One girl on Tour No. 102, wearing a reasonably frilly outfit, wandered into a Leningrad store where second-hand clothing was bought and sold. She said afterward that a number of women there were so enamored of her dress that, in vain attempts to buy it from her, they almost pulled it off her back. Most of the men's suits we saw were of dark and solemn hue, but underneath them—as we learned from observing several fellow train passengers stretch their legs at dawn on a way-station platform—many Russian men wore sleeveless undershirts in pastel shades of green and blue.

Everywhere we went, we passed women who were tidily sweeping the sidewalks or streets with bundles of twigs—the only kind of broom we saw, indoors or out, in the Soviet Union. In Kiev, women were whisking the interstices in the streetcar tracks. (Women operated some of the streetcars, too.) Soviet streets were praiseworthily clean. A block was likely to have several containers placed along the sidewalk, for cigarette butts and scrap paper. In the middle of some of the side streets were narrow, water-filled troughs, shallow enough for a car to straddle without scraping. They were pigeon baths. One should not underestimate a nation that encourages even its pigeons to keep immaculate. Walking along Gorki Street, in Moscow, we had to detour around a squat, slow-moving, bright-red truck that was crawling along the sidewalk—a big vacuum cleaner. But however strong the Soviet passion for health and sanitation, some of its vehicles were strangely behind the times. In Leningrad one day, we watched a small white sedan, with its rear seat removed and red crosses painted on its side doors, screech to a halt before an apartment house. Two white-uniformed men jumped out, carrying a collapsed stretcher, and ran into the building. They soon emerged with a pregnant woman. The driver lifted open the door of the trunk compartment, and the litter-bearers slid their patient through it and into the car. Then the driver slammed down the lid of the trunk, and this awkward and antiquated ambulance chugged away.

WERE THEY VERY ANTI-RELIGIOUS?

Our only Sunday in Russia was spent in Leningrad, and on Saturday afternoon Intourist advised the members of our tour that arrangements could and would be made for us to attend church, if we wanted to. My wife and I were exhausted, and slept late Sunday morning, but several of the tourists took advantage of the offer, out of either piety or curiosity. One Baptist who went to a Greek Orthodox service reported that a collective funeral had been in progress, with five bodies laid out in five parallel caskets. A great many Russian churches were closed and boarded up, and some of these, though they were prominent landmarks, did not rate a mention on the municipal maps a tourist could buy. In quite a few of the churches whose doors were unlocked, no services were being held, and their auxiliary buildings had been converted into apartment houses. When we stopped for a look at the imposing Cathedral of the Smolny Monastery, in Leningrad, the only human activity near the main entrance consisted of some men playing dominoes, a baby boy pounding a tiny milk can against the curb, and a woman beating a rug—a red rug.

The Cathedral of St. Peter and St. Paul, which lies within the five-foot-thick stone walls of the Peter and Paul Fortress, was open, but largely, we gathered, so that Russians could gawk at the tombs of several of their nation's past rulers, among them Peter the Great and Catherine the Great. (Also inside the fortress was a government mint, which at the time of our visit was being guarded by the only soldiers with fixed bayonets we saw anywhere, aside from the Lenin-

Stalin mausoleum. The Communists brook no interference
with the making of money.) Some of the Czars' tombs had
been garlanded by nostalgic citizens with wreaths of fresh
flowers, to which were tied ribbons with Russian phrases
written on them. Peter the Great had an eight-word testimonial attached to his wreath. When we asked Nina for a
translation, she said, after consulting a male guide standing
nearby, that it simply said, "To Peter the Great."

"That's all?" asked the Swedish boy. "Eight whole words
to say just that?"

"That's all," said Nina, with finality.

In Kiev, the main item on our sightseeing agenda was a
trip to a monastery called the *Lavra,* or catacombs. We were
shown around that city by a brusque, businesslike young
woman named Dina. She was married to an Army officer,
and, perhaps because of that orientation, she remarked at
one point that the members of Tour No. 102 were the most
undisciplined gang she'd ever had any truck with. (Dina
wore sunglasses with one cracked lens. An interpreter we
had in Moscow, named Lucy, also had damaged spectacles,
and as for Nina, she had lost her glasses and hadn't been able
to replace them. Either there was a shortage of optical glass
in the Soviet Union or else blurred vision was a condition of
employment by Intourist.) Telling us about the monastery
in advance, Dina said, "It has live monks. Very handsome
monks." From her tone, edged and supercilious, she might
have been speaking of monkeys.

There were actually two monasteries, on two levels. In the
eleventh century, Dina said, monks inhabited the lower one
—a series of caves. By the seventeenth century, the members
of this sect had become extremely wealthy, and they built a
sumptuous settlement on a hill above the catacombs. Now
the lower monastery was the only one operative, though the
monks were not living in the caves, which were filled to capacity with the sanctified remains of their predecessors. Sev-

eral buildings of the upper monastery were in ruins, the result of wartime damage, and one structure that was still intact had been converted into an anti-religious museum; a
sign inside it quoted Karl Marx on religion's tranquillizing
effect on the masses. After walking down a cobbled path, we
entered a cool, dimly lit chamber that led to the caves. A dignified monk, cowled and black-bearded, handed each of us a
beeswax candle. One of the prep-schoolers in our group began to speculate uproariously on what might happen to the
teacher who was shepherding them if, being black-bearded
himself, he held his taper too close to his face. The monk
probably didn't catch the drift of this remark, but its loud-
ness enraged him, and he tried to shove the whole caboodle
of us back outside. Dina calmed him down somehow.

In single file, lighting our way with our candles, we
shuffled silently through the narrow, winding, rock-walled
corridors, stopping occasionally at an alcove to peer at the
mummified corpse of a saint, completely shrouded save for
the shrunken, withered hands. When we came back out into
the daylight, an aged, white-bearded monk was crossing a
courtyard. Dina invited us to take his picture, but the instant
a camera was aimed at him, he pulled his cowl over his face.
We overtook two elderly women who were crossing themselves. Dina gave them a look half indulgent, half contemp-
tuous, as if she were a research scientist observing the behavior of some reflex-conditioned laboratory animals.

WHAT ABOUT THE CHILDREN?

An American could not walk far in a Soviet city without
being approached by small boys (girls did not participate
in the sport), who would badger him for chewing gum, cigarettes, postage stamps, ball-point pens, or, most often,
money. We found Soviet children remarkably familiar with
United States currency; twenty-five-cent pieces were their
favorites, and they had a low opinion of pennies. The chil-

dren who tugged at our sleeves were, by and large, friendly, bright-eyed, sturdy, and cleanly dressed, and if at times they seemed to be violating the first half of Polonius's celebrated injunction, they also engagingly violated the second half. While my wife was chatting haltingly in Leningrad one day with a boy who had started off, modestly, by trying to cadge a dime, he asked her for a ball-point pen. She said she didn't have one, and he thereupon gave *her* a ball-point pen. It embarrassed her to be on the receiving end, and she felt better about the whole business when, a week later, she was able to present the Leningrad pen to an importunate Moscow boy.

Most of the children carried around, as a sort of *quid pro quo,* a pocketful of cheap metal lapel pins, worth perhaps several kopecks apiece. The pins came in a few basic designs —Lenin's head, Moscow University, the letters "C.C.C.P." (the Russian equivalent of "U.S.S.R."), doves of peace, and red stars, or some combination of these symbols. Soviet citizens of all ages were partial to lapel decorations. The first Intourist man we ran into was wearing a pin with a torch on it. He told us it signified his having completed a history course at a university. Boris, our guide in Moscow, had a small gilt canoe riding on his lapel; it was a Swedish boating pin, he said—the gift of some tourists from Stockholm. One Russian student we met, who, like many of his peers, was a rock-'n'-roll enthusiast, had at his throat, instead of a tie, a large silver brooch depicting two convulsive dancers. He was decidedly unlike his peers in that, instead of boasting of his academic accomplishments, he admitted blandly that he had lately flunked an exam. But then he might have been a delinquent; the Communists had not long before announced that one sign of juvenile depravity was the wearing of trousers too narrow to be slipped over shoes, and this fellow had on peg-top pants.

One afternoon, Intourist arranged for Tour No. 102 to

visit a summer camp of the Young Pioneers, the Soviet counterpart, as Boris put it, of our Boy and Girl Scouts—or, as it
might also have been put, of the Hitler Youth. The trip to
the camp, situated fifty miles outside Moscow, was organized
on such short notice that some of us were just sitting down
to lunch when we were told that the bus was set to leave.

We stuffed our pockets with black bread and hurried out
to board it. Boris had with him a foreman from a Moscow
carburetor factory, because this particular camp was reserved
for the children of that factory's workers. We drove out
through flat, open country. Most of the villages we passed
looked seedy, and the houses were rickety frame affairs,
roofed with tin or thatch; to judge by the profusion of out-
houses, very few homes had plumbing. Some of the tourists
tried to photograph this backwardness, but they can't have
done too well, for our driver barrelled along at a bouncy clip,
time and again narrowly missing a startled stroller. Most
Russian drivers, we concluded, regard pedestrians much as
most American drivers regard dead skunks—objects to avoid,
for selfish reasons, but not to slow down for.

After a two-hour journey, we arrived, without misadven-
ture, at the Pioneer camp, which was set in a pleasantly
wooded area permeated with the odor of disinfectant that
one associates with outdoor latrines. A few boys and girls and
a large portrait of Lenin were waiting for us at the entrance
gate. The children wore white shirts and red bandannas—
the official regalia of a Pioneer—and unregimented skirts or
shorts. A handsome, towheaded boy of twelve or so stepped
forward, holding a bugle with a fringed red banner suspended from it. He blew a call—Assembly, I imagine—and
Pioneers converged on us gaily from all directions. A middle-
aged woman official in a severe dark-red suit held the kids
more or less at bay while she conferred with Boris. Then she
told the children to run off and play, or something, and as

they scampered away she led us to a square wooden building, which, Boris said, was a girls' dormitory. "The children are divided into groups, or commands, of ten each," he said. "This dormitory houses one and a half commands."

There was a water cooler on the porch, and next to it a thick china mug with a broken handle. In a room just inside the front door, we passed a tier of tidy little shelves, each containing a towel and a bar of soap. (There might have been a toothbrush in each, too, but I didn't see one.) The dormitory appeared to be of fairly recent construction, the absence of plumbing notwithstanding. One room was filled with suitcases and neatly hung city clothes. Another was a large, lace-curtained sleeping room, with windows on three sides, fifteen brass beds, and three naked bulbs hanging from the ceiling. Jinny said the room was far more austere than any girls' dorm of her previous acquaintance. Aside from the beds, the only furniture was a couple of end tables; there were none of the frivolous knickknacks one might think girl campers would take with them on a holiday.

While we were inspecting this command post, Boris told us that the camp had two hundred and seventy children, ranging in age from four to fifteen. They were attended by a staff of forty-eight adults, including folk-song leaders, folk-dance leaders, and physical-culture leaders.

"Who owns the bedding?" one tourist asked him.

"I know the answer," said Boris, who had informed us earlier that he was an old Young Pioneer himself, "but I will ask her, because you wouldn't believe me."

Boris addressed a few words to the women in red, who nodded, and then he told us that the bedding belonged to the trade-union committee of the carburetor factory. We gathered that this was a notably paternalistic labor organization, for he went on to say, without consulting the woman, that the highest fee any child had to pay for a twenty-six-day vacation was a hundred and thirty-three rubles, and that a good many of the campers paid less, while ten per cent paid nothing at all.

Thus briefed, we went back out, past a raised circular platform, for folk dancing; past a bulletin board on which several weather maps were posted; past a basketball court and a merry-go-round; past a white stone statue of a Pioneer holding a white stone flag; and past a statue of a Pioneer beating a drum. (No sculptors here, either; just statues.) Finally, we came to a wooden reviewing stand confronting an open area planted with flowers. A lofty flagpole, with a red flag fluttering from its peak, occupied the center of this plaza. We mounted the platform and stood there, shoulder to shoulder, while canned music blared forth from a loudspeaker, and then, suddenly and stiffly, from behind a building, the Pioneers marched out, in order of height, the teenagers in the van, the tots at the rear. They halted at attention in the plaza. After a moment, with the blond bugler, a drummer, and a couple of flag-bearers at their head, the whole crowd paraded toward us, and halted again, each command in disciplined formation, thirty feet away. Several youngsters whom we took to be commanders stepped forward and saluted us with raised arms.

One Pioneer, an attractive girl of ten or eleven, came up on the platform, stood behind a speaker's lectern with a microphone on it, and said, in excellent English, "Our dear guests—our dear American friends—we are so glad to welcome you to our Pioneer camp." She apparently hadn't been tipped off that only two-thirds of us were Americans. "We are always glad to welcome people from all over the world," she went on. Not only was she happy to greet us but, what was more, the entire Soviet Union would soon be equally happy to greet Paul Robeson, whom she characterized, nonpolitically, as "the great American singer." "Our life is very interesting, and we're having a good rest here," she said, in conclusion. (My sons have never described their summer camp as restful, but for all I know it may be.) "Now we'd like to hear about your life in the United States, and about your children. Take our best wishes to America."

Suddenly, without any ruffles or flourishes, a bunch of Pioneers swarmed around us and showered us with gifts. Each woman got an enormous bouquet of fresh flowers, and each man a sample of Pioneer handicraft. My present was a deli- cately carved wooden wall ornament, shaped like an oak leaf and painted with acorns. Many of the children, moreover, took off their kerchiefs and tied them around our necks, with what seemed to be, and I hope was, impulsiveness.

When order had been more or less restored, it was up to Tour No. 102 to make fitting response. One of the school- teachers in our group moved to the microphone. "I think all adults love children, and we love you as we love all children," he began. He paused, so Boris could interpret for him, and when the children learned what he had said, they beamed lovingly at us. The teacher talked a bit more, and then our youngest member, Dottie, the seven-year-old Canadian girl, expressed her small-voiced thanks. A sixteen-year-old Amer- ican girl was next. "My name is Grace," she said, "and I'm so *happy* to be here. I'm so *grateful* to all of you." She was close to tears, and had to stop. When Boris translated for her, even his flinty voice seemed tinged with emotion.

I was down at one end of the reviewing stand, where I couldn't see the speakers and had to identify them by their voices. The next voice was instantly recognizable. "My name is Mrs. Kahn," it said, "and I have three sons—eleven, nine and a half, and six." (My sons! Over a loudspeaker in Russia!) I heard a couple of syllables in Boris's by then al- most equally familiar voice, but Jinny, carried away by motherly affection and forgetful of the problems of non- simultaneous translation, plunged on. Boris subsided, and by the time she had finally run out of steam, and out of words about the American way of boys' life, there was nothing the poor man could do but mumble a sorry and emasculated paraphrase of her oration. I was sorry, though I was somewhat taken aback by her peroration, in which she pledged impetuously that our sons would doubtless soon be visiting the Soviet Union themselves.

Then the Pioneers were dismissed, and for the next half hour they swirled around us in uninhibited and touching fraternization. Seven-year-old Dottie was their special pet. Half a dozen young Russian girls, enraptured at meeting a Western contemporary—and one who had her pigtails diplomatically festooned with red ribbons to boot—attached themselves to her, spun her around on the merry-go-round, heaped her with gifts, and every now and then hugged her so heartily that her mother winced. The bugler graciously gave Jinny a Lenin-head pin he was wearing. She reached into her purse for a reciprocal token, and, after coming up with and hastily thrusting down a bottle of vodka, fished forth a French-Line key ring she'd had there for over a year. Another boy started to affix a pin to my lapel. Just as he was fastening the clasp, two swept-wing jet fighters screamed over the treetops, and we both looked upward. When I glanced back down, I saw that what he was pinning on me was a dove of peace. I reached into my pocket, hoping to find some token for him, and came up with a fistful of black-bread crumbs. "I wish I had some coins left," I told him contritely. He smiled and gave me fifty kopecks.

A little later, we were taken—most of us with a Russian child clinging to each hand—into a building that contained a library, several workshops, and an exhibition of the children's handiwork: tooled-leather photograph albums, assorted wood carvings, a globe with an electrically-operated satellite circumnavigating it, and so on. The walls of the corridors were ablaze with propaganda posters and portraits of Lenin and other national pioneers.

"That's Lenin," Jinny's bugler told her.

"Yes, I know," she said.

One of our schoolteachers pointed to a table in the library, on which lay both a copy of *Pravda* and its youth edition, *Pioneer Pravda,* and asked Boris, "What's *pravda* mean?"

Boris was incredulous, as perhaps he had a right to be on being asked such a question by a teacher who'd spent a fortnight in *Pravda*-land.

"Pravda!" said Boris, with unconcealed scorn. *"Truth!* You know *that* word?"

Before too long, it was time for us to head back to Moscow, and the farewell we bade the Pioneers was truly reluctant, for they were as nice and hospitable a crowd of kids as one could hope to meet anywhere.

On the bus, most of us tourists were uncommonly quiet, except for Lester, who could not abide silence. "You know what a Pioneer says when he salutes another one?" he asked Margie, the art teacher. "He says, 'Be ready for the struggle in the cause of the Communist Party!' And when the other one salutes back, he says, 'Always ready!' "

"I don't believe you," said Margie.

"It's true," Lester said. "One of them told me."

"Now you've spoiled everything," said Margie, and, of course, what he had said—I learned later it was true—spoiled something. But, children being children, not everything.

ABOUT THE AUTHOR

A staff writer for *The New Yorker* since his graduation from Harvard in 1937, E. J. Kahn, Jr., has contributed reports to that magazine from such far-off spots as Australia, New Guinea, Panama, Germany, Russia, Japan, Korea, Alaska, and East Rindge, New Hampshire. He is the author of eight books, the father of three sons, and keeps in shape by playing gin rummy.